NEXT QUESTION

D1378352

NEXT QUESTION

AN NFL SUPER AGENT'S
PROVEN GAME PLAN FOR
BUSINESS SUCCESS

DREW AND JASON
ROSENHAUS

BERKLEY BOOKS, NEW YORK

THE BERKLEY PUBLISHING GROUP
Published by the Penguin Group
Penguin Group (USA) Inc.
375 Hudson Street, New York, New York 10014, USA
Penguin Group (Canada), 90 Englinton Avenue East, Suite 700, Toronto, Ontario M4P 2Y3 Canada
(a division of Pearson Penguin Canada Inc.)
Penguin Books Ltd., 80 Strand, London WC2R 0RL, England
Penguin Group Ireland, 25 St. Stephen's Green, Dublin 2, Ireland (a division of Penguin Books Ltd.)
Penguin Group (Australia), 250 Camberwell Road, Camberwell, Victoria 3124, Australia
(a division of Pearson Australia Group Pty. Ltd.)
Penguin Books India Pvt. Ltd., 11 Community Centre, Panchsheel Park, New Delhi—110 017, India
Penguin Group (NZ), 67 Apollo Drive, Rosedale, North Shore 0632, New Zealand
(a division of Pearson New Zealand Ltd.)
Penguin Books (South Africa) (Pty.) Ltd., 24 Sturdee Avenue, Rosebank, Johannesburg 2196,
South Africa

Penguin Books Ltd., Registered Offices: 80 Strand, London, WC2R, 0RL England

This publication is designed to provide accurate and authoritative information in regard to the subject matter covered. It is sold with the understanding that the publisher is not engaged in rendering legal, accounting, or other professional services. If you require legal advice or other expert assistance, you should seek the services of a competent professional. The publisher does not have any control over and does not assume any responsibility for author or third-party websites or their content.

PRINTING HISTORY
Berkley hardcover edition / September 2008
Berkley trade paperback edition / September 2009

ISBN: 978-0-425-22962-0

The Library of Congress has catalogued the Berkley hardcover edition as follows:

Rosenhaus, Drew, 1966–
    Next question : an NFL super agent's proven game plan for business success / Drew and Jason
Rosenhaus.
      p. cm.
    ISBN 978-0-425-22344-4
    1. Sports agents—United States.   2. Football players—United States.   3. National Football
League.   I. Rosenhaus, Jason.   II. Title.
    GV734.5.R667 2008
    796.332'640973—dc22

                                                                                    2008019833

PRINTED IN THE UNITED STATES OF AMERICA

10 9 8 7 6 5 4 3 2 1

From Drew:

I am dedicating this book to my parents, Jill and Robert, and my brother Jason. My mother has given me the greatest gift—love. She is the most loving and caring person in the world. She has made sure that I have a great life. My father is the kindest and most decent man on the planet. He has a great heart. Jason is my best friend. He has been there with me every step of the way. I rely on him for so much and could not have accomplished any of this without him. He is unselfish and supportive. It is a true blessing to have my parents and brother in my life.

From Jason:

For my sweet little Aubrey. As a young agent working with Uncle Drew I learned the saying: "That which does not kill you makes you stronger." As a young husband and father, I have learned from you and your mother, Casie: "So does that which loves you."

CONTENTS

CHAPTER 1

NEXT QUESTION

"DREW, WHAT HAVE YOU DONE FOR T.O. OTHER THAN GET him kicked off the team?"

That's what the reporter rhetorically asked me on Tuesday afternoon, November 8, 2005, in front of my client Terrell Owens. Terrell had just been kicked off the Philadelphia Eagles team for the remaining nine weeks of the 2005 season, costing him $1,720,588. He hired me several months earlier to either get him a new contract or get him traded. Instead, Terrell was punished by his team more harshly than any other player in the history of the NFL.

And now, on a nationally televised press conference, the likes of which the NFL had never seen before, the reporter asked me the most offensive and embarrassing question possible. It was so obnoxious that even Terrell had to laugh.

Put yourself in my shoes for a moment and be a sports agent in the middle of this nightmare. Completely unprecedented, this was the biggest story of the season. The entire sports world had been watching the T.O. saga and it turned into total disaster. After the Eagles announced the suspension, Terrell and I agreed to respond by holding a press conference on his front lawn. We held it there because the media was already camped out by his house, waiting to pounce on us.

I could have done what every other agent would have done—run and hidden—not wanting to be associated with a disastrous situation, but I'm no coward. I was walking into the lion's den and knew it. There was a great deal of public anger, frustration, and disappointment over the way things worked out. Fans and the media pointed the finger at me and came after me, calling for me to be fired.

As I stepped up to the microphones, I reflected on what I could have done differently and thought back to the beginning.

It had all started back on a Saturday, the first weekend in April 2005. My client Willis McGahee was participating in a celebrity ESPN bowling event in South Florida. Always making the effort to be on the job for my clients, I went with him to the event. My brother Jason and our partner Robert Bailey, who handles the marketing for our clients, were there with me.

It turned out that Willis wasn't the only NFL player there; Terrell Owens was also doing some bowling. After Terrell was done bowling, a friend of his came over and said Terrell wanted to talk to me. It seemed Terrell's friend was very familiar with me and Willis McGahee. He told me that Terrell was not happy with his agent and his contract situation with the Eagles. He wanted me to address those issues with Terrell and at Terrell's request, I was more than happy to do so.

Once Terrell initiated the communication regarding his contract, I went to work. Jason was Johnny-on-the-spot with compelling information. The same year Terrell signed his contract with the Eagles, we also negotiated a contract with them for Pro Bowl defensive end Jevon Kearse. Jevon's contract was very impressive. It was an eight-year deal worth $62.6 million. The first year, Jevon would earn $16.535 million. The second year he would earn $3.015 million. The third year he would earn $4.2 million and the fourth year $6.325 million.

To compare Jevon and Terrell's contracts—both signed in March 2004—after the first year Jevon's earnings would total $16.535 million versus Terrell's $9.16 million. The second-year earnings would total $19.5 million for Jevon and $12.41 million for Terrell. The third-year earnings would total $23.75 million for Jevon and $20.68 million for Terrell. The fourth-year earnings for Jevon would total $29.075 million and $26.18 million for Terrell.

So over the first two years, Jevon's contract compensated him close to $20 million versus Terrell's $12 million and Jevon's guaranteed money was $12 million compared to Terrell's $2 million. Terrell was coming off of a Pro Bowl year, several of them in fact.

Don't get me wrong, the Eagles did not overpay for Jevon. There were other teams willing to compensate him with a similar contract. Jevon did a fair-market-value deal. The point was that Terrell did not get a fair-market-value deal.

Terrell did not have a fair-market-value deal because his former agent failed to get him on the 2004 free-agent market.

There was a big scandal around that 2004 negotiation, as Terrell's previous agent dropped the ball—big-time. Terrell was originally scheduled to become a free agent in early March 2004 and be able to control his own destiny. As a free agent, he could field offers from other teams and choose the highest bidder. However, his contract required that he send in notice to his team (the San Francisco 49ers) by a certain date, voiding out the remaining years of his contract.

Unfortunately, the date necessary to send in the notice was changed by the NFL and the NFL Players Association (NFLPA), but Terrell's agent did not send in the notice in accordance with the change. He missed the deadline. The NFLPA insisted that they notified Terrell's agent of the date change but the agent denied it. The end result was that Terrell was still under contract at the start of free agency. Consequently, the 49ers traded Terrell under his still-existing contract to the Baltimore Ravens. Terrell had three years remaining on his contract and would be paid a $5.3 million salary in 2004. Terrell was outraged because he wanted to be a free agent and make twice that amount. Terrell also wanted to choose the team he would play for and he wanted to play for the Eagles with Pro Bowl quarterback Donovan McNabb. He did not want to play for the Ravens because the Ravens had quarterback problems. Terrell wanted to play for the Eagles and receive a new contract with a big up-front bonus.

To defend Terrell, the NFLPA filed a grievance against the team in the effort to make Terrell a free agent even though he missed the beginning of the free-agency period. The problem with missing the beginning of the process is that teams with money to spend do it quickly, and after the first week or so, all the money is spent.

Once the hearing got under way, it seemed the NFLPA was going to win the case for Terrell. To avoid losing Terrell without any compensation, the 49ers agreed to trade him to the Eagles and the Eagles gave him a new contract that would make him $9,160,000 that first year.

The problem with Terrell's deal is that he would have gotten much more in the first two years of the deal if he had been a free agent at the start of March like Jevon Kearse was. I believe that if Terrell had been a free agent in 2004, there would have been a good chance of him landing a Jevon Kearse type of contract.

I had a very good relationship with the Eagles. Shortly after I concluded Jevon's negotiations with them, Joe Banner, the team's president, told the *Philadelphia Inquirer,* "We have a long history of dealing with Drew. He's intelligent. He knows what he's doing. He closes deals, and his players [often] re-sign with the same team."

After discussing all of this, Terrell said that he wanted to meet with me again after he talked to his agent. I sensed that Terrell felt betrayed by his original agent for a lot of reasons. Terrell was moving on and I happened to be in the right place at the right time. However, if I had decided not to work that day and visit with Willis, I would not have signed Terrell, which I did about a week afterward in April 2005.

To understand why Terrell was unhappy with his situation heading into the second year of his contract, you have to look back at his first year with the Eagles. The 2004 season was a remarkable year for Terrell as he helped the team get to the Super Bowl. Terrell and Donovan were a dynamic duo as they put up a lot of points together. Toward the end of the season, the Eagles were the hot team in the NFC, and Terrell suffered a severe ankle injury. It was the type of injury that takes players ten to twelve weeks to recover from. Although it seemed Terrell's season was over, he vowed to be ready in six weeks if the Eagles could make it to the Super Bowl. The Eagles had gone to the NFC Championship Game the past three years and lost. They'd brought Terrell in to get them into the Super Bowl, which he did. Once the Eagles got there, the question was would Terrell be ready to play. The medical experts said no, as no player had ever recovered from that type of injury in less than ten weeks. One thing about Terrell is that he is a very determined individual once he puts his mind to something. Terrell slept day and night in an oxygen chamber and did everything else the Eagles' training staff suggested he do. Before the game, Terrell's doctor refused to clear him to play, as the risk of injury was too great. If Terrell reinjured that ankle, he would never be the same and his career could be over. His doctor advised him not to play and warned him that if he played despite the doctor's objection, he would be jeopardizing his career.

Terrell promised everyone he would play and he delivered. When game time arrived, number 81 went out there and put together one of the greatest performances of his career. Although the Eagles didn't win, Terrell was a fan favorite for putting out a tremendous effort.

The problem was that after Terrell made over $9 million in his first year, he was scheduled to take a serious cut in pay at $3.25 million in 2005. Having risked it all, and because he felt he had outperformed the contract, Terrell believed he deserved to make more than the $3.25 million. And I agreed 100 percent. The bottom line was we wanted to bust the contract and get more money—that was the job I was hired to do.

The original plan was to quietly negotiate with the Eagles behind the scenes, but it didn't exactly happen like that. As soon as Terrell hired me, I went to meet with the Eagles to state our position. The Eagles told me that they could not redo Terrell's contract just one year into a seven-year deal. The Eagles explained they could not afford to set that precedent. We were at an impasse. I anticipated that would be the case but had confidence that somehow, someway, we would find a way to work it out. As I left the building, the media swarmed all over me. It didn't take Sherlock Holmes to realize that we wanted a new contract.

Here was perhaps the most popular player in the NFL, with the most well-known agent, at a standoff with the toughest front-office negotiators in the league. The media had a field day. Although I would not comment on the negotiations, that didn't stop the media from doing so.

On April 6, the *Philadelphia Daily News* reported:

Eagles president Joe Banner will meet today with Drew Rosenhaus, new agent for wide receiver Terrell Owens. There is an unmistakable hint of trouble brewing between the Eagles and the superstar. Banner said he isn't sure what to think about Owens' sudden ditching of agent David Joseph in favor of Rosenhaus. "I'm not going to get into the specifics at this time," said Rosenhaus. "Whenever I begin representing a player, I always like to sit down with a team and discuss my client's contractual situation." Asked what Owens didn't like about the deal, which is said to pay him about $13 million over the first 2 years and $8 million in the third year, Rosenhaus said, "That's really between me and the team."

At that point, I wanted the negotiations to stay behind closed doors. As far as we were concerned, Terrell was entering his tenth year that 2005 season and had survived a career-threatening situation. He had no job security whatsoever, as his contract was not guaranteed. Terrell originally signed in 2004 a seven-year $48.6 million contract. However, the contract was structured so that Terrell would get the second big bonus in the third year. That way, the Eagles would pay Terrell $3.25 million in the second year, and if things went well, they would pay him his third-year compensation amount of $8.27 million. But if Terrell got hurt that second year, they would not have to pay him the third year and they would basically get Terrell for cheap that second year.

Publicly, there was a mixed reaction to the situation. It was the hot story at the time and everybody had an opinion. Do you blame Terrell, a veteran of ten years, for wanting to get one last big bonus before being too old or injured to command another big-money deal? Didn't he deserve to make more than the $3.25 million that second year since his two-year compensation did not put him among the top ten highest-paid receivers at his position? On the flip side, the Eagles just paid Terrell over $9 million to sign a seven-year contract. (Do you blame a team for refusing to set the precedent of a player being able to renegotiate his deal after only one season with six more years to go under contact?) Then again, Terrell had a great year for the Eagles, as the team had the kind of chemistry it takes to get to the Super Bowl. They came very close to doing it. Terrell gave a one-of-a-kind performance. Wasn't it worth it to make a special exception for a special player? There was merit to both sides.

The Eagles made it very clear to me behind closed doors that they would not renegotiate the deal. Nevertheless, I still felt that, as the midnight hour approached at the start of the season, the Eagles would be willing to compromise. My brother and partner Jason believed the key to getting something done was to keep everything as low-key as possible. I agreed and was optimistic.

Although neither Terrell nor I was talking, the media was all over the situation.

Tony Kornheiser, on his ESPN show *Pardon the Interruption*, said, "You don't hire Drew Rosenhaus to restructure... you hire Drew Rosenhaus to rip up and get more."

ESPN insider Sal Paolantonio is the media guru on the Philadelphia Eagles. After my meeting with the Eagles, Sal reported the following on April 12:

PHILADELPHIA—It has been five fun-filled days of sports talk in this town since Terrell Owens dumped his longtime agent and friend, David Joseph, and hired the intrepid Drew Rosenhaus, who showed up at the Eagles Novacare Complex last week as if he were Ashton Kutcher in the hit movie, "Guess Who."

And just like in the film, the first meeting was cordial but awkward, short but according to script.

The Eagles—it has been written and said over and over again—as a rule do not renegotiate contracts. Have a nice day, Mr. Rosenhaus.

But in this little drama that will certainly take months to unfold, everybody is missing one big, important point: Throughout his nine-year NFL career, one thing has been clear about the mercurial, flamboyant and quite fabulous football player named Terrell Owens.

T.O. does not make rules. He breaks them.

Consider the following:

When he wanted out of San Francisco, he appealed to the NFL's special master to annul a trade to Baltimore. Voila, T.O. was wearing Eagles green—just like he said he would.

When Owens showed up in Philadelphia, he didn't follow the unwritten rules of the Andy Reid way. No, Owens flaunted his style and name—from overshadowing Donovan McNabb in training camp, to mocking Ray Lewis, the Ravens' revered middle linebacker.

Not done, Owens defied Mother Nature—not to mention his own doctor. One of the planet's renowned surgeons repaired Owens' broken leg and sprained ankle and told No. 81 that it was not a good idea to push it to return for Super Bowl XXXIX.

So what did Owens do? He started the game and was the Eagles' leading receiver. Had the Eagles beaten the New England Patriots in Jacksonville, Owens might have been the MVP.

So, about that contract.

On Wednesday, Rosenhaus met with Eagles president Joe Banner. Owens' current contract, which runs through 2010 and which Owens signed last year, is worth about $6.9 million per year, about the third-highest average salary for a wide receiver (behind Marvin Harrison and Randy Moss). But, after making about $9 million last year, Owens is due about $3.5 million in 2005.

And in 2006, when Owens will be turning 33, he will be due bonuses totaling about $7.5 million. No one believes the Eagles will fork over that money to a player that age...

After the meeting with Banner, Rosenhaus was unusually untalkative...

"I met with Joe," said Rosenhaus, who has a great working relationship with the Eagles. "It was positive. We'll meet again." That's all Rosenhaus said after the meeting, which apparently lasted less than 10 minutes.

Banner released a short statement: "I had a brief meeting this afternoon with Drew Rosenhaus, who now represents Terrell Owens. We discussed his new representation of Terrell, as he does often with teams of new clients. We are not prepared, at this time, to discuss any other details of the conversation."

Typical Banner. Just ask the agents for Jeremiah Trotter and Duce Staley, or Bobby Taylor or Troy Vincent or Ike Reese. All were extraordinarily productive and wildly popular, but once they reached 30, they had to get their money elsewhere (Trotter may be back in Philly, but Banner never gave in).

Sal summed it up best when he wrote, "And in 2006, when Owens will be turning 33, he will be due bonuses totaling about $7.5 million. *No one believes the Eagles will fork over that money to a player that age...*"

Having realized how quickly his career could end, and after coming off one of the best seasons of his career with a team he helped get to the Super Bowl, Terrell became convinced that he deserved a new deal and was determined to fight for it. He knew that there was a good chance, as Sal suggested, that the Eagles would use Terrell up in 2005 for $3.25 million, and when it was time to pay him the big bonus in his third year, the Eagles would likely release him. If Terrell got hurt his second year, he would never see the big money. As a matter of principle, Terrell wanted the new deal and felt he was right to fight for it, as did I. But when the Eagles let it be known that they were not going to give him the new deal, he was understandably upset.

When the start of the voluntary off-season program began, without any show of good faith by the team, Terrell and I saw no reason for him to risk injury and participate. The media and fans criticized Terrell, questioning his conditioning, his work ethic, his performance, and his desire to play the game. Insulted, Terrell responded on April 12 in a conversation with ESPN reporter Len Pasquarelli:

As always, there is a lot being written and [reported] without anyone talking to me. I mean, I can't do right and I can't do wrong. It's getting, in some ways, like it was for me in San Francisco.

But the one thing that won't change is that I'm going to show up to play and to win. No one can ever [debate] that...

No one can ever accuse me of not being in great shape. Andy [Reid] knows that. My teammates know that, when I show up, I'm ready to go. The biggest concern should be winning a Super Bowl. That's what I show up to do. I've never been out of shape. I mean, this is my [livelihood]...

[Regarding the Super Bowl] I was trying to inspire myself. I wanted to prove to myself that I could do it. But why did I want to do it? To win a Super Bowl for the team, for the fans, for the city. I did everything they asked me to do. I played every snap they allowed me to play. I wasn't even running until, like, two weeks before the game. But I made sure I was in the best shape possible. I wasn't the guy who got tired in the Super Bowl.

The media and fans reacted as if Terrell personally insulted Donovan. Because Donovan was televised vomiting at the end of the game, everyone assumed Terrell was taking a shot at his quarterback. Terrell told me that he never mentioned Donovan's name because he did not intend to talk about Donovan or insult him. One thing Terrell has never done is lie. His biggest fault is his honesty. He is always going to speak his mind and can't be a politician about things. He didn't know how to compromise and be politically correct. For doing nothing more than speaking his mind, Terrell has paid a huge price. If Terrell says he did not mean to insult Donovan, then that is the truth. But the fans and media didn't see it that way and neither did Donovan.

The truth of the matter is nobody knew that Terrell and Donovan were no longer the best of friends. A rift had developed between them, as Terrell felt Donovan had stabbed him in the back. The two biggest egos on the team were headed for a collision course that would destroy the team.

Almost overnight, Terrell went from being a Philadelphia favorite to one of the most vilified. I was pretty high on that list as well. The situation had spiraled out of control between April and August, at the start of training camp, as there was one controversy after another. Terrell and Donovan gave some quotes to the media that further escalated the situation.

At that point, Terrell and I publicly stated our position and the Eagles stated theirs. Both sides had dug in and neither was going to compromise.

As training camp approached at the start of August, the big question was whether Terrell would report or hold out. It was very hard for him to report. He was very emotional about it. If he reported, then the Eagles would have little incentive to give him a new contract. If he showed up, why would they pay him more than they were contractually obligated to pay?

The other option was to hold out. We knew that if the team was going to have any success in 2005, they needed Terrell. We also knew that if Terrell held out, they would need to make an example out of him and fine him thousands of dollars for every day he missed. Despite all my efforts to persuade Terrell to report, he still struggled with the decision, but in the end decided to report.

When we arrived at camp, I arranged for a meeting between Terrell, Eagles President Joe Banner, Coach Andy Reid, and myself. I hoped that we could reach some kind of positive understanding that if Terrell got off to a good start or had a productive season, they would consider renegotiating the contract to provide him with some kind of guarantee or long-term security. The Eagles would not agree to any of this, so Terrell became infuriated and walked out of the meeting. Things were just going from bad to worse. Nevertheless, Terrell did not say one word to the media and went about his business.

The media was all over Terrell, so in order to shield him from as much heat as I could, I made the following statement to the members of the press:

All the talk, all the rhetoric in the off season is meaningless...He's here. He's not happy with his contract, but he's a professional and he'll do his best to help the Eagles win a championship... Terrell is here to play football, he's very serious and businesslike... Let me and the Eagles handle his concerns over his contract... We're not here to negotiate in bad faith or threaten to walk out... This isn't about leverage.

After a couple days of practice, Terrell's groin became inflamed. Some members of the media had the nerve to accuse him of faking it, as if he were trying to withhold his services in order to pressure the Eagles into giving him a new contract. You can imagine how upset Terrell was to have to listen to this at the same time as he was getting injections in his groin to ease the inflammation and help him return to training camp.

Coach Reid, who at that point was not on the best of terms with Terrell, had no reason to defend him, but he's a stand-up guy. He straightened the media out by saying: "It's a legitimate injury. This guy would never do that. He's not that type of guy. He would never go in that direction... I'm being cautious with it. I don't want it to get worse. It's a constant battle."

Although Terrell felt physically better over the next week, his relationship with his coaches did not improve. He and his offensive coordinator (currently the head coach of the Minnesota Vikings), Brad Childress, were not getting along. Terrell felt the coach was antagonizing him on purpose by saying "Hi, Terrell" despite the fact that Terrell did not respond to him. Eventually Terrell told the coach to stop talking to him.

This did not go over well with Coach Reid. It wasn't long before Coach Reid and Terrell got into it. On Wednesday August 10, after a practice, Terrell was directed by the trainer to go get some rehab on his groin. However, it was Terrell's turn to sign autographs for the fans. Coach Reid has a rotating system in which certain players sign autographs for the fans at practice on certain days. Although it was Terrell's turn, he wanted to go straight to rehab after the practice. The first preseason game was coming up and he wanted to do everything possible to get ready. He wanted to get working on his rehab immediately.

Coach Reid wanted Terrell to sign the autographs first and then go. Terrell's problem was that he didn't want to sign for just a few minutes and then leave the other kids disappointed. Had he gone over to the fans, he would have to stay there for an hour, which would have been counterproductive for his rehab.

From Coach Reid's perspective, it was Terrell's turn and he expected Terrell to sign like everybody else. When Coach Reid told Terrell to sign autographs, Terrell told him he wanted to go straight to rehab. One thing led to another and Coach Reid told Terrell to shut up. Terrell got offended and told him to shut up. Coach Reid walked away, sending Terrell home for the day.

After taking a shower and doing his rehab, Terrell drove home. Coach Reid said after practice to the media, "I did send him home. He's expected to return next Wednesday. It's in-house business and it's going to stay in-house. I'll work it out with T.O. I'm not going to sit here and turn it into a bash session."

By the time Terrell pulled into his driveway, the fans and the media were all over his front lawn. Jason and I flew in immediately. As we drove up, Terrell was shooting hoops with fans and media all around him. Next Terrell was doing biceps curls with the fans counting each repetition. Then Terrell started doing crunches with the camera focused on his abs while the news-station helicopters flew overhead. It was an absolute circus.

At that point, the Eagles were not going to do a new deal no matter what. They had drawn a line in the sand and that was that. But perhaps they would be willing to trade Terrell to another team that would give Terrell a new contract. By demonstrating how irreconcilable the differences were between the two sides, we hoped that maybe the Eagles would agree to trade Terrell away.

So we decided to state our case on TV. Terrell and I went on *Pardon the Interruption* with Michael Wilbon and Bob Ryan. We also went on the halftime show live with Chris Berman during ESPN's Thursday-night NFL preseason football game between Green Bay and San Diego on August 11.

Terrell said to Wilbon and Ryan, "My attitude is not going to change. I came into training camp [and] was working toward being diligent and honoring my contract. I did that. As far as me going in and changing, nothing's going to change. I will not go out and try to be somebody I'm not."

When they asked Terrell about his argument with Coach Reid, he responded, "In the midst of that he told me to shut up. I just told him, I'm a grown man, and I told him the same, I told him to shut up.

That was it. Everybody knows he's a controlling guy. He wants to be the main guy."

When they brought up McNabb, Terrell answered, "Everybody's calling me a hypocrite, [but] he's the same hypocrite. It was reported that he doesn't want to talk to me privately right now. Then I get to my dorm room, and he has his brother call a friend of mine to talk to me on the side. I have no desire to talk to Donovan."

When they asked Terrell whether Donovan and he could play together, he said, "I don't think so. I'm just being honest."

I suggested on TV that a solution could still be reached either through a trade or through negotiations. I tried to keep the door open. The media responded by saying that the Eagles had no choice but to trade Terrell or else the team would implode. But almost immediately, the team responded by telling the media that there would be no trade. They were determined not to let Terrell have his way.

The situation was impossible. No options were left on the table to broker a trade or a new contract. There was nothing left but a lot of bad will all the way around.

The next day, August 12, 2005, Mike Florio of ProFootballTalk. com wrote:

> The problem at this point is there's no exit strategy for Owens that allows him to get back onto the field while at the same time feeling like he's received fair consideration. Stuck in his mind is the belief that he's underpaid, and his fear that the Eagles wouldn't pick up his $7.5 million option and roster boni after his current contractual year is satisfied has created a set of circumstances in which the team *never* will pay the money.

And the thing that Owens doesn't realize is that no one else will, either.

The media was now saying that no team, not just the Eagles, would ever pay Terrell the kind of money he was scheduled to make, let alone the new contract he wanted.

After all that, Terrell, Jason, and I knew that there was only one course of action left—for Terrell to have an excellent season on and off the field. There was still a way to come out on top. We could still win this battle. After all the ill will, we knew the Eagles would not pay Terrell the big money the following season and he would be a free agent then. The problem was that Terrell would have to take the risk of playing the whole 2005 season without getting seriously hurt. Jason and I were confident that if he put together an outstanding performance on the field and just kept to himself, we had a good shot at getting him released by the Eagles and getting an improved contract. Those were some big ifs, though.

The first four games went great. Terrell put up big numbers, catching thirty-two passes for 506 yards and four touchdowns, and helped the team get off to a 3–1 start. From there, things started to get a little rocky.

The Eagles lost the next game to the Dallas Cowboys. Terrell, paying tribute to his friend Michael Irvin, who, as an ESPN commentator, had been the only high-profile member of the media who took up for Terrell, wore Michael's throwback Cowboy jersey to and from the game. Looking to stir it up after a loss, the media tried to make a big deal out of it. Coach Reid responded by actually defending him, saying, "He's a big Michael Irvin fan. On the way home, I give these guys an opportunity to wear comfortable clothes. I have done that since I have been here, and he's very close with Michael. I don't think it's that big of a deal."

There was a bye week and the next game was against the San Diego Chargers at Philadelphia. I decided to go up for that game along with Terrell's publicist at the time, Kim Etheredge, as this was going to be the game in which Terrell caught his hundredth career touchdown pass. That is a Hall of Fame–caliber achievement, as only five other players in the history of the NFL have accomplished such a feat. When Terrell scored, he celebrated by taking out his towel, folding it over his left arm as if he were a waiter, and lifting the football up in his right hand as if he were carrying a dish.

At that point in the season, Terrell had shown a lot of maturity by burying the hatchet and being a productive player on the team. He had conversed with Donovan and his coaches. He even celebrated with Donovan after scoring one touchdown. Things were going in the right direction. After his hundredth touchdown, Terrell rightfully expected some kind of announcement or congratulatory acknowledgment by the team. Why not build on the positive momentum by doing something to credit Terrell? When this failed to materialize, it was a slap in the face and a shot to the gut. Terrell felt like the team hit him a low blow. The team went on to win the game, but it was a bitter victory.

At 5–2, the Eagles were still doing well but had a tough road game against the Broncos coming up. Although the team lost, Terrell turned in a spectacular performance by catching a short pass at the line of scrimmage and faking out Pro Bowl cornerback Champ Bailey and running for a ninety-one-yard touchdown. That would be the last touchdown Terrell would ever score for the Eagles.

On the plane ride home—one week after Coach Reid had

reminded the guys about dressing professionally and wearing suits after the games instead of jeans—Terrell wore a tuxedo with sneakers. It was pretty funny stuff, even the coaches thought so.

After the game, the ankle Terrell had injured the year before swelled up. He got treatment day and night on it, trying to get ready for the next game. When asked about the injury, Coach Reid said, "He is hurting…He is sore. It's going to be a fight to get him there for Sunday. We're taking it day by day. He's made progress the last couple of days."

Terrell worked with Eagles trainer Rick Burkholder (who is among the best in the business) day and night. Nevertheless, the media and some fans unfairly and inaccurately speculated that he was faking the injury. For some reason, after listening on the morning radio show to people accusing Terrell of faking it, Hugh Douglas believed the rumor to be true. To be fair, Hugh is a former client of mine and I think he's a great guy, but in this case, his emotions got the best of him. Hugh used to play for the Eagles, and when his age caught up to him, Coach Reid, who loves Hugh, hired him to work for the team as an ambassador to the players.

Hugh walked into the training room screaming and yelling about there being fakers on the team. He seemed to be looking for a fight. Being called a faker is one of the worst things you can accuse a player of. Those are fighting words, and Terrell had to stand up for himself if he was going to retain any respect in that team locker room. That's just the way it is.

Although Hugh, a former defensive lineman, was much bigger than him, Terrell got out of the whirlpool, put his slippers on, and confronted Hugh.

Hugh was all hyped up and so was Terrell. One thing led to

another and Hugh took a swing at Terrell. Terrell ducked under the punch and the two locked up. Terrell was verbally assaulted and physically attacked by a member of the Eagles' management. Hugh was wrong and he knew it.

When it was over, Terrell finished his rehab and practiced as best as he could that afternoon. There was no apology or even concerned conversation from the coaching staff or management about what had happened. Despite being very upset, Terrell didn't say a word to the media or complain to anyone, not even me.

When Terrell got home, he was understandably irritated and not in the best of moods. A few weeks earlier, he agreed to let a kid he knew back from his days with the 49ers interview him. The kid's name was Graham Bensinger, and he was a freshman at Syracuse University. Graham contacted Terrell directly and did not go through me, Terrell's publicist Kim, or our marketing president, Robert Bailey. To help him out, Terrell agreed to give him an exclusive for ESPN .com. Terrell should have canceled on him under the circumstances, but he didn't have the heart to take away the kid's big break. Disaster ensued.

Graham interviewed Terrell for fifty-seven minutes with an ESPN camera crew there to film it. It was just supposed to be in print for ESPN.com, but the kid, who was anything but naive, tried to manipulate and exploit the situation to make a name for himself.

For the most part, Terrell was very positive toward the team. But Graham needled and needled him. Unfortunately, in an interview, you can say nine positive things and one negative thing, and it will be that one negative thing that stands out. Well, after Terrell had been positive in his answers, Graham hit him with a follow-up, and he couldn't help but speak his mind. Maybe it was because he was in a bad mood after the fight with Hugh or maybe it was the frustration over not getting any recognition from the team after scoring his hundredth touchdown, but Terrell got it off his chest.

After asking Terrell how much it meant to him to score the touchdown, Graham asked: "Obviously, it's not necessary, but everybody likes to be complimented, everyone likes to be congratulated for accomplishing something. And you did something that only five [other] players in the history of the NFL have done. So, how surprised were you then when the Eagles just made no public acknowledgment of it?"

Terrell responded:

Probably just like the statement that I said a while ago: If you align expectations with reality, you will never be disappointed. You know, their reaction shows you the type of class and integrity of an organization that they claim not to be. You know, they claim to be first class and the best organization. I just felt like it was an embarrassment. It just shows the lack of class that they had. My publicist talked to the head PR guy, and he made an excuse about [how] they didn't recognize it, or they didn't realize that it was coming up. But I know that was a blatant lie. If it would have been somebody else, they probably would have popped fireworks around the stadium...

Right or wrong, Terrell told what he saw as the truth of the matter.

Graham asked: "Your friend Michael Irvin recently said that if Brett Favre was the starting quarterback for the Philadelphia Eagles, they'd be undefeated right now. What do you think of that comment?"

Terrell answered: "That's a good assessment, I would agree with that."

"How so?" Graham asked.

Terrell answered: "I just feel like just what he brings to the table . . . I mean he's the guy. Obviously, a number of commentators will say he's a warrior. He has played with injuries. I just feel like [with] him being knowledgeable about the quarterback position, I just feel like we'd be in a better situation."

What happened here is that over a period of twenty-four hours, Terrell was wrongfully accused of faking an injury, got into a fistfight with a former player who took a swing at him, and then a few hours later did an interview where he was goaded into agreeing with an ESPN commentator's opinion that the Eagles would be better off with legendary Green Bay Packer quarterback Brett Favre than with their own quarterback. Considering that Brett Favre is considered a future Hall of Famer and one of the best quarterbacks to ever play the game, just about everyone would share that opinion. Nevertheless, that remark was the straw that broke the camel's back. Terrell had no idea that the interview would be a big deal. Again, this was supposed to be a small-time interview with a freshman from Syracuse University.

The next morning, as Terrell drove to the facility, he had no idea that the interview had created such a fervor. The town was in an uproar and the Eagles organization was put in a very bad position as the public perceived the interview as another verbal jab at Donovan and the team. Coach Andy Reid called Terrell into his office and demanded that he make a public apology on national TV. I spoke with Coach Reid and told him that I would draft an apology for Terrell. I worked with Kim Etheredge to put it together. When Terrell reviewed it, he

wasn't comfortable with the apology to Donovan and crossed it out.
Terrell read the following apology on TV:

> I've had an opportunity to talk with the Eagles organization
> and I have learned that the team does not recognize individual
> achievements. It has been brought to my attention that I have
> offended the organization and my teammates. Therefore, I would
> like to apologize for any derogatory comments toward them.

There was obviously no mention of the quarterback. The media
called the apology insincere.

Coach Reid called Terrell back into his office and told him that
if he did not personally apologize to Donovan, the coach would have
no choice but to send him home for the weekend and miss the game.
He gave Terrell the choice of missing the game against the Redskins
or apologizing.

Terrell called me and we talked it over. I did everything I could
to persuade him to make the apology, but I knew he wouldn't. It was
a matter of principle to him, and he felt he had already apologized.
Terrell is an extremely proud person, which fuels his passion to be the
Pro Bowl player that he is, but that pride also comes at a price. He just
couldn't bring himself to apologize to McNabb.

Trying to salvage the situation, I called Coach Reid and pleaded
with him to give Terrell some time to cool off and let him reach out
to Donovan in his own way. But Coach Reid and the organization
were out of patience and he told me that if Terrell didn't apologize he
would sit him down for the Redskin game. There was nothing more I
could do. Terrell was sent home for the weekend.

Our plan had been for Terrell to have a Pro Bowl year, and once the Eagles released him the following March rather than pay him the big bonus, he would be a free agent and get a blockbuster deal. Now that he'd been suspended for one game, this looked a lot harder to accomplish.

It turned out that although the Eagles lost the game to the Redskins, Donovan still made the following remark afterwards:

Obviously it is tough losing a guy of his caliber, his ability, but *I think we might be better off.* I think what we did tonight, we showed that we played well together. I think we also showed that when given the opportunity, guys can make plays for us. We're 4–4. We're not 1–7. I think that is the way to look at it. For the guys in the locker room, we win together and we lose together... It was unfortunate that we didn't win this game, but I think it may be a stepping stone for us to move forward. [italics added]

When I saw Donovan's comment, I realized there was a possibility that the Eagles could decide to suspend Terrell for the four games and not just for that weekend. I didn't think they would do it, though, because it would be suicidal for the team. With Terrell, they were still winning; without him, they had no chance. Everyone else pretty much thought the same thing and assumed Terrell would be back. Everyone but the Eagles...

The media jumped all over Donovan's comments and put a lot of pressure on the team to suspend Terrell for the rest of the season. I called Coach Reid and pleaded with him not to suspend him. As for Terrell, he had no idea that he would be missing more than that one game. He was hurt anyway, and probably couldn't play, so missing that game was not the end of the world. If Terrell had been given any indication that he was risking suspension for the rest of the season, he would have found a way to square things with Donovan. Neither he nor I ever saw it coming.

And on Monday morning, November 7, Coach Reid called a press conference to announce that Terrell was officially suspended for four games without pay and would be placed on the inactive list for the rest of the season.

Coach Reid stated that he was suspended because of a "large number of situations that accumulated over a period of time" and that he "had been warned repeatedly about the consequences of [his] actions."

Coach Reid added, "We gave Terrell every opportunity to avoid this outcome…The league has been notified by the players' union that they will be grieving our right to take that action. Therefore, there is nothing more that I can say at this point."

We and the rest of the NFL world were shocked. The Eagles had decided to send Terrell home for the rest of the season. Terrell was devastated. He wanted to play football and win with that team. From the start of the regular season, he'd done his best to be a good football player for the Eagles. And now it was all over with eight games to go in the 2005 season. He was crushed.

Terrell turned to me to take action. How were we going to get a big contract now? We had had a chance to beat Terrell's contract with the Eagles if he finished with a tremendously productive season, but now that he was out for the year, this seemed almost impossible. I called Coach Reid to see if there was any way to work this out and he told me there was nothing we could do.

As my competitors reveled in this disaster for me and Terrell, I had to do something. The plan was to make another apology, one that would placate everyone and persuade the Eagles to take Terrell back. If that didn't work, and we knew it was a long shot, we would file an appeal with the NFLPA to overturn the suspension. I talked with the NFLPA and they told me that we had an outstanding chance of success with the appeal. But first we had to face the media and make the apology.

Jason worked with Terrell on the apology. He also knew that the media would obviously come after me and suggested answering "next question" to any inappropriate remarks.

The worst thing about it was that it looked like I had failed my client. It looked like Terrell's career was in jeopardy and he could lose millions of dollars. All over the Internet, there were demands that I be fired, sued, and lose all my clients. My competitors all felt this situation would put me out of business.

Mike Florio of ProFootballTalk.com, on November 7, 2005, wrote:

The bottom line for Owens is that his conduct could end up costing him $2,489,705 in past bonus money and 2005 salary. In order to merely break even as to where he would have been if the team had exercised its March 2006 option, Owens needs to pocket $9,989,705 on his next contract.

And we'll bet $9,989,705 that it won't happen...

Current speculation in league circles is that the Broncos will offer him a one-year, short-fuse, incentive-laden deal once he's on the market.

Instead of Terrell making $8.3 million in 2005, it looked like he was going to be making the minimum. We were in a nightmare.

I was the guy that everyone pointed the finger at. And as horrible as the situation was, I could have hidden and sent Terrell out there on his own, but above all else, I stand behind my clients. Above all else, I am accountable. If my clients know one thing about me, it's that they can always count on me to be there for them, fighting in the trenches until the end. Say or think what you will about me, but you don't see other agents stand by their clients when they get into an unpopular mess, do you?

When Terrell and I walked outside his front door, the media and angered fans were all over the place. It felt like we were surrounded by an angry mob. There were cameras everywhere and you could feel the contempt in the air. Terrell stepped up and read a sincere apology to the Eagles, to Donovan, and to the fans. It was humble and heartfelt. There was nothing to criticize. After he finished his statement, it was my turn.

I didn't read a statement, I took on the media's questions. It was really a gut check, as we were in a brutal position. It's one thing to do a national press conference when you've just negotiated a huge contract for your client; it's another thing when your client has just gotten suspended and stands to lose millions.

In front of a frenzied national media, I fielded tough questions, one after another. There I stood, knowing that the Eagles were going to fine Terrell $1,720,588 for the nine weeks lost plus try to recover more. There I stood knowing that the Eagles were not going to pay Terrell the $8 million the following season. There I stood having to face the uncertainty of what would happen. The media was already arguing that Terrell would be lucky to get the minimum salary next season, saying no team would touch him for big money. There I stood knowing my competitors and detractors were loving every minute of this ordeal and were convinced it would put me out of the business. They were convinced I would lose not only Terrell but all my other clients. There I stood as the media, analysts, experts, my competitors, and the majority of the fans out there charged me with ruining my client's career. There I stood facing that adversity and it was all being broadcast live on national TV.

There I stood, knowing that my family, my clients, the NFL world, and all the college players would be watching when that one reporter tried to humiliate me, shouting: "Drew, what have you done for T.O. other than get him kicked off the team?"

It was a slap in my face. I could have gotten angry and lost my composure. I could have reacted a hundred different negative ways. And yet my response was without hesitation.

"Next question!"

"Next question" was more than my answer, it is my philosophy. Since 1988, Jason and I have enjoyed tremendous victories and suffered devastating losses. We have started from the absolute bottom and fought our way to the top in one of the toughest, most competitive businesses by adhering to a code of principles that we live and die by.

"Next Question" is rule number one. It means that no matter what, no matter how impossible the situation appears, always believe that with hard work and smart work, you will find a way to succeed. The principle is to have the unyielding confidence in yourself and the strength of heart to move forward by asking yourself, "What do I do next in order to win?" You've got to have the toughness not to panic, not to fear the consequences, and not to feel sorry for yourself. What "Next Question" comes down to is believing in yourself, and believing that by continuing to fight, you will eventually see your opportunity and then seize it.

On that day, during one of my darkest hours, with question after tough question coming at me, I fought back, repeatedly answering, "Next question." I was adhering to the "Next Question" principle, not ducking a question—I was doing the exact opposite.

This book is about what Jason and I have learned the hard way through battle after battle. I am going to share with you in detail where we went wrong, how we overcame our mistakes, and how we were able to learn from them to come out on top. I will take you back to the days of my youth when I took on legendary coaches like Don Shula and Jimmy Johnson all the way through to my recent dealings with Cowboys owner Jerry Jones and NFL executive Bill Parcells. Over the last twenty years, I have fought so many wars against other agents and had unbelievable adventures with the greatest personalities in the NFL. In the coming chapters I will go over with you the principles that have rewarded me when I applied them and punished me when I discarded them. If you have the discipline and determination to apply them, they will serve you well.

CHAPTER 2

NEXT QUESTION PART II

TO RECAP, MY CLIENT HAD JUST BEEN SUSPENDED WITHOUT pay for four games and was being deactivated for the remaining five weeks. Overall, Terrell stood to lose a total of $2,489,705. The suspension without pay would cause him to lose checks for four games, amounting to $764,705, and the Eagles would be able to recover an additional $1.725 million. The Eagles could get back $1.725 million because the suspension would trigger a clause in Terrell's contract forcing him to pay back $1.725 million of his original signing bonus in 2004. Although the Eagles said they would pay Terrell for the remaining five weeks after the suspension, they withheld his checks for the remaining five games as payment toward the $1.725 million. The total of the five checks they withheld was $955,882. (Note: In January of 2008, the Eagles got a judgment for the remaining $769,118 balance of the $1.725 million.) The bottom line is that the Eagles would be able to keep a total of $1,720,588 worth of Terrell's paychecks, plus collect an additional $769,118, bringing the total amount to $2,489,705—unless we reversed the suspension on our appeal at the arbitration. Adhering to the philosophy of "Next Question"—that is, focusing on what you should do next to win—I told Terrell that we would fight back through the appeal. I told him we still had a chance to get him back on the field and make things right.

Everything was at stake for Terrell in the appeal. If we won the appeal, then the fine would be reduced and the Eagles would not be able to claim Terrell triggered the clause in his contract allowing them to go after $1.725 million of his 2004 bonus. More important to Terrell, if we won the appeal, the suspension would be reversed and the Eagles would be forced to either take him back or release him.

At that point, after having the weekend to remove himself from the situation and calm down, he wanted more than anything to get back on the field. He woke up that Monday morning having no idea the Eagles would kick him off the team. It pained him deeply not to be able to play, and when you add on the monetary loss of $2,489,705, plus the media's stinging criticism and the fans' animosity, he was in a world of hurt. But he showed an incredible amount of inner strength by staying strong and positive through it all.

It would have been real easy for Terrell to fire me and throw me under the bus as so many people publicly urged him to do. It would have been very convenient for him to make me the scapegoat; but Terrell showed a lot of character (and intelligence, if I might humbly add) by being loyal and staying with us.

In order to prevail, we needed to win that case and reverse the suspension. If we accomplished this and the Eagles took Terrell back, the plan was to make things right with the team so that Terrell could get back on track. If he could finish the season at a high level, perhaps we could land a good contract after the Eagles released him the following March.

If they were to release Terrell, he could catch on with a new team, play well, and put us in a position to get a new contract.

While in the midst of the storm, I looked to the horizon of winning that appeal. I told Terrell we would have our appeal ASAP and he wouldn't be home for long.

The first thing I did was get Terrell on the phone with the NFLPA legal department. They were all over this case, since for several months, despite our best efforts to walk the fine line and prevent this, we knew there was a strong possibility that we would have to fight it out in court (arbitration hearing technically). The NFLPA immediately set a date for the hearing—November 18–just ten days later. The idea was to get a hearing date and decision well before the four-week period of the suspension expired so we could reverse it and get back on the field.

I could not have been more pleased with the fact that the NFLPA had the ultimate law firm, with attorneys Jeffrey Kessler and David Feher heading the case.

The NFLPA was excited that arbitrator Richard Bloch was assigned to the hearing. He had a reputation as a fair arbitrator who ruled consistently in accordance with established labor-law rules and precedents. He was viewed as a guy who went by the book.

The next day, the Eagles sent me a letter stating the six reasons why Terrell had been suspended.

1. The ESPN.com interview with Graham Bensinger
2. Failure to apologize to the satisfaction of Coach Reid

3. Being late to a mandatory offensive team meeting

4. Failure to comply with the team rules regarding travel attire on every road trip despite numerous reminders from Coach Reid in team meetings

5. Parking in reserved, handicap, and coaches' spots that he was not permitted to park in

6. Being involved in a fight with an employee in the training room

Those were the reasons the Eagles were trying to discipline Terrell more harshly than any player in the history of the NFL. When you take into account that Terrell was fined more than any other player and look at those reasons again, I ask you this:

Did Terrell physically hurt another player, or get arrested for a DUI, or get busted for drug possession, or cheat with steroids, or assault or rape a woman? Did he commit vehicular manslaughter? Not one of the NFL players who got arrested or charged with the above violent offenses was fined a fraction of the money Terrell was fined or suspended for as long. Do any of the six offenses listed above compare to the crimes other players were convicted of? The NFL CBA (Collective Bargaining Agreement) and federal labor law required that all players be treated in the same fashion.

Whether you like Terrell or not, he was not getting a fair shake. Not to mention that there were rules in place and those rules were very clear. The NFL Players Association was adamant that the Eagles could not send Terrell home for the rest of the season because the CBA specifically states that a player cannot be disciplined for detrimental conduct for more than a maximum of four games. The Eagles were trying to suspend Terrell for four games and deactivating him the remaining five games. NFL case law had established that sending a player home and preventing him from playing, although with pay, was still a disciplinary measure. In fact, it was Arbitrator Bloch himself who helped in part to establish that precedent. For those reasons, it was an absolute slam dunk that we were going to get the suspension reversed. The only question was whether the suspension would be reduced from four games to two games or one.

Nevertheless, when Jason, Terrell, and I went to meet with the attorneys the night before the hearing, even though it was obvious we were going to reverse the suspension, Jason urged Terrell to try to work things out with Coach Reid and avoid the hearing altogether. Terrell agreed.

Terrell's teammate and Pro Bowl linebacker Jeremiah Trotter came over to visit with Terrell and told me that Coach Reid would take Terrell back if he talked to the coach and promised him he would make things right. Terrell called Coach Reid and they talked for a long time, late into the night. After listening to everything Terrell had to say, Coach Reid decided to play it out with the hearing. I had hoped he would allow us to forgo the aggravation of a hearing, but we had no choice.

The next morning, Jason and I went to the hearing with Terrell and our team of attorneys. As Arbitrator Bloch walked in, he was very cold toward Terrell, but when he saw Coach Reid he acted like he was meeting his boyhood idol or something. I suddenly got a bad feeling. Fortunately, as the hearing went on, everything went our way. NFLPA general counsel Richard Berthelsen and attorney Jeffrey Kessler were dominant.

They cross-examined Coach Reid for hours. Coach Reid was very impressive as he testified honestly, fairly, and accurately, and would not be manipulated into saying something he did not want to say. However, Kessler got him to admit that the reason Terrell was being sent home after the suspension was for conduct detrimental. When that happened, our team of attorneys knew they had the case won because the rules are clear that the most discipline a team can mete out is the four-game suspension; they could not discipline Terrell any further after that. The Eagles' legal team actually argued with a straight face that Terrell had not been sent home as a form of punishment since they were going to pay him (which they did not do).

Kessler and Berthelsen countered and crushed that argument by citing a previous case decision by Bloch that set the precedent according to which deactivating a player is considered a form of punishment. Kessler and his partner David Feher went through each of the six reasons why the Eagles suspended Terrell and made them each look minuscule.

The case law was overwhelming. An NFL player, Bill Romanowski, started a fight with a teammate, ripped his helmet off, punched the guy in the eye, broke his face, and ended the guy's career right on the spot. His punishment was a fraction of what the Eagles were trying to do to Terrell. When an NHL player attacked another player from behind with his hockey stick and broke the guy's neck, he wasn't punished as severely as Terrell. And when the Indiana Pacer players jumped into the stands and started attacking the fans, they weren't disciplined as severely as this. Considering that Terrell never punched anyone, considering that Terrell was the one who got punched at, this was ridiculous and every legal expert knew it. You might not like Terrell's defiant behavior, but this is still America and the rules should apply fairly to everyone regardless of race, religion, or personality.

That's why our attorneys could not have been happier or more confident as they concluded the thirteen-hour hearing. That's why the other legal counsel looked miserable and knew they were beaten.

The day Bloch's decision was due, a prominent reporter for *Newsday*, Bob Glauber, broke the story, writing that arbitrator Bloch had decided to reduce Terrell's suspension to one or two games and he would be immediately reinstated. ESPN's Sal Paolantonio, the Eagle insider, reported that if the suspension was reduced as expected, the Eagles were going to cut Terrell.

As Sal reported, the Eagles were all set to release Terrell, and although Terrell actually preferred to go back and play for Coach Reid and the Eagle fans, he wanted most of all to play football. I was desperate to see him get back on the field and reestablish his market value. I did not want to be facing a one-year deal for the minimum with incentives for Terrell. I knew that if he could finish strong for another team, we could resurrect his career.

And then in the afternoon, as we were waiting on the good news, I got a call from our attorney Jeff Kessler. He was hysterically upset and told me we lost on everything. He was enraged, Terrell was in shock, and I felt like I got kicked in the balls.

Terrell looked at me like, "What do we do now?" What was our next move? How do we get Terrell back on the field? How am I going to get him $10 million now? How could this happen? Wasn't there something we could do?

The decision was final. There was no further appeal. Terrell's 2005 season was over. We had no leverage. The Eagles and the rest of the NFL world were stunned and thrilled at the same time. It seemed that the NFL bad boys were finally being taught a lesson. The big deal looked impossible now.

Being an attorney, Jason looked carefully at Bloch's reasoning in the decision, and if what he read didn't make him physically ill, I think he would have laughed. The beginning of Bloch's decision stated:

For the reasons to be discussed, the findings are (1) the four-week suspension was for just cause and (2) there was no contract violation inherent in Club's determining that Owens should not return to the team. Resolution of this dispute requires recognition of *the highly unusual nature of this case,* the existing boundaries of applicable CBA language and, above all, *a clear understanding of the facts.* [italics added]

The key phrase here is the "highly unusual nature of this case." By writing that the decision was based on the "highly unusual nature of this case," Bloch was able to completely discard the rules of the CBA and case-law precedent. The gist of it was that the rules and rights guaranteed to all NFL players applied to everyone but Terrell because of the highly unusual nature of the case.

Throughout Bloch's decision, in which he reversed his previous precedent and all others by saying that deactivating Terrell and preventing him from being able to play was not punishment, he justified his reasoning by stating that the decision was tied to the unique, particular facts of the case. So in Terrell's case, the rules don't apply, but they still apply to everyone else.

No one saw that coming, not even the Eagles. Len Pasquarelli, in his column for ESPN.com, wrote:

"It was even better than we thought it might be," said one Philadelphia management official, trying hard not to gloat too much, Wednesday afternoon.

Truth be told, here's what the Eagles figured as their best-case scenario, as they assessed Bloch's options: The arbitrator would uphold the four-game suspension but order that the team permit Owens to report back to work after Sunday's game against Green Bay, the final week the franchise was allowed to sanction him under the parameters of the catch-all charge of "conduct detrimental to the team." And then, forced to have Owens back at the facility, lifting weights and on the practice field, the team would have to decide whether to keep him around as an expensive "scout team" player or simply release him.

The Eagles had no idea that they would win the case and the NFLPA was completely livid. NFLPA General Counsel Richard Berthelsen admitted he was "shocked," and said:

> I think the arbitrator chose to accept not only the Eagles' version of the evidence, but I think he went even further and pieced the evidence together in a way that it really didn't evolve...We are obviously very disappointed with Arbitrator Bloch's decision. His ruling...ignores the obligation a club has to either provide employment to a player or allow him to play somewhere else. We are confident that we put on a winning case at the hearing last Friday, and we still believe Terrell Owens had a right to a legitimate reinstatement.

Gene Upshaw angrily responded, saying, "One thing I can control is that he will no longer be an arbitrator in any more of our cases. Under the [collective bargaining agreement], either side has a right between Dec. 1 and Dec. 10 to dismiss an arbitrator, and we are going to dismiss this one."

Gene kept his word and Bloch never heard another NFL case after that. Would you believe that Bloch actually became a professional magician in Vegas? We sure as heck wanted to make him disappear!

Within hours of the decision, we got a fax saying that the Eagles were going to go after the signing bonus they paid Terrell by withholding the remaining paychecks left that season.

We were screwed and the whole world knew it. We had no other options. How were we going to come out on top now? Our Next Question motto was put to the ultimate test.

I knew we had to provide Terrell with something positive to look forward to. But what? Jason had the solution. What we did next was strike a deal to write a book about the whole story from Terrell's perspective. Jason and I thought it would be very therapeutic for Terrell to sit down and tell his side of the story. We also knew it would bring him a very lucrative endorsement deal, which he would need with the Eagles withholding all his remaining paychecks for the season.

So over the next couple of months, Jason and Terrell sat down and Terrell told his story. Jason coauthored the book, and by the time it hit the stores, Jason would be a *New York Times* best-selling author and Terrell would rake in some big bucks.

The book and two national commercials got Terrell through the remaining six weeks of the regular 2005 season, plus the playoffs and the Super Bowl. With the 2006 free-agent period approaching on March 3, 2006, Terrell was expecting me to get him a $10 million contract. Never mind that he'd been suspended for the second half of the season. Never mind that every expert in the world predicted he would get a one-year deal for less than $1 million plus incentives. Never mind that every single head coach and general manager around the league were scared of the controversy. They were afraid that if they went to their owner and told the owner to write a big check to Terrell and it all blew up, they would get fired. They didn't want to risk it. Never mind all of that, I had to answer to Terrell.

Terrell did his part to help me. From the moment he was suspended, he handled himself in a completely professional manner and wasn't involved in a single controversy. I needed to be able to point to the maturity of his handling of the suspension in order to persuade the teams that he had learned from this experience and would conduct himself in a professional manner with his new team. Terrell understood this.

As it turned out, the rest of the season was no party for the Eagles, either. The team were still in the mix at 4–3 when they sent Terrell home. After that, they went 2–7 as Donovan got hurt, and finished 6–10 overall. At the end of the 2005 season, everybody ended up losing—the team, Terrell, his teammates, the fans, the NFL, me... everyone except my competitors, who jumped all over this to criticize me. Other agents figured they finally had the goods on me to take me down.

Looking to minimize the collateral damage, the Eagles agreed to my request for permission to talk to other teams about working out a trade for Terrell. A trade would benefit the Eagles in two ways. First, they would get some kind of compensation for Terrell in the form of another player or a draft pick. Second, they would have some control over what team Terrell went to. This mattered because once the season was over, the team wanted Terrell to go away and disappear. They didn't want him to sign with a team in their NFC East Division and have to play against him twice a year.

So when I told the Eagles that the Broncos had an interest in trading for Terrell, they were more than willing to facilitate the process since the Broncos were in the AFC West. Although the Eagles could technically trade Terrell without his consent, they needed our involvement for two reasons. First, no team would trade for him unless he wanted to be there because they didn't want the headache of dealing with an unhappy player. Second, if the Eagles traded Terrell, they would also be trading his contract, and unless a team was willing to pay him the $8.27 million compensation he was scheduled to earn in 2006, the team would need him to renegotiate the deal. If Terrell refused to renegotiate, a trade would not happen. The bottom line is that we had control over a trade.

What we didn't have control over was getting a team to fork over $10 million, but we could try our best to be persuasive. I saw the Broncos general manager, Ted Sundquist, at the Senior Bowl in late January 2006 and he told that they were interested in trading for Terrell. I was happy to have a lead when Ted told me to expect a call from Coach Shanahan. Denver had made bold moves for big money in the past, so I knew they were the type of team that had the guts and the deep pockets to come after Terrell.

When the coach called, he invited Terrell and me to visit with him in Denver. The next week, the Broncos flew us in and picked us up at the airport. We went to Coach Shanahan's house and had the pleasure of meeting his wife. They were very gracious and gave us a tour of their beautiful house. We sat down in his living room and it was very casual.

Shanahan primarily talked about the Bronco team and why Terrell would make such a good fit. Although he did ask Terrell about why things had unraveled with the Eagles, he was not stern or authoritarian. He was a gentleman, and I could sense that although it seemed like they were recruiting Terrell, the coach was really trying to decide whether or not the trade would work.

We left Denver cautiously optimistic that they would offer us the big deal. Two weeks later I saw Coach Shanahan again in Hawaii at the Pro Bowl. When I asked him about Terrell, he was lukewarm, and I didn't get a good feeling about it. Shortly thereafter, Ted called and said the Broncos would like to do a one-year deal around the million-dollar mark but with incentives. Very disappointed, I told him that Terrell wanted a big signing bonus and it just wouldn't work out for everybody unless he was happy with his contract. He told me that they were not interested in doing a big contract but would keep in touch. They were the only team that approached me about Terrell at all. If they weren't going to do the big deal, I didn't know who would.

When I told Terrell about it, he took it in stride. Always optimistically pointing to our next move, I thought something would happen for us at the NFL Combine in late February, just a few weeks away.

The NFL Combine is held every year in Indianapolis. It is the event where the teams bring in the top prospects from around the country for April's draft. There, they medically examine the players, put them through agility drills, have them run the forty-yard dash, and subject them to intense interviews to evaluate their intelligence and character. Every team is there with an arsenal of coaches, scouts, and executives not only to look at all the draft prospects but also to meet with agents.

The teams meet with agents because free agency begins about a week after the Combine. Agents communicate with teams at the Combine about their upcoming free agents so they can gauge their clients' market value. Free agency is the process by which a player who is a veteran of four years or more, and whose contract has expired, can go to whatever team he wants.

For instance, if I have a veteran player with the Patriots who is about to become a free agent at the start of March, I need to know what other teams are interested in him and to what extent. If, say, right before the start of free agency in March, the Patriots were to make me an offer to keep my player on the team, I need to know if there is a better situation out there. If there is, then I will not do the deal with the Patriots but will take the player into free agency. If there isn't a better situation and the player wants to stay in New England, I will do the deal with the Patriots in February before free agency starts.

If there are teams interested in my hypothetical Patriot client who is an upcoming free agent in March, I will communicate with them in person in February at the Combine so I will know the player's market value when we make our decision to stay or enter free agency.

At the Combine, I make it a point to discuss my upcoming free agents with every team. However, there are tampering rules that do not allow teams to discuss potential free agents on other teams with me. I can only discuss the players on that team with that team. However, hypothetical conversations happen and the point gets across. Fortunately for us, we had permission from the Eagles to talk to other teams about a trade for Terrell, so we did not have to deal with that difficulty.

While at the Combine, Jason and I walked around with an index card listing our upcoming free agents for all the teams to see, and yes, Terrell's name was on it.

I knew that I had to make something happen at the Combine. While there, I had two phone conversations with Dallas Cowboys head coach Bill Parcells, who vaguely expressed interest in Terrell. We did not discuss a contract. He wanted to know about Terrell. I assured him that Terrell would love to be a Cowboy and it would work out.

Afterwards, Jason and I walked all over Indianapolis, looking for Jerry Jones and his son Stephen. When I saw Jerry, he was very friendly and suggested that we meet to talk about Terrell.

The next day, I had lunch with Bill Parcells. The media saw us at lunch and went crazy. From there, I walked with Coach Parcells to get on the Cowboy bus to meet with Jerry, Stephen and Bill. It looks a lot like John Madden's bus, but is more like a mobile office. The bus was super cool, as was Jerry Jones. The guy always looks like a million bucks and Coach Parcells always looks like an NFL icon. Jerry is smooth, charismatic, and persuasive. Coach Parcells is straightforward, commands your respect, and can come across as intimidating, but I've had a long history with him and can't help but like him.

We had a long meeting and I explained that Terrell would want to be a Dallas Cowboy and that it would be a huge success.

At that point, I explained that for it to work out, Terrell needed to feel positive about his contract as well. I told them that Terrell needed to beat the Eagles contract for him to be happy and be at his best. They had to be in all the way or not at all.

Although Jerry and Bill did not indicate if they were in or out, I walked out of the meeting and called Terrell to tell him that we had a shot there. I told him I was confident something would happen in Dallas or elsewhere despite the suspension because he was too good a player. To hedge our bet, I also talked with the Kansas City Chiefs and the Green Bay Packers about Terrell. They were both interested, but like Dallas, it was hard to tell if they would make the big offer.

The problem was that no one would trade for Terrell because they didn't want to pay him the $8.3 million. The reason was simple: any coach or GM who went out and gave Terrell the big bonus after the implosion at Philly would lose his job if it didn't work out. And if they weren't going to pay him the $8.3 million in a trade, how were we going to get the $10 million in free agency?

Here was the crux of our problem. Any coach or GM who would persuade his owner to pay Terrell $10 million would be fired by his owner and crucified by the media if it didn't work out. That was a risk no GM or coach was willing to take. So I ask you, what is the solution to that problem? The answer: if a coach or general manager wouldn't take the risk of getting fired by his owner, perhaps the owner himself would. Let's see…what owner out there is enough of a maverick to take that chance? Jerry Jones?

We would have to wait a week until free agency began to find out—or so I thought. Free agency was supposed to begin on March 3, but of course things could not be as simple as that. Terrell's contract required the Eagles to pay him a $5 million bonus if he was on the team's roster on the fifth day of the 2006 league year. The league year was scheduled to begin on March 3, so they would have to release Terrell by the fourth day or else he'd be entitled to the bonus. We therefore expected Terrell to be released by Monday, March 6.

However, there was a serious problem. The Collective Bargaining Agreement (CBA) was set to expire on March 2, and if a new deal to extend it was not reached, the salary cap would be approximately $94.5 million. The league owners and the NFLPA had reached an impasse in the negotiations. The cap number of $94.5 million was not big enough to provide a lot of teams with cap room to go out and do big deals, plus if no deal was reached, there would be rules making it more difficult to be creative in dealing with the salary cap. However, if the two sides could do a deal to extend the CBA, it would add about

$8 million to the salary cap and eliminate some of the onerous rules prohibiting creativity with respect to the cap. A new deal would mean big deals for a lot of players in free agency, and we needed that boost.

As the midnight hour approached, the two sides agreed to extend the deadline from Thursday evening to Sunday evening. Sunday afternoon it was extended again until Wednesday evening, with a stipulation that if the owners did not accept the NFLPA's final position by Wednesday evening, free agency would begin at 12:01 A.M., Thursday morning. Come Wednesday night, the owners agreed and the new salary cap figure was set at $102 million and free agency would begin 12:01 A.M., Friday morning.

In addition to the bigger salary-cap number, the NFLPA made sure another decision like Arbitrator Bloch's could never happen again. They did this by including new language in the CBA that stipulated that deactivating a player is a form of discipline that counts toward the four-week maximum discipline provision. The CBA was also changed to include player-friendly language regarding progressive discipline and bonus forfeitures for discipline.

Free agency began Friday morning, but Terrell still had to wait the four days. Just before 4 P.M. on the following Tuesday, I was watching ESPN and saw it reported that the Eagles had released Terrell. Okay, there were teams out there with cap room and now Terrell for the first time in his career was a free agent.

I hoped the phone would ring off the hook immediately with teams bidding in a frenzy to sign Terrell. Despite the fact that every expert predicted it would take a long time, possibly months, for a deal to get done for anything other than the minimum $810,000 contract plus incentives, I told Terrell that I believed the big deal was out there and was going to happen soon.

However, my confidence was put to the test when the phone did not ring one time for Terrell that first night after he was released. To say I was disappointed is a gross understatement.

Teams like Kansas City, Green Bay, and Denver were interested, but only at the $810,000 level plus incentives. Terrell was originally under contract with the Eagles to make $8.3 million in 2006, $5.5 million in 2007, and $6.5 million in 2008. And now the top experts in the business were predicting that I was only going to get a salary of $810,000 this year? That wasn't going to get it done. Usually, when a team wants your client bad enough to write a big check, they call immediately. If you have to call them, you are in big trouble. That night, I felt the heat, but I kept the faith and focused on what I could do next.

The next morning I took action and called Coach Parcells. He told me to sit tight, that the Cowboys were interested and would get back to me. Later that day, two teams called and were interested at potentially big numbers. One of those calls was from Stephen Jones— Jerry's son. I talked with Stephen and told him that for the situation to work out, Terrell needed to make the big money that he felt he deserved. I explained to him that if Terrell felt the team went all out for him, he would do the same for them. That was the only way it could work. Stephen said he would talk it over with his people and get back to me. We were alive! There was a real shot at making it happen and I could see that victory was within our grasp.

As soon as I got off the phone with Stephen, I called Terrell and discussed the Cowboys and the second team that was heavily interested in him. Terrell explained to me that if Dallas were to make the big commitment to him, he'd want to be a Cowboy. At that point, my adrenaline was pumping and I was in my deal-making mode.

There are two dangers at that stage of a free-agency negotiation.

The first danger is being too aggressive. If you are too aggressive, you can scare a team off. If you scare them off, they will sign another player and you are finished. The second danger is not being aggressive enough and leaving money on the table. An agent's job is to act in the best interest of his client. That means being able to know instinctively when to pull the trigger for your client.

As I waited for Stephen Jones to call back, I wondered if I'd been too aggressive. What if the Cowboys were willing to pay medium-range money and I scared them away and we were stuck with rock-bottom offers? What if I could have gotten a B-plus-caliber contract for Terrell and blew it by being too aggressive and telling Stephen we needed the $10 million?

I realized that if I could have smacked myself for even questioning my actions, I would have. I knew that I had done it right. The Cowboys were either going to make the deal or not. There was no in between. They were either all in or going to walk away. That next phone call would determine everything.

So when the phone rang and the caller ID said it was Stephen Jones, I was ready. Stephen and I went back and forth for hours exchanging proposals and counterproposals. The pressure was intense, but Jason and I were focused on the task at hand. We knew where we had to be and weren't going to stop until we got there. So, when the Cowboys offered us $10 million that first year, with a total of $25 million over the three-year contract, I remained calm and professional, but wanted to jump through the roof. We pulled the trigger and told Stephen we had a deal!

After having the numbers charted, Jason officially declared: "We did it! We won! We got the winning contract!" Jason and I hugged like only brothers can do.

We won for our client. It wasn't that we beat the Eagles. We had nothing but respect for Coach Reid, Joe Banner, and Howie Roseman. It was all about Terrell getting the kind of contract that he felt he deserved and that he'd gone through so much adversity for so long to achieve. The only losers were my competitors and the people out there rooting against us.

For months now, I'd known that when the moment of truth arrived and I told Terrell what the best offer would be, he would break down either because the deal was so good or because it was so bad. So when I found myself on Jerry Jones's private jet with Terrell and saw tears in his eyes, I knew that we had done the impossible.

Terrell was en route to Dallas to sign a three-year $25 million contract. Terrell would make $10 million the first year, $8 million the second year, and $7 million the third. When you do the math, if Terrell had stayed with the Eagles and been a model citizen, and if the Eagles had paid him the big bonus (a big if), he'd have made $8.27 million in 2006 plus he would not have lost the $1,720,588 in withheld paychecks from the suspension in 2005. The total with the Eagles would have been $9,990,588. Instead, Terrell was going to make $10 million with the Dallas Cowboys. Keep in mind there is no state income tax in Texas, so Terrell also increased his net earnings. Additionally, he made more money in endorsements as a result of the book and two national TV commercials in the second year than he did during his first year with the Eagles. In 2006, Terrell's endorsements with the Cowboys exceeded his first year with the Eagles as well. Any way you slice it, Terrell came out on top financially that first year.

As for the second year, by the end of the 2007 season, Terrell would have made $13.77 million over the remaining second year of his

Eagle contract versus the $18 million he made with the Cowboys. At that point, the difference was over $4 million!

And as for the third year, assuming Terrell did not do an extension prior to the expiration of the 2008 season, he would take home $25 million with the Cowboys versus $20.68 million with the Eagles. Taking into account that Terrell in 2008 will have paid the Eagles the remaining balance of $769,118, the total compensation with the Eagles would have been worth approximately $21,449,118. In the end, $25 million is a lot better than $21.45 million. The verdict came in and it was in our favor!

As I watched Jerry Jones talk with Terrell on the jet and tell him how he started with nothing as a college kid, worked his way up, making millions and losing millions, and I saw Terrell realize that his dream had come true, I knew that this was a special moment.

After the deal, Bill Parcells had this to say about me:

> I like Drew a lot. He's a self-made guy and I have a lot of respect for what he's accomplished. He has more clients than anybody in the NFL and he works out of an office with two people with him and when the phone rings he answers and I respect that. We have a difference of opinion from time to time but you would with any agent...Drew is someone that I would say...I have a very good relationship with...and I've done a lot of business with him before...I do trust him...He's never told me anything but the truth. That's important. And that's not always a common thing among agents, I gotta tell you that. So the ones that are that way I have a high regard for.

At the press conference, I watched the big smiles as Jerry and Terrell shook hands, and I couldn't help but think about all the adversity we'd endured along the way. I thought of how good it felt to come through for Terrell, who never quit on me no matter what. I thought of all the times Jason and I refused to hang our heads and kept our chins up. I thought of all the times we believed in ourselves when it seemed like the world was against us. I thought of all my competitors who were laughing during the "Next Question press conference" and I knew that on this day, they were sick to their stomachs to see me and my client come out on top. I thought of how I felt at the press conference on Terrell's front lawn versus this one. And then I thought of that reporter who asked me what I had done for Terrell other than get him kicked off the team.

I'd like him to ask me that question now. Ironically, if he were to do that today, my answer would still be "Next Question." It always will be.

What came next was another press conference on June 3, 2008, where Jerry Jones announced a new deal we negotiated for Terrell.

The new contract was a three-year extension where over the four-year period Terrell would earn $34 million. Thus, from 2006 through 2008, Terrell will have earned in excess of $31.73 million versus the $20.27 million he would have earned had he stayed with the Eagles.

By becoming a Dallas Cowboy and busting the Eagles contract, even after the fines and forfeitures, Terrell profited by a staggering $9 million. Ladies and gentlemen, I rest my case.

CHAPTER 3

SELL YOURSELF,
NOT YOUR SOUL

AT APPROXIMATELY 1:30 P.M. SATURDAY AFTERNOON ON
November 10, 2007, a sixty-seven-year-old fierce warrior known
as Young Soo Do stood in the back parking lot of his tae kwon do
school in North Miami, when from a distance of about ten feet, a
professional hitman emerged out of nowhere, shooting him once in
the hand and three times in the stomach with a high-powered, fully
automatic assault rifle.

Within minutes, my karate teacher was airlifted to the trauma
center at Jackson Memorial Hospital. I got the call while I was driving
with Jason. We raced over to the hospital not knowing all the facts.
As we pulled up, we ran over to his son, Ricky Do, whose karate uniform was covered in his father's blood.

In shock at the sight of the dark red stains on Ricky's uniform,
we asked him what was going on and tried to encourage him to hang
in there. He was there with Police Sergeant Peter Cruz, who'd been
like a son to Young Soo Do for the last twenty-five years. Peter, who

was in charge of the violent crimes division for Miami Dade Police Department, told us the following:

At the time of the incident, Ricky was teaching a class and Grand Master Young was outside while another man named LeClerc Prosper was washing his car. Without making any demands, a six-foot-tall male with a medium build and short hair fired four rounds from a fully automatic high-powered assault rifle at Young Soo Do. After shooting Grand Master Young, the gunman fired one round at LeClerc Prosper, striking him in the lower extremities while he was running way.

As Ricky ran out toward his father, he saw the gunman run away. At the neighboring Farm Store market, a video surveillance camera showed a 2003–2005 four-door Mercedes-Benz C Class black vehicle drive off. There are over 3,700 vehicles matching that description in Dade and Broward counties.

After two days and numerous surgeries to repair his intestines, they had to be entirely removed. Grand Master Young was in and out of consciousness. By Monday afternoon, November 12, fluid was filling his lungs and his heart was failing. Despite the pain, he was a fighter to the end. As he took his final breaths, Jason was there with him. Holding Grand Master Young's hand while it was still warm, tears streaming down his face, Jason swore he would honor his teacher by taking care of Master Young's family and by promising to do his best to emulate the brave, noble, strong man Grand Master Young always was. As Young Soo Do passed away, Jason as well as his wife, son, and two daughters, and an overcrowded room full of friends and students erupted in tears and sorrow.

Even the nurses and doctors were crying as Jason said his good-bye, stood up, wiped his tears, and walked out. He had to leave the room. He couldn't stop himself from violently shaking with the agony of the anger and loss.

Jason went from the hospital straight to the funeral home with Ricky Do and took care of the funeral arrangements. They picked out funeral plots for both Young Soo Do and his wife. As Jason stood there looking at what would be the final resting place of Young Soo Do, he thought back to when we started going to karate school.

When I landed in Miami after being out of town on business for less than ten hours, I called Jason for the update and he told me, "Bad news. It is with great regret that I inform you that Young Soo Do has passed away."

It meant a lot to me that Jason was there with him at the final hour.

On my way over to the hospital, I thought of what Young Soo Do had meant to me and my family. Since Young Soo Do had been a father figure to me, I couldn't help but think of my own dad.

I flashed back to being a kid in Miami in the 1970s. I was born in 1966 in New Jersey, but my parents moved to Miami in July of 1969 shortly after Jason was born. My dad supported us by running a manufacturing business. He owned the company with his two brothers, and it was all about sales. He would go to various department stores to sell his products. He was manufacturing synthetic marble items—bathtubs, ashtrays, desktops, picture frames, all kinds of things.

My dad was a great salesman—but with one caveat. He had to believe in his product. He couldn't sell products that were overpriced, of poor quality, or just not right for the customer. My dad grew up in the 1940s when the Nazis were the bad guys and the Americans were the good guys. Things were clear. Whether it was cops and robbers or cowboys and Indians, he always wanted to be the good guy.

By the time he became a businessman, he had a big conscience and a good heart. Unfortunately, while trying to build a business, he could not make the coldhearted, bottom-line decisions that were necessary to turn a profit.

My father wanted to be an honorable man in a ruthless business. He tried to manufacture products of the highest quality, built by first-rate workers, that were completed to perfection. He paid the workers much more than his competitors.

He promoted one of the guys to a managerial position and paid him handsomely. My dad brought him by the house all the time. We all called him "Uncle Willy." My dad was a muscular guy who worked out in a gym, but Uncle Willy was a giant compared to him. Jason and I really liked and admired Uncle Willy. We considered him family. His skin color was irrelevant to us.

Everybody loved working for my father at the factory because there they were all friends. My dad led by example, working as hard as anyone and doing whatever manual work was necessary. He produced the ideal product. Unfortunately, doing so was overly expensive and the price became too high to be profitable.

My younger brother Jason and I (our little sister Dana, too) loved going to the factory. My father was always working with the men and he was always jovial. That is, until one day in 1983 when he told us that he was going out of business. I didn't really apprehend the significance of that day, but I soon would.

My dad was heartbroken. My mom was scared. He had to find a new line of work to support the family. I wasn't too young to understand the anxiety in their faces.

All through my years in junior high and high school, my parents suffered over paying bills. We were constantly harassed by bill collectors over the phone. And yet all three of their children had been provided with braces on their teeth, nice clothes, an allowance, and cool cars. I still don't know how they did it. I do know that it took a heavy toll on them.

Rather than making them closed, distant, or mean, the pressure made them more loving and caring than ever. My dad would tell us not to be kindhearted like him. He told us that we had to be tough. Now, you have to understand my father was a muscular guy with a temper. Growing up, I knew I had the toughest dad on the block because he got into more fights than anybody. So imagine the guy you look up to as the toughest person in the world telling you that you have to be tougher than him.

He told me to still be the good guy but to be tough and ruthless at the same time. Most of all, he and Mom emphasized that we had to have a profession—like a lawyer, an accountant, a doctor, an engineer...

It was a lot like growing up with Ralph Kramden, the Jackie Gleason character from *The Honeymooners* TV show in the fifties, as your dad because he was always trying to start this business or do that deal, and no matter how good it looked, it invariably fell through at the last minute for one unlikely reason after another.

He tried and tried, but could never catch a break. That made me very angry with the business world. I had previously grown up thinking that life was fair and there was justice. I quickly realized that life was not a Disney movie where everything automatically had a happy ending.

I had lost the innocence of youth, where happiness is the norm since you don't know better. I remembered when things were good for my parents and became motivated to make them better any way that I could.

Around the time my dad lost his business, something else happened to me. For some reason, another kid in the neighborhood wanted to fight me. I think it was over a girl who liked me instead of him. He was bigger than I was and I was scared to fight him. But my friends told me I had nothing to worry about because they had my back if he tried anything. His friends told him the same thing. It looked like there was going to be a big rumble. I was about twelve or thirteen.

After all the talk in school, he was waiting for me by my house. My friends and his formed a circle around us. He was talking trash and so were my friends. And then he got up close to me. My friends did nothing. They sold me out. I was on my own. Jason, who was three years younger than I, wasn't there because he was at an elementary school; otherwise he would have been right next to me.

The kid pushed me and I did nothing. I walked away. I left. I was too scared to fight him. The kids were teasing me for chickening out. As humiliating as it was, the worst part was going home. I knew I had to tell my dad what happened. I was terribly ashamed.

My father was the toughest guy in the world to me. I admired him for that. As his son, I felt like an embarrassment and thought he would be disappointed in me. But he wasn't. He told me that everyone is afraid to get into a fight and that I was no different. He explained that all I needed was training and confidence.

It turned out that over the weekend we went to an awesome Chuck Norris karate movie. The very next day my dad took Jason and me to a tae kwon do school. The place was a tiny hole in the wall. It smelled of sweat and dirt. There was neither an air conditioner nor a water fountain like there was at school. There was a class going on.

There might have been a dozen students. Being Jewish and wealthy, compared to the other kids in the class, I was out of place.

Those kids looked poor, mean, and tough. I wanted to leave, but my dad was too excited with what he saw.

There was a small office. Inside there were pictures of a young South Korean man kicking and doing all kinds of amazing things. The desk had a glass top with pictures facing up underneath. There were photos of the same man training American soldiers in a Vietnam camp base. Apparently he'd been a member of the Korean Special Forces unit in Vietnam known as the Blue Dragons. He later became a mercenary for the U.S. government in Vietnam and trained American soldiers in hand-to-hand combat. He was the real deal.

There were pictures of the guy breaking all kinds of objects with his hands, feet, and head. In one picture, he was pulling a truck with a rope with his teeth. Another photo had him chopping off the tops of wineglasses without knocking over the bottoms (something very few men in the world can do).

Throughout the class, the instructor, Grand Master Young Soo Do (pronounced "Doe" as in John Doe), a sixth-degree black belt at the time, was yelling loudly and energetically. He was a not a tall man, but his yell was crazy with energy. It fired the students up. When he yelled, the students exploded with energy. Before I knew it, I was fired up. Every time he yelled, it really made you want to punch, jump, or kick something.

After the class was dismissed, he walked over to us. He shook hands with my father, who was thrilled to meet him. My dad instantly took a great liking to Master Do and the feeling was mutual. My dad explained what had happened to me and had one request.

"Make my boys tough!"

At that moment Young Soo Do turned to me and looked me in the eyes. He smiled and shook my hand. "Hello, boy!"

No matter how well I describe his greeting, it won't do it justice. He didn't just say hello, he yelled it with a smile. And it wasn't a smile, at least not like anything I had seen before. It was a look of friendship, but at the same time he had the scariest look I had ever seen. He had dark eyes that looked a hundred years old, a smile that looked like he could bite your throat out at any moment, a handsome face, long black hair like a lion, and a hand that felt like stone. Despite all that intimidation, there was something very welcoming and likable about him. In a nutshell, I thought he was super cool and belonged in the movies as Chuck Norris's archrival.

I looked at his hands and saw layers and layers of dead skin that had formed a huge callus on his hands and over his knuckles. I couldn't believe this guy was human. He smiled the same way at Jason and we were both fascinated and terrified of the guy.

My father signed us up immediately and paid him extra to take care of us. And Young Soo Do took care of us all right. He didn't go easy on us, he did the opposite. He beat the hell out of us. It wasn't just the money. For whatever reason, he took a special liking to us and our dad. A good thing, too, for my father, because one day his temper got him into real trouble.

I don't know if you've seen the movie *Cocaine Cowboys* about Miami in the early 1980s, but that's really how it was. It seemed like in every gym or blue-collar business you went to, someone somewhere was involved with drug trafficking, either marijuana or cocaine. Whether it was smuggling, dealing, enforcing, or collecting, there were badasses everywhere. People were getting shot and killed regularly and it became no big deal in the news. There were just certain guys you did not mess with.

Less than a year after we joined the karate school, my dad had already become lifelong friends with Young Soo Do. One afternoon, my father got into a confrontation with a guy at the local gym. The guy insulted my dad, so he naturally shoved the guy.

His face all red, huffing and puffing, the guy threatened my father—"You're dead"—and walked to the locker room. The owner of the place, like almost everyone else there, was a friend of the other guy. The owner told my father that the guy was the wrong guy to push. The owner made it clear that the guy was seriously going to try to hurt my dad and had probably gone to the locker to get his gun. He told my dad to get away fast.

My father was not armed and knew a better option than to go to the police. He could think of only one thing to do. He jumped into his car and raced out of there. In his rearview mirror he saw the guy with two other bad-news-looking dudes get into a car and follow him. My dad raced over to Young Soo Do's school.

Since it was in the middle of the day, no class was scheduled, so Young Soo Do was on a break. Let me tell you his idea of taking a break. There is a doorway in the back of the school by a parking lot. It is a concrete doorway with a steel frame. It is a perfectly symmetrical doorway with one exception. About five feet up, there is a huge dent in the steel and a break in the concrete. That is because every day for I don't know how long, Young Soo Do smacked his hand into the steel and concrete. He chopped it, punched it, and knife-handed it (folding the thumb in and straightening the index finger, thus using the opposite side of the hand for a chop). The purpose of the exercise was to maintain the callus mass on his hands and knuckles. His knuckles had bubbles of callus on them. This way, when he punched something hard, the object shattered instead of his own bone. He did the same thing to his heels. His hands and feet were literally like hammers.

That's how you know if a martial artist is legit or not in my opinion— look for the callus.

My father jumped out of his car as the car behind him pulled in. He ran over toward Young Soo Do and told him the problem. Young Soo Do continued to smack the steel, making a loud noise.

The three men got out of their car and approached. Stopping within five feet of Young Soo Do, the guy my father had pissed off threatened my dad again.

All three guys had handguns tucked into the front of their pants. My dad recognized the other two guys and knew they were steroid muscle for drug dealers. My father had heard that they were killers. Flashing their guns to intimidate Young Soo Do, though, they had miscalculated.

When they showed their handguns, he stopped hitting the concrete and actually smiled.

With his Korean accent and broken English, he inquired very politely and with a smile, "You have guns... You shoot me?"

Before they could respond and break the dead silence, he let them know in no uncertain terms, "You shoot me... I kill you."

Whether it was the smile or the look in his eyes, they knew he meant it and they lost their resolve. It suddenly wasn't worth it to them anymore.

It was the scariest thing my dad ever witnessed, and growing up in Jersey, he'd been in more than his share of action. Just like that, upon hearing "You shoot me... I kill you," the other guys weren't so tough anymore. They froze, looked at one another, nodded to Young Soo Do as if they had an understanding, and left. That's what happened.

I learned something about friendship, courage, and loyalty that day. From then on, I had the ultimate respect for Young Soo Do. I was no longer afraid of him. I was too hungry to win his respect. Earning his approval meant so much to Jason and me that we were happy to get injured just to show him and my father that we were tough, too. Cuts, bruises, broken toes, and dislocated fingers became accomplishments. Blisters were great. Whenever we got a blister on our feet or hands, we would show him immediately. He had this rusted, dull pair of scissors the sharp ends of which were broken off. When we showed him our blisters, he would cut them off and enjoy it.

Fear soon became a challenge to us, a chance to know the thrill of getting crazy and testing ourselves. Over time, Jason and I both became second-degree black belts. We learned a great deal from the master: discipline and mental toughness. Although we were not big, strong, or overly athletic, we were mentally tough.

Our karate teacher had a saying that he made us repeat: "Strong mind . . . strong body." The meaning is that a strong mind makes for a strong body. Young Soo Do had done what my dad asked; he made us tough-minded.

Now, we weren't going to walk into a bar all of a sudden and kick everyone's butt. We knew that karate didn't turn you into Bruce Lee, but it does improve your self-confidence and make you more of what you are. I walked into karate class as someone who was ashamed and afraid to fight. That fear never left, but I gained a desire for self-respect and accomplishment that overcame it.

Along the way, I developed a fear that motivated me. I became afraid of not being the winner that I wanted to be. Out of that fear, I developed a hunger to compete and win. There are few things more competitive than an actual hand-to-hand fight. It is a real battle between two competitors. I wasn't the best fighter, but I was the best competitor. Every time I would fight, I wanted to win so bad that I trained hard and fought harder. I hated the embarrassment and failure of losing and I loved proving that I was better than my opponent in front of Young Soo Do. Along the way, it became more important to prove to myself that I was better than my opponent. I didn't win every fight. There were guys who kicked faster, punched harder, and were just more athletic than I was. But I always gave superior effort. Whoever went up against me knew they were going to get hit.

I was an effort guy who made himself into a talented martial artist. Jason was more of a bad-temper type of student. He also gave tremendous effort, but he really liked to fight. Young Soo Do had one student (out of hundreds over the years) whom he didn't like. The kid had a bad attitude, was a bully, and had a big mouth. He beat up a lot of students. But he always listened to Young Soo Do and was an excellent fighter. So Young Soo Do decided that Jason, who was half the kid's size, was the answer. Jason was faster, tougher, and meaner.

Jason really hated that other kid and wanted to fight him every day. Jason couldn't stand him and couldn't wait to fight him. Jason won most of his fights. But this one time, he was really angry and lost the fight. After they bowed when the fight was over, Jason pushed the kid in the back of the head and wanted to street-fight him. That was something the other kid would do. Young Soo Do got furious with Jason and punished him by making him do push-ups on his knuckles while smacking him repeatedly on his heels with a hard wooden club. Then he made Jason throw kicks and punches in the corner until he vomited.

At first, Jason didn't understand why his teacher who loved him and disliked the other kid had gotten so angry about it. Afterward, I told Jason that it was because Young Soo Do did not want to see him act like the other kid. Jason learned never to lower himself to the level of his opponent again—a valuable lesson that we abide by every day in our business.

Other agents break the rules all the time and cheat because they can't beat me on a level playing field. And when they lose, they cry wolf, claiming that I cheated. I pride myself on not lowering myself to their level.

At Young Soo Do's funeral, Jason told the story of his fight with the bully as he, my dad, and I all had the great honor to speak. There were a lot of people there with hate in their hearts over the injustice of the murder of such a great man. That hate can turn you into a lesser person. Young Soo Do would not want that to happen.

As I sat there at the funeral, hundreds of memories flashed through my mind. I remember one afternoon, Young Soo Do had me do a separate workout to accommodate my after-school schedule. I was supposed to do a certain number of a difficult type of kick. He asked me how many more I had to go. I was tired, I had homework to do, and I wanted to move on to the next exercise. He had been in his office and it was impossible for him to have watched me or kept count. I don't know why, but I told him ten kicks remaining even though I probably had forty.

Somehow, someway, he knew. He looked at me and smiled a smile that let me know he knew. I thought he was going to crack my neck or smack me on the heels with a stick as I did push-ups for being dishonest. The way he looked at me, I felt guilty and would have been okay with taking a beating. But instead, he just said to me, "Not for me, boy, for you..."

I realized that anytime I do something halfheartedly, I am hurting myself. From that day on, I believed in working harder than the next guy and always trying my best. I developed a work ethic throughout junior and senior high school that was second to none.

When I was a freshman in high school, I had a friend who was flunking out. He and I were close and in similar situations. I was at a crossroads. I could have followed my friend's path of spending all my time chasing girls and rebelling, or I could choose to make myself into a winner.

At the time, my dad was going through hard times trying to support the family. He would tell me that he didn't want me to struggle like him. He would tell me that I had to get good grades, go to college, and become a professional. I saw my mom and dad deal with anxiety over paying their bills. I saw them suffer. I wanted to help them and the best way I could do that was to become successful.

Getting outstanding grades would make them happy and that's what I wanted to do. It was an automatic transition for me to apply the discipline I learned as a black-belt karate student to making myself into a straight-A student. I studied and studied like a fanatic. I started competing to get the highest scores on exams and wanted to be the best in the classroom. A-minuses were unacceptable as I took pride in setting the curve on exams. It was the discipline and the competitiveness that I learned in karate that allowed me to sit at a desk for hours and study.

As I sat there staring at the casket, the memories kept coming back to me. I was proud of the fact that even though I stopped training with Grand Master Do after I graduated high school and began at the University of Miami, I still visited with him. Jason kept his training going while he was in high school. Although I wasn't at karate class, I still felt like I was training every day. Going to the library every day was like going to karate class. It took discipline and mental toughness. I felt my teacher's presence and teachings with me as I studied hard to become an excellent student at UM. I realized that everything about my youth had prepared me for the moment I walked onto the campus as a freshman in the fall of 1984.

Listening to Ricky Do speak at the funeral about his father, I was amazed at his composure and how strong he was for his family. He had his mother and two sisters looking to him to lead the family now. My dad was sitting right next to me and I thought about how much I loved him, how much he had done for me.

I know he is proud of me, Jason, and my sister Dana, who is also an attorney. My parents should be proud of themselves for raising three lawyers (that is a good thing these days, right?).

I wondered if my dad knew what a huge role he played in my becoming an agent. You see, my dad became a monster Miami Dolphins fan in the early 1970s when they were Super Bowl champions. He had season tickets for years and took us to every game once we were old enough. Watching the Dolphins play on Sundays and *The Don Shula Show* on Monday nights was our favorite thing in the world. My father's father, Irving Rosenhaus, used to play college football at Rutgers in the early 1920s and was a big Giants fan all his life. Living in Florida, it was only natural for our dad to become a Dolphins fan and for us as well. In the early 1980s, my dad had become friends with some of the players, including tight end Joe Rose, who is now a very successful sports-talk radio and TV personality in South Florida. Joe and some of the other players often came over to our house on Tuesday nights for a home-cooked meal. As a kid, I read up on their backgrounds and watched their performances closely so that I could make conversation with them at the dinner table. Before long, I was a natural at communicating with the players. It was a thrill to talk football with them.

Being twelve or so, I was really starstruck. It was tremendous fun watching the same Dolphins who'd been over at our house playing football on TV, and it was even more fun to talk with them on Tuesday nights at dinner. I developed a sense of admiration for these giants who were super tough, athletic, and talented.

It was the process of natural evolution that matured me into an aspiring agent. First, from my father I had a passion for the NFL and a tremendous respect and admiration for the pure toughness and incredible athleticism of football players. As my dad brought Dolphin players over, I developed an interest in football and an ability to communicate and build a relationship with players. Factor in the discipline, dedication, determination, mental toughness, pride, and competitiveness that I learned from Young Soo Do. Add in the hunger to be successful that became ingrained in me watching my parents suffer through financial hardship. Then came the transition from karate student to academic student. That translated into working as hard as I could to be an outstanding student in high school, studying anywhere from four to twelve hours a day.

At the University of Miami, I was surrounded by the best college football players in the country. I planned on becoming a lawyer and making big money to help my family. The ingredients for a sports agent were there.

Having the ability to communicate with football players as well as a tremendous respect for their toughness, I naturally became friends with several players on the University of Miami Hurricane football team, including wide receiver Michael Irvin (now a Hall of Fame member who played for the Dallas Cowboys). Whenever we hung out, it was one laugh after another. I really knew how to make the guys crack up. At the same time, I was an exceptional student due to my hard-core work ethic. The way the players worked on the field and in the weight room was how I worked in the library—dedicated. Next thing I knew, Michael Irvin suggested to me that I should become a sports agent.

I hadn't thought much about it before, but I instantly recognized that was what I wanted to do for so many reasons.

The idea of being an NFL agent seemed incredibly exciting and fun. Working with superstar players, dealing with coaches, and negotiating with NFL teams was everything that I dreamed of doing before I knew what an NFL agent was. There was also big money, fast action, competition, and beautiful cheerleaders...

But there was also something else. It always seemed wrong to me that my father had struggled financially because he was an honest man with a good heart who couldn't compromise his principles and sell anything but the best product. No matter how hard he worked, doing the right thing was too expensive. He wouldn't cut corners like the competition and was eventually forced out of business. Ruthless and unscrupulous competitors put him out of business. I saw what the business world did to good men like my father and would never forgive or forget.

Being a sports agent was different. The harder I worked, the more honest I was, the greater I fought for my clients—the better job I did for my friends—the better job I would do for my career. I saw that dishonesty, cheating, cutting corners, and giving anything less than my best effort would not work in the long run.

By being THE sports agent, I saw how I could bring justice back into my world. As an agent, I could do what my father did—work hard, do right by my customers, and deliver the best product. From my father, I developed a passion for becoming a sports agent and the desire to be successful. For my father, I could crush the unscrupulous competition and make them suffer.

Early on in college, I had a focus and plan to become a dominant sports agent. While the rest of the students were out getting drunk at frat parties, I spent my nights in the libraries making myself into a machine.

To become a sports agent, I knew I had to be impressive enough to convince players that they should hire me to negotiate their NFL contracts. I had to be able to persuade the players to put their careers in my hands.

Imagine that you are a college football player getting ready to enter the NFL draft. You come from a background where your parents worked hard to put food on the table and pay the bills to barely get by. And now you have this one chance to get drafted and make millions of dollars. You have to trust one person to help you get drafted high and to negotiate your contract. You can make enough money with that one contract to provide you and your family with financial security for the rest of your life. Are you gonna hire some kid still in law school? Are you gonna hire someone your age?

No! So what was my solution to get players to hire me? How could I accomplish the impossible while competing against established, experienced agents twice my age? Why would anyone hire me to be their agent while I was still in law school? They would if I was the best agent out there.

Like my dad, I wanted to sell the best product. From Young Soo Do, I learned the self-confidence and acquired the work ethic to make myself into the best. I believed that if I worked hard to become the agent most determined to make his client succeed, I would be the best agent for that client. I knew that if I could make myself into the best agent, I would be able to sell myself.

The principle here, the key focus of this chapter, is to make yourself into the best at what you do, whatever it is, so when you sell your product or services, you are selling the best. The idea is to not sell your soul or sell out by being a cheat, a swindler, a fraud, or a crook. Those guys will eventually fall, and in turn, you will eventually rise.

That's a nice concept, but the hard part is making it a reality. How could I make myself into the best agent? With the best training, of course. I had already been trained to be a hard worker, to be mentally tough, and to compete from karate. From my parents, I learned to be honest and to do right by the people who believed in me. What I needed to learn was how to be an agent. First, I had to get the academic training. Second, I had to get some experience.

The best academic training for an agent at that time was, in my opinion, at Duke Law School in Durham, North Carolina, which had an outstanding sports-law program. In order to get into Duke, I studied at UM as hard as the Hurricane players trained. I studied harder than any other student I knew. By taking an accelerated course load, I graduated UM in three years and headed off to Duke.

When I left UM in May of 1987, Jason entered as a freshman, so we kept our presence alive at the school. Jason's mission was to maintain the relationships that I cultivated and build new ones so that when I was ready to be an agent, they would give me a meeting.

But before any of that could happen, I needed to work for an agent. The best agent training I could get was with a local South Florida agent named Mel Levine, who was the dominant agent at UM. Mel represented Michael Irvin. After I finished my first year of law school at Duke, I called him over and over again to get a meeting. When that didn't work, I went to my friend and his star client, Michael Irvin. Michael helped me get the interview. When I got my shot with the guy, I hit him with everything I had.

I knew that everything I wanted to accomplish would depend on that interview. I sold Mel on my work ethic—that I would work my butt off day and night for free. I sold him on my hunger—that I would fight, scratch, and claw to persuade players to sign with him. I sold him on my talent to develop strong relationships with the players to help keep them happy. I sold him on my resourcefulness to find the right players to recruit. I sold him on my ability to find a way to win against other agents. I sold him on the value my excellent academic background and training would have as a contract negotiator. I sold him on me.

He hired me on the spot. During my second year of law school, I was working for Mel. I sold players on the combination of my determination to work hard for them and Mel's experience as a contract negotiator. After a few months on the job, I succeeded in signing players and getting close to them. I soon realized that I was capable of being their contract negotiator, too. I honestly believed, even though I didn't have any experience, that I would be a better agent for my guys than Mel.

I told the guys that what I lacked in experience, I more than made up for with hunger, hard work, and a determination to succeed for them. I sold myself and guys went with me.

Shortly after I went out on my own and was preparing to compete against Mel Levine to take over UM, Mel got into trouble for ripping off his clients. He eventually went to jail and his business was finished. I gained numerous clients who left him. Over the years, scores of players left their agents to hire me because their agents were either lazy, poor negotiators, greedy, crooked, cheap, or not on the ball. The competition beat themselves. By being honest, hardworking, and producing for my clients, I picked up client after client.

Year after year of working hard, fighting to represent my clients to the best of my abilities and to protect their best interests, vaulted me to the top. Along the way, Jason and I never forgot about the man who cared about us when we were just kids. We never forgot who recognized that we could be special.

Every year since I started with Young Soo Do in 1980, he would put on an exhibition in which he would break bricks with his hands, feet, and head. Forget about the fancy jumping spin kicks or breaking boards. What impresses me is brute toughness such as sticking your index finger through a frozen watermelon, smashing a river rock with your bare hands, smacking your head into a brick, or kicking concrete reinforced with steel rods. He started with a small school and a small event, but he built up his school to become a big school with a big event in the community.

Young Soo Do had taken so many youths off the street and given them the direction, the desire, and the discipline they needed to become professional and productive members in society. He helped teens become doctors, lawyers, police officers, firefighters, and even sports agents. Eventually, his annual exhibition became the top local martial-arts exhibition, as he was an icon in the community.

Jason and I not only helped sponsor the event, as Chairmen of the school, but participated as well. Toward the end of the night, after the black belts did their testing and sparring, Young Soo Do and his son Ricky would do the big finale. It was a great honor for us to be invited to go out there with him.

Dressed in suits or casual attire, he would bring us onto the stage to do something special. Each year he would have us karate-chop something and he made the assignment more difficult each time. This one year, in 2003, Jason brought his new girlfriend Cassandra ("Casie"). He wanted to impress her. He told her that he was going to karate-chop five concrete blocks. Well, I do a local sports show every Sunday night for the local Fox affiliate, WSVN. I serve as an NFL insider on the show. They decided to send a TV camera guy there to cover us breaking the concrete.

Young Soo Do decided that since the TV camera guy was there, Jason and I should do two different things to mix it up. I didn't think much of the idea at the time, but I soon would. I went first, and right after I chopped my right hand through the concrete blocks, Young Soo Do told Jason it was his turn. As Jason lined up and measured his hand in the center, Young Soo Do stopped him and yelled, "No, boy! Punch!"

Okay, now Jason and I, as well as other black belts, had karate-chopped the concrete blocks with our hands before, but never punched. Only the crazy badasses did that. Punching something hurts—a lot! Punching is also much more dangerous, as you can break your hand more easily since there's no soft flesh to absorb the concrete impact on your knuckles.

I told Jason to chop it. But with Casie there, I knew he wouldn't back down. He looked at me and I knew that look. He was snarling. He intentionally lost his temper, got all jacked up, looked Young Soo Do in the eyes, and waited. He was waiting for Young Soo Do to start yelling. Young Soo Do smiled that crazy smile of his and yelled with every ounce of breath in his lungs. Grand Master Do stomped his right foot as Jason yelled with him, punching the concrete blocks as if his life depended on it.

That's what Master Young did for us—he gave us courage. From that courage we believed in ourselves and gave our best effort. Never mind that Jason smashed his knuckles along with the concrete; he did something he will always be proud of.

Ironically, on a Friday night less than fifteen hours before the shooting, Jason and I lamented about how this year there wouldn't be an exhibition. It turned out that Young Soo Do was trying to move the school out of North Miami, but the deal fell through. If only he had moved. If only...

One week later, this great, all-powerful man, whose energy was like none I had ever seen, was lying in a casket. Thousands of people were there. I saw faces that I hadn't seen in over twenty years—guys I went to junior and senior high school with.

When it was time for my dad to speak at the funeral and pay tribute to Young Soo Do, he said that Young Soo Do took his sons and changed them from soft, weak-minded mama's boys into hardworking, mentally tough, and successful competitors.

When Jason spoke, he concluded by having everyone stand up and, at Ricky's count, yell their karate yell as loud as they could so everyone above would know who was coming their way. Every man, woman, politician, and child in that building, whether they were a karate student or not, yelled their good-bye at the top of their lungs.

When it was time for me to speak, I said that I was proud to be Young Soo Do's student and thanked him for making me into the person I had wanted to be. I said that he taught me if you try to be your best, you will be your best.

It was because of him that I became the best. It is my sincere hope that as you read this, you think of the person who has helped you to become who you are today. I hope you think of the people in your life who helped you to become who you want to be. I hope you thank them and let them know how much you love them.

I hope you do all of this because I can never again see Young Soo Do's scary smile. I can never again hear his energetic yell that would make me want to break bricks even now. I can never again thank him. That hurts me to the core.

But I take solace in knowing that I am my best and knowing that he was very proud of Jason and me. It is an honor to him that I am the best NFL agent in the business. More NFL players have chosen to put their trust and careers in my hands than any other agent because they believe in me and Jason. Even our competitors can't deny that we are the hardest workers in the business and negotiate outstanding contracts on behalf of our clients. We are the top agents in the business for one simple reason—the same reason that accounts for twenty years of success—because we sell ourselves, we sell the best.

CHAPTER 4

BET ON YOURSELF!

IF YOU DON'T BET ON YOURSELF, WHO WILL? THE WAY I SEE
it, you have to go for it in life to make it happen. You can't just play
it safe all the time. By working hard, you will eventually come across
opportunities. And when opportunities present themselves, you have
to take a chance and bet on yourself to succeed. Otherwise, you can't
get to where you want to be.

Where I want you to be is in the shoes of someone else for a
moment. Imagine that you are a college football player. You're not just
any football player; you are the MVP running back for the University
of Miami Hurricanes, and right now you are playing in the National
Championship Game.

You are a chiseled six-one and 225 pounds. In addition to being
the most athletic running back in college football, you are also the
best, with an incredible combination of power, speed, and elusiveness.
Even though you are a junior, at twenty-two years old, you are ready
to enter the NFL draft.

You are projected by most experts to be the second overall pick in the upcoming draft and get a bonus of $15 million. Can you imagine being twenty-two years old and about to get a $15 million paycheck because you are a young stud? Think about that. Life is good.

You have come out of nowhere to win the starting job and have had a record-breaking season. You set single-season school records at UM by rushing 282 times for 1,753 yards (6.2 average) and twenty-eight touchdowns. And now you are playing in the last game of your college career, the National Championship Game.

It's the fourth quarter with only a few minutes left to play. Your team is down 17–14 and has the ball deep in its own territory. It's up to you to lead the team. After you have a couple of good running plays to move the ball to midfield, the quarterback throws you a short pass.

As soon as you catch it, you turn to run upfield. However, right before your front left leg can plant, your knee takes a direct hit. While your front leg is in midair, the force from the defender's helmet actually bends your knee backward as your lower leg dangles forward. Your knee is grotesquely dislocated. The ligaments that keep your knee together are ripped apart. The pain in your knee is excruciating, but what brings tears to your eyes as you are carried off the field is the fear that it's all over.

With an injury that ugly, you don't need to be a doctor to know instantly that the knee is blown out and will require major reconstructive surgery. You tore three ligaments in your knee. That typically means a yearlong process of grueling rehabilitation. That also means the $15 million check is gone. Your career is in total jeopardy and may be over. Not so fun and exciting anymore, is it?

That's what happened to a young man named Willis McGahee.

Jason and I were at the game on January 3, 2003, between the

Miami Hurricanes and the Ohio State Buckeyes at Sun Devil Stadium in Tempe, Arizona. When I saw Willis's knee bend backward, I was sick to my stomach. Although I hadn't had the opportunity to meet Willis yet, I sure was planning on it. It was a foregone conclusion that Willis as a junior was going to leave UM a year early to enter the 2003 NFL draft and be a top five draft pick. I couldn't wait to recruit him. With him being from Miami and me being based there, coupled with the fact that I had represented numerous Hurricane first-round picks over the years, including guys who were Willis's friends and former teammates, I made a lot of sense for him. I was confident that I would make him a client.

I had not recruited any other running backs that year and was focused on representing Hurricane rookies. He was my top target. Sure, when I saw the injury, I was disappointed that my top recruit was now out of the mix. But what bothered me the most was seeing a nice kid come so close to making it big and then having it taken away from him. Over and over on ESPN, I kept seeing video of Willis in tears and agony as he was carried off the field. Whether you knew Willis or not, you couldn't help but feel sorry for him.

It reminded me of another UM running back—Melvin Bratton. Heading into his last college game, Melvin was an outstanding player, projected to be a high first-round pick. Just like Willis, he blew out his knee on a short passing play in the fourth quarter of the big game. The situations were eerily similar.

Melvin had to have major reconstructive knee surgery and it caused him to drop from the first round to the sixth in the 1988 draft. He was drafted by his local team, the Miami Dolphins, even though he wouldn't be able to play that season. The Dolphins offered him sixth-round money, but he and his agent reasoned that if he couldn't get third-round money, he would wait until the next year's draft. He decided to turn the Dolphins down and reenter the NFL draft in 1989. He ended up being drafted in the seventh round by the Denver Broncos. He took the seventh-round contract and managed to stay in the league for three years. Unfortunately, his career didn't last long enough to qualify for a pension; he was only three games shy. Melvin never overcame the injury.

That was fifteen years ago. I knew Melvin. We were at UM together, but he was a few years older. He had already left UM for the pros when I became an agent in 1989.

I had hoped that things would be different for Willis, who used the same surgeon as Melvin—Dr. John Uribe. The doctor's reputation and his success in performing knee surgeries were outstanding. Since the medical and rehabilitation fields had progressed so much over the last fifteen years, I knew Willis would be in good hands and had a shot to come back strong from the injury.

Willis was a junior and therefore had his entire senior season to rehab his injury. Maybe, just maybe, he would be able to come back in time to have a productive senior season and prove he was still the same talent. Maybe he could put together a strong enough senior season to get drafted high.

Needless to say, when I found out a few days later that Willis had decided to come out early even though he was severely injured, I was surprised. Like almost everybody else, I just assumed he would stay in school. And then, when I heard that Willis had already signed with an agent, I was even more surprised. It turned out that Willis signed with an agent the night of his surgery, as he was lying in his hospital bed.

It was a big story that Willis came out. The media and draft experts were critical of his decision. I figured at that time—early January 2003—that if things went well with his rehab, he would likely be drafted in the middle rounds. The reason why he wouldn't be a high pick anymore is that with an injury like that, he would not be able to play his rookie year.

With serious knee injuries, there are no guarantees the player can come back well enough to play in the NFL. Willis was damaged goods. Coaches need to win now or they lose their jobs. No coach was going to draft a player high who wouldn't be able to contribute that first year, if at all. A coach can afford to invest a middle-round pick in a guy who may not play the first year but has big potential. Middle-round picks get a few hundred thousand to sign, not big money in NFL terms.

Any coach who drafted Willis high would be in serious jeopardy of losing his job if Willis didn't pan out. There are plenty of first-round picks who turn out to be a bust. Drafting first-round picks is risky in the best of circumstances. But a coach who drafts a guy high with a surgical knee is really putting himself in a position to be either vilified or glorified, taking too much of a risk. That's why the draft experts had Willis projected in the fifth or sixth round when the news of his decision broke.

Sixth-round picks in 2003 would get an average up-front bonus of $64,000 versus the $3.5 million first-round picks averaged. There are seven rounds with thirty-two picks in each round. In the first round, there was about a $10 million discrepancy between what the first pick gets up front to sign versus the thirty-second pick.

That year, we represented several of Willis's Hurricane teammates who were also entering the draft. To build a close rapport with our rookies, Jason and I would go out to the Hurricane training facility almost every day that the guys were out there. (Note: We would do so in compliance with UM's policy toward agents and not converse with underclassmen.) We were out there because we liked to be very hands-on and provide our rookies with personal attention. That is a major reason why players at the University of Miami are such a great fit for us.

As I was waiting for the guys, I bumped into Willis. We made small talk about the attractive, athletic girl I'd seen him talking to earlier but didn't talk any business. The conversation was brief and I didn't think much of it. Later that day, the guys told me that Willis said he wasn't happy with his agent and that he asked them about me. I became very interested in Willis. I hoped he would follow up with me.

About a week later, with only a week left before the guys headed out to Indianapolis for the NFL Combine, Willis and I bumped into each other again while I was waiting for my clients. This time he initiated the conversation and talked business. He told me he wasn't happy with his agent and was meeting with other agents. He expressed an interest in meeting with me. He suggested I call him over the next day or so to set up a meeting.

Knowing how talented Willis was before he got hurt, I knew that if he could make it back, he would be a great player. So I called him as he suggested, but he didn't commit to the where and the when of a meeting. I was disappointed that as the week went by, I didn't get a sit-down. I knew if I got my shot, I could make it happen.

When I went up to the Indianapolis Combine, I heard that Willis had fired his agent and was all set to sign with a different one. I assumed he had his mind made up and that was why he didn't meet with me. I was disappointed, but you can't win 'em all, so I moved on.

While I was meeting with a team executive at the Combine, Jason was grabbing dinner with one of our rookies who was also in Indianapolis. As they ate, our client complained that he wasn't getting any sleep because of his roommate's snoring. Jason asked who his roommate was. It turned out that it was Willis. Sensing an opportunity, Jason persuaded our client to do his best to have Willis call us. Jason figured that since Willis had not yet signed with another agent, he was still fair game and maybe there was a chance he would call.

When Jason told me about the conversation, I didn't think much of it, since Willis had never followed up with me and I had heard he was a done deal with another agent. Needless to say, when Willis called me later that night from his hotel room, I was pleasantly surprised.

We met early the next morning since he had to catch a flight back home. Even though it was early, I already had a current update on Willis's situation from the NFL teams who'd medically checked him out. It turned out that his injury was unique in that the ligaments were a clean tear and the doctor said the surgery had gone exceptionally well. The teams were very impressed that Willis, in late February, was already off the crutches and walking with a minimal limp. He was way ahead of schedule. I could sense among the teams that there was a quiet buzz of excitement and optimism surrounding him.

To start our conversation off on the right foot, I told Willis the positive feedback I'd heard from numerous NFL scouts. Willis said that he wanted to move on from his agent because there was not much of a relationship between them. He wanted an agent whom he could be close to so that he could see for himself what was going on.

I complimented him on doing a good job of promoting himself at the Combine. With the media, he was very positive: "My mind-set is that I can do anything I want to do, which I am doing. I'm walking right now. I'm not using crutches or a brace. I'm getting around pretty good. The doctors say they've never seen anything like it. They're very surprised."

I assured him that my approach was going to be even more positive. I explained to Willis that I believed he had a good chance to be a first-round pick and be the first running back selected in the draft. I told him that we needed to go on a media blitz to make everyone else believe it. I sold him on the belief that if we sell, sell, and sell, the teams will buy.

Additionally, since I was already at UM every day to visit my other Hurricane clients, I would without a doubt be there to visit with him every day, too. Being locally based, I would be in constant communication with Dr. Uribe and Willis's rehab physical therapist Ed Garabedian and could thus convey his excellent recovery progress to the teams with firsthand information. Then Jason showed him several charts illustrating our recent rookie contracts. He was so interested that we continued the meeting while driving with him to the Indianapolis airport.

Willis hired us as soon as we won over his mother and grandmother. My first order of business was to get his promotion going in the right direction. A couple of weeks earlier, on February 12, the *Miami Herald* had come out with an article titled "McGahee's First NFL Contract Might Be Unique." The article said that Willis's agent at that time "has a challenging job" because "McGahee, once considered a top five pick, is now projected by most draft analysts to go between the third and fifth rounds. So to decrease the financial loss McGahee will take, his rookie contract likely will include voided years and several performance based incentives." The main point of the article was that because Willis was going to be drafted in the middle rounds, he would need a unique contract with extra incentive bonuses so that if he returned to form and played like a top five pick, he'd be paid like one as well.

Willis's previous agent said that it was too early into his rehabilitation to predict how the injury would affect his draft position. He was quoted as saying: "I've heard that he's going in the first round. I've heard that he's not going to get drafted. I've heard that he's going in the middle of the rounds. People are saying a lot of things. And instead of saying anything at this point, I just wanted to make sure that we follow what the doctors are saying."

The very first day I signed Willis, I took a different approach. Rather than play it safe and sit on the fence, I picked up the phone and made a lot of calls to the media.

Two weeks after the *Miami Herald* article, a second one came out. Titled "Draft Hopes Up, McGahee Picks Rosenhaus As Agent." The article detailed the twists and turns in McGahee's draft hopes.

Drew Rosenhaus will have his work cut out for him before and after the NFL draft in April. In the Fiesta bowl last month, McGahee tore ligaments in his knee after a devastating hit by Ohio State's Will Allen. The injury was initially deemed so severe that there was speculation McGahee's career could be over...

Less than two months later, he walks without crutches—and he walked with only a trace of a limp last weekend at the scouting combine in Indianapolis.

McGahee now is predicted to go in the third round. Rosenhaus, however, is more optimistic.

"I'm confident that with the way Willis is recovering, he can be a first-round prospect."

For the first couple of weeks, the media kept portraying Willis, based on NFL-team sources, as a third-round pick. The teams form their own independent evaluations. They do not communicate with one another and share opinions. Thus, teams often develop very different opinions on players. I knew that if I kept saying teams were telling me Willis was going in the first round, they would believe it and realize that Willis's stock was rising. Every single day I talked to the teams and told them they needed to take Willis in the first round, that if they waited until the second, it would be too late.

About a week before the draft, I put together a special workout for Willis at the University of Miami. The teams came to watch him put on a show. He did a forty-yard dash at a fast jog. His build was sensational. He bench pressed 225 pounds 22 times. He did squats at 225 pounds. He did leg curls and other exercises illustrating the strength in his knee. It was a far cry from a typical workout, where the guys sprint—not jog—forty yards, but it was an impressive performance nevertheless.

ESPN was all over the workout. They did a feature on Willis's recovery and projected draft status. I went on national TV and said that Willis was going to be drafted in the first round and that he would be the first running back taken in the draft.

Let me repeat that. I said on national TV that Willis was going to be drafted in the first round and that he would be the first running back taken in the draft. I didn't say maybe or probably or likely. I left no doubt and appeared supremely confident even though the media was now projecting Willis had a shot to be a second-round pick and would be drafted after Penn State running back Larry Johnson.

I knew that if Willis wasn't a first-round pick and wasn't the first running back drafted, I would be vilified by the media and every agent in the business. I knew it was a big risk. I knew I would lose all credibility and be humiliated on national TV if, on draft day, I was still sitting there with Willis at the end of the first round waiting for the phone to ring.

My competitors and many members of the media were thrilled that I made that prediction. They couldn't wait for Willis to go in the second or third round so they could blast me and call me every name in the book (behind my back, of course). They were waiting for me to fall flat on my face in front of the ESPN cameras on draft day.

But where other agents are scared to fail, we are hungry to succeed. I had the guts to go on national TV and promote my client to the best of my abilities. I didn't play it safe. I did everything within my power to succeed for Willis. I bet on him and me to come out on top. The stakes were high.

Draft day, Saturday April 26. I set up the draft headquarters at my house in Miami Beach. I had two clients over with their families. Jerome McDougle, a UM defensive end, was drafted with the fifteenth pick in the first round by the Philadelphia Eagles. Jerome's family was in the living room and we joyously celebrated when he was picked. Right after Jerome was picked, the draft continued, and while I was ecstatic about Jerome, in the back of my mind, I was feeling the heat.

Willis's group was in my office area. He was sitting at my desk with me and Jason. The way the draft worked in 2003 was that each team got a pick in each round. Since there were thirty-two teams, there were thirty-two picks in the first round. Each team had fifteen minutes to make their selection in round one. There were a total of seven rounds, and the teams had ten minutes to decide in the second round and five minutes in the third through seventh rounds.

The draft format has since been changed to ten minutes per pick in the first round and seven minutes in the second round, and five minutes per pick thereafter.

It looks like a team is going to take you when the phone rings and the team is on the other line saying they are going to pick you. But it's not final and for sure until you see the NFL commissioner on TV announce that the team has selected you.

With each draft pick in the first round, the up-front bonus decreases hundreds of thousands of dollars. Falling several picks can cause a player to lose millions of dollars. During those fifteen minutes, you stare at your phone and wait for it ring. With all that money on the line, it is a long fifteen minutes. The reality is that if the team doesn't call after the first ten minutes, they are not going to call at all.

With Jerome being picked fifteenth, we watched and waited as the sixteenth, seventeenth, eighteenth, nineteenth, twentieth, twenty-first, twenty-second... We hoped that Willis would come into play once we got into the twenties. That's when it got extremely intense. We didn't want to be waiting for the call once it got into the thirtieth pick.

The Buffalo Bills had the twenty-third pick. They already had a very good running back in Travis Henry and had expressed nothing more than a casual interest in Willis leading up to the draft. They were not a team that we considered to be hot for Willis. Not one draft expert or reporter in the world remotely predicted the Bills would be interested in him.

During those fifteen minutes, ESPN (who, along with a dozen other stations, had a camera crew at my house) kept flashing live shots of Willis and me waiting for the call. No one was expecting us to be drafted this early or by this team. However, I wanted us to look busy and productive. I didn't want my client to be seen on national TV just sitting around with his thumb up his butt. And maybe, just maybe, if a team saw us on the phone, they would think we were talking to another team that was trying to trade up so they could draft us.

My thinking all along was that by saying over and over again that Willis was going to be a first-round pick, any team who wanted him and thought they could wait until the second round to get him would believe that they had to trade up or take him in the first round to get him. I wanted the teams to think I knew something they didn't. I wanted the teams to think there was another team out there that they had to beat to the punch by taking Willis as early as possible in the first round. That was my objective from day one. I promoted my client.

So while we were waiting for the phone to ring, I wanted us to look busy. I wanted a team to think we were on the phone with another team. I wanted teams to think we were in play and it was time to make their move to get Willis.

So while we were on TV, I called Willis, who was sitting right next to me, and we started talking to each other on the phone. It was funny. Next thing I knew, Willis's phone rang and it wasn't me on the other line. It was the Buffalo Bills calling.

No way! I thought to myself, not so much because the twenty-third pick was too high for Willis but because it was the Bills who were calling. The Bills had the twenty-third pick and they were on the phone with Willis. At first I wasn't sure they were going to take him. A lot of time had passed on the fifteen-minute clock. But when I realized that the head coach and general manager were on the phone, I knew it was going to happen.

And then on national TV, NFL Commissioner Paul Tagliabue

announced, "With the twenty-third pick, the Buffalo Bills select Willis McGahee, running back . . . University of Miami."

"YES!" I yelled as I grabbed Willis. The crowd erupted in cheers. The room was insane. I looked at Willis hug his mother with tears of joy streaming down their faces and it got me. It got everyone. Willis was crying, his mom was crying, his family was crying, my family members were crying, even the media was crying. Jason and I hugged each other with the thrill of victory.

We did it! When everyone else said Willis was going in the third round, I had the guts to say to the national media that Willis was going to be a first-round pick and the first running back taken. I gambled on Willis and myself and we won! Big-time!

But, as always, there was a bit of controversy. The media claimed that by staging the phone call, I hoodwinked the Bills into taking Willis. Maybe I did, maybe I didn't. Who knows? I don't think the phone antics hurt the situation, but I believe that the Bills would have drafted Willis whether we did it or not.

The bottom line was that I was on cloud nine. I thought back to when Willis was being carted off the field in tears after suffering that horrible injury. Then I looked at the way he hugged his mom. The sheer happiness of it all felt good.

Sure, I took a little heat for the phone ploy, but it didn't faze me. I did right by my client and that was all I cared about. I promoted Willis to the best of my abilities with the goal that he would be a first-round pick and that's exactly what happened. Did I get Willis drafted in the first round? No. But I did my job and then some of helping him get drafted to the highest of his potential. For that, I earned a lot of respect.

Even the toughest critics, like Mike Florio of ProFootballTalk

.com, who took a shot at me for wearing an orange shirt on draft day, wrote:

> Although we've taken our share of shots at Drew Rosenhaus over the past month or so, we've been very impressed by the level of loyalty and support that Rosenhaus has displayed for his client. The guy believes in and fights for his clients. Sure, those qualities will tend to piss off from time to time the front-office types who don't want to pay Rosenhaus's clients the amount of money that Rosenhaus wants. But even the things that some folks have labeled as goofy—such as making an in-house phone call to McGahee in order to create the impression that he was on the horn with an NFL team—are proof positive that Rosenhaus has a true passion for his clients' interests.
>
> In the end, everyone wins on this one.

That's what happens when you take a chance and bet on yourself.

CHAPTER 5

DISTINGUISH YOURSELF

WHEN COACH JIMMY JOHNSON LED THE UNIVERSITY OF
Miami Hurricanes to the national championship in the 1980s, there
was something special about that team. They were the most intimidating, the roughest and toughest team I had ever seen in college
football.

Walking around that campus, the players looked mean and scary.
One of the harshest characters was defensive lineman Dan Stubbs.
Dan played in the NFL a few years and was an outstanding college
player. He was six-four and 280 pounds. He had a very pronounced
forehead and long arms. His voice was deep and his laugh sounded
evil. This was the guy other players didn't mess with.

That's the way it was at UM. They were crazy, reckless, and fearless. That group of Hurricanes established a tradition of winning
through toughness that they took pride in. They wanted to see the
tradition continue with the incoming freshmen.

It was all about respect. Freshmen, no matter who they were or how big, would have to treat seniors with respect. It was always the seniors first and freshmen last. To keep rebellious freshmen in line, seniors tried to break their will. After practice, they would slap a guy in the back of the head, push him down, and berate him. Then they would make the freshman carry a senior player's helmet and shoulder pads off the field.

If a freshman was too big and strong for one guy to handle, the seniors would group together, wait until the freshman was alone in the locker room, and then jump him. Freshmen were always getting ganged up on.

This was by design. The freshmen were all assigned lockers in the back of the locker room by the bathrooms. The lockers were dirty and nasty. The players called that section of the locker room the Ghetto.

Every day, there was some kind of fight going on—mostly wrestling matches where you did everything but punch the guy in the face. When guys got into an argument or fight at practice, they took it into the locker room to finish it. There, team members formed a circle around the two guys, who would either fistfight or wrestle to settle their dispute.

That team comprised the toughest guys the NFL had ever seen, players like DT Warren Sapp, DT Jerome Brown, WR Michael Irvin, RB Melvin Bratton, RB Alonzo Highsmith, current UM head coach Randy Shannon, S Bennie Blades, LB Bernard "Tiger" Clark, DL Jimmie Jones, LB Rod Carter, WR Brian Blades, WR Brett Perriman, current FIU head coach Mario Cristobal, and LB Jessie Armstead. Those guys were all great players and the list goes on and on.

To keep the tradition of toughness going, upperclassmen who'd paid their dues would form a circle around the Ghetto. One of the seniors would stand in the center of the circle and say to the freshmen: "Who is going to get in the middle?"

It was a challenge that only true badasses accepted. Once a freshman was man enough to jump in, a wrestling match would ensue. They would slam each other on the ground, into the lockers, and choke each other until someone quit or was out.

At that time, all the players lived in their own apartment complex. There were numerous three-story buildings with three bedrooms in each apartment. The guys were always together and always fighting for dominance among one another. That building complex was out-of-control with wild fights, parties, and girls galore. In the mid nineties, a player, Marlin Barnes, was beaten to death there by outsiders, and after that, the complex was closed down and the players were sent off to live among the other students in the various dormitories.

But that's how it was from the early 1980s to the mid-1990s. That was a big part of the reason the Hurricanes won national championships and set an NCAA record for fifty-seven consecutive home-game wins.

It was that Hurricane swagger and attitude that distinguished them from every other team. The seniors were the leaders, and in 1987, Stubbs was the alpha male. That was the code and anyone who bucked the code had to answer to him. One freshman in particular, Robert Bailey, started to stand out. Robert was a little guy at five-ten and 175 pounds. He was small but he had the biggest heart out there.

Robert showed it every day in practice. Freshmen play on the scout team. The role of the scout team is to practice against the starting unit. Their purpose is to mimic the opposing team and help prepare the starters for the upcoming game. The way it works is the starting offense goes up against the scout-team defense and vice versa. The value of these practices is if the scout-team players get hurt, the team doesn't lose a starter. The freshmen are expendable.

The starters are supposed to pound on the scout team. As a freshman, Robert was on the scout-team defense. Robert was a cornerback, who is typically the smallest player on the field. Every single day at practice, Robert hit the wide receiver or running back as hard as he could. He kept hitting the starting players so hard that guys were getting pissed off and fighting him on the field. No matter who it was, no matter how much bigger they were, Robert kept slamming into the guy full speed. Even though it was just practice, Robert played with the intensity of a real game. After every hit, Robert got up, yelled at that guy, and talked smack. He was a true headhunter and Head Coach Jimmy Johnson loved him!

Jimmy was so impressed with Robert that he did something he very rarely did; he made an exception and played Robert in actual games. And Robert didn't let him down. He flew to the ball with reckless abandon, hitting everything he could as hard as he could.

When guys got into the circle at the Ghetto, Robert always jumped in and loved every minute of it. Since there was no punching to the face, it wasn't a real fight, and for Robert, it was a lot of fun to dive in there and mix it up. When one of his fellow freshman got into the circle and started losing, Robert jumped in there and turned it into a rumble.

After Robert made some plays in the games, he was respected on the team. Since he was rising up the food chain, Stubbs took it upon himself to keep him in his place. After a practice, Stubbs walked up to him and yelled out in front of the whole team, "You are going to bring my helmet into the locker room!"

"Okay," Robert calmly answered.

But instead of doing this, Robert walked over to the sandpit, filled Stubbs's helmet with sand, and threw it over the fence, onto the track field. When Stubbs saw what Robert had done, he ran out onto the field. Robert was holding his own helmet, ready to hit Stubbs upside his head with it. Even with the helmet as a weapon, Robert knew Stubbs was going to be tough to beat.

Stubbs approached Robert and said, "It's like that."

Robert answered, "You won't ever ask me to carry your helmet in again."

Now, Stubbs was six inches taller and 110 pounds heavier than Robert. He could have taken Robert's head off if he wanted to. Instead, he laughed that deep, evil, scary laugh of his and walked away. Some other freshman picked up his helmet and cleaned it for him— not Robert. Evidently, he liked Robert's bravado—so did Jason.

In 1987, while I was at Duke Law School, Jason was a freshman at UM. He and Robert became best friends. In fact, when Robert was drafted in the fourth round by the Los Angeles Rams in 1991, Jason negotiated his contract.

What made Robert special is the uncanny ability he had to distinguish himself. Distinguishing yourself from your peers is what this chapter is all about.

The harsh reality for Robert was that he was too small, not fast enough, and too light to be a starter in the NFL. He just wasn't blessed with the physical ability necessary to be a great player in the NFL. But what he lacked in height, weight, speed, and strength, he made up for with intelligence, effort, and toughness.

The average NFL career lasts three seasons. So when Robert was released by the Rams after his fourth season, he had done well for himself. By playing more than three seasons, he qualified for his pension.

After a couple of weeks without a job, we signed him with the Washington Redskins at the start of the 1995 season. Unfortunately, the Redskins released him a little over a month later. At that point, in his fifth year, it looked like his career was coming to an end.

Drew and I were okay with this because we had earmarked Robert as the only person on the planet who could work with us whose last name wasn't Rosenhaus.

It wasn't that Robert was the only player who had what it took to be part of our company—there were several others—but only Robert was perfect for several reasons. First, he is extremely prideful—not arrogant, but determined to be the best at what he does. Second, Robert is very clever and always sees the angles. Third, he is a worker. He loves to work just like we do. Fourth, his loyalty and character had already been proven and were beyond question. Being competent and of high character, though, is not what separated him from many of our other clients. The single factor that separated Robert from the other players was that he was never a starter, so he didn't make the big money.

Robert never developed the complacency that can come with big money. And because he was always making the minimum salary, he had to work to pay the bills. Add the fact that Robert loves to work and be successful, plus his character and competence, and you have the ultimate partner.

Thinking there was a good chance that Robert's NFL career was done, Jason and I were all set to bring him into our company. The next day, the Dallas Cowboys called. Their defensive coordinator, Dave Campo, had been Robert's position coach back at UM. Coach Campo and the staff wanted Robert and gave him another chance.

Robert capitalized on the opportunity and completely resurrected his career. That year, 1995, he played on all passing downs and performed very well as the Cowboys went on to win the Super Bowl under Coach Barry Switzer.

The next year, 1996, Robert's old college coach Jimmy Johnson took over Don Shula's job as head coach of the Miami Dolphins. Jimmy loved Robert and signed him to the Dolphins. Unfortunately for Robert, his defensive coordinator, George Hill, did not share those feelings. Consequently, after he played for them for one year, the Dolphins let Robert go.

If you listen to Robert, he has an entertaining explanation for why Coach Hill soured on him, but I'm not sure I buy it. One morning Jason got a phone call from Stuart Weinstein, the Dolphins head of security. Stu is a great guy who is respected around the league and throughout South Florida's police stations.

Apparently, the police contacted Stu because Robert had gotten into an altercation. He was involved in a minor fender bender with some big country dude in Davie, Florida. The guy had a bad case of road rage and called Robert the N-word and pulled a tire iron on him. Big mistake.

When the guy swung the tire iron at Robert, Robert managed to duck under the swing, grab the guy, and wrestle the tire iron away from him. He punched the guy and stopped at that. Because the other guy attacked Robert, he was the one who got into trouble (Robert decided not to press charges).

However, although he himself did not get into trouble with the law, according to Robert, he was late to Coach Hill's meeting and from then on he was in the doghouse. Like I said, I don't think that being late was the reason Robert fell out of favor with Coach Hill; he probably likes an excuse to just tell the tale of his pugilistic adventure.

In any case, the Dolphins cut him in March of 1997, and at that point, Robert had been released three times. Jason and I realized that his career could finally be coming to an end, but the guy just kept on going like the Energizer bunny.

He went on to play three more seasons for the Detroit Lions as a defensive cornerback on passing downs and as a special-teams player. Along the way, he set a record for the longest punt return in NFL history. The play won him an ESPY Award and it personifies Robert's career.

The play started off like any other punt and ended up as the most bizarre punt return ever. The punter kicked the ball into the back of the end zone. Robert was supposed to block for the returner. The ball bounced high and looked to everyone like it was going to bounce out of bounds. Instead, it just kind of died in the corner of the end zone. Robert's teammate who was supposed to return the ball walked off the field.

Robert noticed that everyone else had presumed the ball was going out and that it was so deep in the end zone anyway that no one would be dumb enough to even think about returning it. Robert peeked left and then right, seeing that the players from both teams had stopped running, turned around, and started walking off the field. Before the referee blew the whistle, Robert scooped up the ball and started running by everyone. By the time the other team noticed him running, he had already passed them and returned the punt for a 103-yard touchdown. That play was voted the most outstanding play of the entire season and has become a staple for viewing at special-teams meetings in high school, college, and the pros.

When Robert's contract with the Lions expired in 2000, the Baltimore Ravens knocked on the door. Robert only played one year with them, but in that year, they won the Super Bowl. Does this guy have lady luck in his corner or what?

After the Super Bowl, Robert, who made a few notable plays in the big game, was released. He played one more year with the Lions in 2001 and, due to a neck injury, retired. The guy was more than just lucky; he was pretty smart, too. To prove it, he was one of the few players to both purchase and collect on a disability insurance policy that he acquired at the start of the 2001 season.

Smart, fearless, loyal, tough, proud, competent, aggressive, hard-working, hungry, and retired (finally), he was perfect to team up with Jason and me. And in Robert's first season, he did an awesome job of promoting Jeremy Shockey, Warren Sapp, Zach Thomas, and our other clients as well.

We didn't hire Robert because he was a tough guy. We brought him into our company and made him a partner because no matter where he went, he managed to distinguish himself from his peers.

We look for that quality in all our clients. The 'Canes used to be loaded with supertough players who excelled like that. Over time, they lost that edge. Hopefully Coach Randy Shannon, who was part of those championship teams, can bring them back. Until then, instead of there being a whole team full of winners, now there are just a select few in the group. But those select few are something special.

Sean Taylor was special. From day one as a freshman, he was a man among boys. At six-three and 220 pounds, he was not only the biggest safety on the field, but he was also the fastest. Never before had college football seen a safety that big and strong who hit that hard and ran that fast. He was truly an exceptional athlete.

But because Sean was only twenty years old when he left UM to enter the draft as a junior, he was wild. He had it all. Handsome, tall, athletic, smart, funny, charismatic, brute toughness—he was a projected top ten pick in the 2004 draft.

He had a very pretty girlfriend and came from a good family; his father was the police chief of his South Florida hometown, Florida City. I think because Sean had so much going for him, he had a hard time yielding to the system.

Sean played the game with everything he had. He threw his body around like he was made of steel. He worked hard and liked to party hard. He liked to have a good time—what college kid doesn't.

Recruiting Sean was tough, but we got it done. Jason, Robert, and I worked hard to keep Sean happy and on course. We knew he had a shot to be the fifth pick of the draft by the Redskins and I was in constant communication with their owner, Dan Snyder, Head Coach Joe Gibbs, and Executive Vice President of Football Operations Vinny Cerrato.

The whole time leading up to the draft, no matter what I said or did, Sean kept me at a distance. I tried to become one of his friends, but he wouldn't let me: I was a business associate—not a teammate, not a partner, not a comrade. It was frustrating for me because I need to have a close relationship with my clients so that I can trust them. I need to trust my clients because friendship and respect is all I have. My clients can all fire me tomorrow and I would be out of business. There are agents out there right now calling my clients, approaching my clients, trying to bribe my clients to fire me and hire them. The only thing that stops them from switching agents is our friendship and their confidence in me to succeed for them. One without the other isn't enough to keep a client in the NFL.

With Sean, I knew he had confidence in me, but I also knew we weren't close. On draft day, in April 2004, Sean, his friends and family erupted in celebration when he was the fifth overall pick taken in the first round by the Washington Redskins. Sean wanted to be the fifth pick. He was competing against his former UM teammate Kellen Winslow II, who ended up being drafted sixth by the Cleveland Browns. Sean told me he wanted to go fifth and to the Redskins. I worked hard to make that happen, and when it did, I thought Sean would finally break and let me be one of his friends. It didn't happen that way.

I hugged Sean and congratulated him when we got the call, but he still seemed distant. I figured in time, we'd get tight. The next day, we flew out on Snyder's private jet to the Redskin facility, where they held a big press conference for Sean. At the conference, Coach Gibbs specifically thanked me for my hard work during the entire draft process. They were counting on me to help manage Sean.

That day, I played racquetball with the team's owner, Dan Snyder. I thought with my relationship with the owner and head coach, and with the success we'd had on draft day, Sean would never fire me. I thought wrong. Within a few days, I got a termination letter faxed to my office from Sean. I couldn't believe it. I was devastated.

I'd worked so hard to help Sean become the fifth pick. I was sick over losing a great player and humiliated that the news he fired me was all over the national media. I was angry about it, but I kept my composure. From time to time, Sean called me to say he was thinking about rehiring me. I told him if he wanted me to negotiate his contract, I would get the job done for him. In late July, Sean had a new agent and had that agent negotiate his contract. A few days later, Kellen Winslow signed his contract.

One morning I was out at the Dolphins' training facility watching a training-camp practice. My phone rang and it was Sean. He told me he was upset that his contract had come in below market and he said he wanted me to be his agent. He apologized for what had happened and promised that it would never happen again.

From then on, Sean was great to me. Before, he looked at me as someone to use for a purpose. Afterward, he looked at me as his friend. It finally happened, we grew close. And although I didn't make any money on the deal since another agent negotiated it, I was thrilled to represent Sean. I like money as much as the next guy, but money isn't enough reward for what I give.

As hard as I try, I can't tell you how much fun it was for me to watch Sean play. He was such a hard hitter, such a tough guy among tough guys, that his Redskin teammates nicknamed him "The Meast" for being half man, half beast. Almost single-handedly, he turned that Redskin defense into one that was feared by opposing offenses.

I watched Sean play like a monster for four seasons and loved it. Most of all, I enjoyed watching him turn into a man. His first year, he skipped a mandatory rookie symposium. He was fined heavily but didn't care. He was not going to do something he did not want to do.

In 2005, his second year, Sean was involved in a serious situation. On June 5, 2005, it was reported that he had allegedly caught a couple of shady characters who had apparently stolen his two ATVs; he tracked them down, and allegedly pulled a gun on one of them and punched the other guy in the face.

It was reported that Sean was charged with aggravated assault with a firearm, a felony, and misdemeanor battery. For that, if found guilty, he was looking at serving sixteen years in prison.

When he called me, I never asked him what happened. My job was to help him find legal representation and that was what I did. His trial was scheduled for after the 2005 season, which allowed him at least to play out the year. With the specter of jail hanging over his head, Sean had an excellent 2005 season. After a protracted legal battle, the felony charges were dropped.

With that case behind him, Sean went on to have his best year in 2006 and was voted into the Pro Bowl. The 2007 off-season was his best. He had a baby girl with his beautiful longtime girlfriend, Jackie Garcia, the niece of the movie star Andy Garcia, and it profoundly changed his life.

Sean became something of a recluse. No more parties, no more nightclubs, no more going out. He was all about his family and his profession. He even got rid of his gun. He was all about his daughter and being the best football player he could be. He was poised for a great 2007 season and *Sports Illustrated* named him the hardest hitter in the NFL. He worked very hard in the summer to be in great shape. He even worked out with me, running wind sprints, to have fun with his training.

He got off to an unbelievable start and led the NFC in interceptions before missing two games with a knee injury. On Friday night, November 23, 2007, he called me to say he was thinking about coming to Miami. He told me that he wasn't going to play in the game against the Tampa Bay Bucs and that he wanted Dr. John Uribe to look at his knee. I told him to let me know and I would clear it with the team and have his flight set up for him. As I hung up the phone, I told him, "I'll talk to you later."

Those were the last words I said to him. Two nights later, at 1:45 A.M., Sean heard burglars breaking into his South Florida house. He was in bed with his girlfriend and daughter. Since he no longer kept a gun, he grabbed a machete, told Jackie to hide under the bed, and went out into the living room. He startled the four robbers. One of them apparently panicked and shot Sean in the upper inside left leg. Tragically, Sean was shot in the femoral artery near his groin.

Jason and I got the call in the middle of the night. His dad told us that Sean had been shot in the leg. We raced over to the Jackson Memorial Trauma Center. We had been there before. Just ten days after Young Soo Do's funeral, we were there again waiting for word on Sean.

Jason called Robert and he raced over there, too. The Redskins owner Dan Snyder, Vinny Cerrato, and running back Clinton Portis all flew in immediately on Snyder's private jet.

We learned that Sean had lost a tremendous amount of blood. He was in a coma after the surgery from all the blood loss. His heart had stopped twice during the emergency surgery.

To replace the lost blood, they pumped him full of "foreign" blood, which his body rejected. That Monday night, he took a turn for the better. Sean squeezed the doctor's hand and showed signs of recovering consciousness. When the doctor came out and told us this, we all rejoiced. The Redskins asked me to make a statement to the media about the positive development, but I just couldn't do it. For the first time in my life, I couldn't face the cameras. It just didn't seem right for me to talk about my friend who was fighting for his life. I asked the Redskins to do it for me and they were gracious enough to do so.

I left the hospital late that night feeling optimistic. I went to bed hoping for the first time in my life that the phone wouldn't ring. I didn't want bad news. Then, a few hours later, I got the call I was dreading. Sean had passed away at three-thirty in the morning.

Jason, Robert, and I were shell-shocked. Just two weeks after losing Young Soo Do, we had lost Sean as well. Those were two of the most indestructible men I ever knew. It turned out that the panicked burglar who'd shot Sean was some seventeen-year-old punk. It was sheer chance that the bullet struck the femoral artery. Man, if only Sean had never gotten injured or hadn't made that trip to Miami... If only...

It just makes me sick to think that some seventeen-year-old coward with a gun could kill someone so strong, tough, and full of life. Nowadays kids are buying false bravado from drugs and guns instead of developing bravery from within. It is senseless, heartbreaking, and unjust to think a beautiful little girl will have to grow up without her father. She and her mother will have to live the rest of their lives with the horror of knowing that Sean was shot in the groin and bled to death in terrible pain. Why?

Shortly after Sean passed away, I got a phone call. It was from someone who'd heard someone talking about the burglary. He told me that he suspected that a guy he knew was involved. I put Sean's father Pete on the phone with him and it led to the arrest of the four killers. Although it was a small part, I take a great deal of satisfaction in knowing that I did what I could to bring those murderers to justice. I wish I could do the same for Young Soo Do, whose murder remains unsolved.

It was disgusting to me the way the media speculated about the circumstances surrounding Sean's shooting while his family was praying for him to recover and then when they were mourning his passing. Report after report speculated about how Sean's off-season troubles had caught up with him and contributed to his shooting.

The four teens who broke into Sean's home didn't know him. Someone who knew Sean bragged about his wealth in front of those four hoods. They thought Sean was out of town since the season was going on and it was a Sunday night. They weren't looking for him and Sean did nothing to bring this upon himself. But that didn't stop the media from speculating in a manner that showed no consideration toward Sean or his family. And people call me a bad guy? You didn't see my face on TV talking about Sean, even when his team and family asked me to do so. You didn't see me until I spoke at Sean's funeral. Shame on the media; they made me sick.

At the funeral, I was with so many of my clients…Redskin running back Clinton Portis, Redskin wide receiver Santana Moss, Redskin linebacker London Fletcher, Redskin running back Rock Cartwright, Redskin defensive end Demetric Evans, Giants receiver Plaxico Burress, Giant tight end Jeremy Shockey, Cardinal running back Edgerrin James, Cardinal defensive back Antrel Rolle, Bronco linebacker Nate Webster, Bronco center Chris Myers, Panther linebacker Jon Beason, Panther defensive tackle Damione Lewis, Buccaneer cornerback Phillip Buchanon, Steeler running back Najeh Davenport, Giant running back Reuben Droughns, Bears defensive tackle Tommie Harris, Eagles defensive end Jerome McDougle, 49ers running back Frank Gore, Giant defensive tackle William Joseph, Bengals receiver Chad Johnson, Eagles defensive end Jevon Kearse, Bears linebacker Darrell McClover, Saints cornerback Mike McKenzie, Giants cornerback Sam Madison, Giants linebacker Antonio Pearce, Bengals linebacker Lemar Marshall, future Giants safety Kenny Phillips, Rams tight end Randy McMichael, Giants wide receiver Sinorice Moss, Bears tight end Greg Olsen, Saints tight end Buck Ortega, and Bills wide receiver Roscoe Parrish.

Every single one of those guys who was there, without exception, shed tears throughout the service. I myself broke down when

I addressed the crowd, and during Sean's eulogy, I thanked him for being a hero and saving Jackie and his daughter's lives.

I couldn't believe the class of the Redskin organization. Not only did Dan Snyder fly the whole team and organization down on a charter jet for the funeral, but he donated $500,000 to a trust fund for Sean's daughter. And he did more than give money. As I walked over to him, I watched him wipe tears from his eyes. He is truly a great owner whom Redskin fans should be thankful for.

All in all, it was a brutally sad day and it was hard to watch the Redskins play the rest of the season without Sean. One thing about him that I know is that he would want his friends to learn from his mistakes. He would want other young kids coming out of college to learn what he learned.

What Sean learned is that it's never too late to enjoy your life and appreciate your blessings. It's never too late to make things right and become a better person. As a Pro Bowler and a safety, Sean distinguished himself as the hardest hitter in the game. On the football field, he'd distinguished himself since high school. But from the moment his daughter was born, Sean learned to be something more. Before it was his time to leave this world, he learned to distinguish himself as a person, as a father, as a teammate, and as a friend. In the end, he did it right. Rest in peace, my friend, rest in peace. We'll be with you down the road...

CHAPTER 6

DISTINGUISH YOURSELF
PART II

IN THE LAST CHAPTER, I EXPLAINED HOW SEAN TAYLOR and Robert Bailey distinguished themselves. In this chapter, I am going to tell you how I did it. I did it by being the good guy!

Okay, I know, that's pretty ironic considering that in 1996 my face was on the cover of *Sports Illustrated* with the title "The Most Hated Man in the NFL." I know that a lot of people find it amusing that I consider myself the good guy, but as Jason (who's read five books on Einstein's theory of relativity) likes to say, everything is relative.

Sure, my competitors despise me. Being fired is a terrible experience to have to go through. Keep in mind that out of our 110 NFL clients, 81 of them fired their previous agent in order to hire us. That's a lot of pissed-off agents. And when you take into account all of the agents who have been fired over the last twenty years or so by players who hired me, there are a lot of agents out there with an ax to grind. But that's their fault. Most of the time, you won't get fired if you do a good job and work hard. Sometimes it's just bad luck that gets you fired. Either way, it's easy to blame me. And they want to because getting fired in this business is especially tough: not only do you lose a client whom you've worked so hard to sign (as well as the income you would have derived from that client), but you get it rubbed in your face every time you see that ex-client play on TV, knowing that your rival agent is now enjoying representing him instead of you. It's very painful, but it is a part of the business that happens to every successful agent, including me. It's terrifying to lose a client because it creates insecurity among other clients. And your competitor agents use it against you in recruiting. When it happens to me, because I am high profile, it is splashed all over the media, so it is embarrassing to boot. I like to think I am fearless, but the truth is I do fear failure and especially getting fired.

I know how much it hurts to lose a client. That's one of the reasons I work so hard to keep my clients happy and loyal. That's also the reason dozens of other agents who have been fired by my clients have so much animosity toward me.

Fans get mad at me because oftentimes, when a player wants more money or to be traded, it's frustrating for them. Almost all of my dealings with the teams are low profile and positive. However, when that rare situation arises where the player and the team are at a total impasse, and there is no other alternative, sometimes the media's involvement is a necessary evil. When the dispute becomes public, everyone gets a black eye, but I do what I can to take the punch for my client. By my being visible, the fans become angry with me instead of my client and that's how it should be. It's better that the complaints are directed at me.

If you talk to my competitors and the fans (in certain situations), I may be labeled the bad guy, but to my clients and their families, I am the hero. To the rich Normans of England, Robin Hood (a Norman himself) was a villain who robbed them. To the poor Saxons, Robin Hood was a hero who took from the rich and gave to the poor. To my clients and their family, I work hard to get them the kind of money that can provide them with lifetime financial security. To them, I am the good guy. It's all relative, depending on what your perspective is. And the perspective that matters the most to me is that of my clients and my family.

I don't want to be a villain. I want to be the good guy, like Batman, Conan, Bruce Lee, and Rocky. In this business being the good guy means representing your client in the best interest of the client. I realized that if I outwork the competition to produce better results for my client, other players would see it and want to work with me. This was 1989. They weren't just the days of *Miami Vice* for the drug-smuggling industry, they were *Miami Vice* days for sports agents, too.

The sports-agent business was dirty. Today, the NCAA, state legislation, and the NFLPA have cleaned it up tremendously, but back then it was very shady. At the time, two NFL agents (Norby Walters and Lloyd Bloom) had just been convicted of federal charges in connection with a scheme to defraud several universities by paying cash to athletes in exchange for signing improper contracts, and then threatening to harm them if they tried to renege.

Walters and Bloom signed more than forty athletes by paying them cash before they were through playing college football. Agents are not permitted to give any type of benefit to a college player until they have played their last college game. Walters and Bloom signed players to contracts before their college season was over and then, when players tried to back out of the deal, they threatened to have the Mob break their legs. Even though their convictions were later overturned on appeal, the situation led to many states passing laws that make it a crime for agents to sign players before their collegiate season is over. If I were to buy a college football player a cup of coffee today in Florida, I could go to jail for a year since I would be guilty of a felony.

Although Bloom's conviction was overturned on appeal, he didn't walk away from his past. In August 1993, he was shot several times in the chest while in his own home. There were no signs of forced entry and no weapon was found. It was an obvious Mob hit. You play with fire...

That being said, I believe in being aggressive, in taking chances, and in betting on yourself but only in the best interest of your client and always in playing by the rules. I have been taking chances and betting on myself from day one. Sometimes that is the only way to distinguish yourself from your peers. My very first draft, in 1989, presented me with a once-in-a-lifetime opportunity and I wasn't too scared to take it.

As I mentioned earlier, I started working for another agent, Mel Levine, in the summer of 1988, and by January 1989, I had signed several good rookies to join the firm. We had a lot of success my first year. To keep me with the firm, Mel offered me a big salary and bonuses in addition to paying my expenses. He told me that when Jason was ready, he'd bring him into the firm as well. He offered me everything I could ask for. The future looked very bright for me and I would have no financial pressure at all.

But I wanted to be my own man. I didn't want to be Mel's junior partner. I believed that I could break out on my own, start my own firm, and take my top recruit, Robert Massey, with me. I didn't think Mel could help me anymore and I believed I could sell myself and build my own company from the ground up. The problem was I had no money and was still in my second year of law school at Duke. Plus, Mel had a strong grip on the University of Miami, representing many great players like Michael Irvin, Brett Perriman, Bennie Blades, and Brian Blades. Competing against him would be very difficult. I was tempted to stay on another year, learn from Mel, and break away only when the time seemed more propitious. When you have a good thing going, why screw it up? Because I didn't want a good thing: I wanted something great. Jimmy Johnson, when he coached the Miami Dolphins, had a saying: "The enemy of good is great." I think Jimmy got that quote by paraphrasing Voltaire, but I can't prove it. Anyways, I love that quote. Good makes you complacent and eats away at your drive to be great.

I remember talking to Jason about whether I should stay with Mel or go out on my own. He just laughed, saying, "Drew, you already know what you are going to do, so why are you asking?" He knew my aggressive nature; he knew I was going to go for it.

I didn't want to be a small fish in a big pond. I wanted to be the biggest fish in the biggest pond. I wanted to distinguish myself. So I decided to leave the firm. I made my decision right before the draft. I didn't think it would be fair to Mel to stay on another year, all the while plotting to leave him.

In making my move, in order to make it work, I knew I would have to distinguish myself from Mel and all the other agents out there. So I came up with the idea of inviting ESPN to my apartment in Durham, North Carolina, to televise Robert Massey getting drafted. I sold them on the idea that Massey would be chosen anywhere from the late first round to the beginning of the third round. I sold them on the angle of the youngest agent in the history of the business (twenty-two years of age) representing a player in the draft. I sold them on the idea of an unknown, up-and-coming agent representing an unknown, up-and-coming player. Massey didn't have a big name because he played for a small school—North Carolina Central. I sold myself, I sold Robert, and they bought it. They ended up doing a feature on us that they showed on draft day.

ESPN sent a camera crew to my apartment on draft day and they kept shooting live video of us and interviewing us all day during the draft. We got incredible, one-of-a-kind exposure. We made a huge splash.

With Robert Massey coming out of North Carolina Central, an extremely small school with zero exposure, he needed all the hype he could get. And guess who else made a name for himself—me. Every single college player who watched the draft saw me all over the TV. All the players I went to school with saw me on ESPN. Every agent in the business, including Mel, watched me (some twenty-two-year-old law student) on ESPN, promoting my client on draft day. Other players entering the draft were pissed off at their agents, asking why they weren't on TV instead of Massey. Every other agent was aggravated with me, wondering how the hell I got on ESPN. As for Mel, he wasn't too happy to see me on TV saying Robert was my client instead of his. I called him right afterward to tell him I was leaving and taking Robert with me. He wasn't happy, but it was business, nothing personal. I had to do what was best for my future, not his. When he asked me why I waited until then to tell him, I explained to him that I couldn't risk him sabotaging my big move until after I made it.

It was all a big gamble, but sometimes that's what you have to do to distinguish yourself. Had Robert not been drafted pretty high, I would have looked bad. Not only would I have been embarrassed, but I would have had a hard time selling rookies to sign with me next year. It's not like Mel would take me back if I fell flat on my face. But I had confidence that Robert would be drafted in the second round and that's exactly what happened. I took a gamble and won. So did Robert. He got exposure to help him with his marketing opportunities in New Orleans, where he was drafted. We were no longer unknowns.

That took guts on my part. To walk away from a good thing and put everything I had on the line on national TV, it was nerve-racking. Rather than be scared, I was excited about succeeding. In hindsight, it turned out that I wasn't walking away from such a good thing, as Mel was busted for ripping his clients off. As I mentioned, he was sentenced to thirty months in federal prison for committing tax and financial fraud with his clients.

It seemed to me that if the agents in the business weren't crooks, they were cows. They were soft, lazy, or greedy. I knew that if I busted my butt for my clients, acted in their best interest, and did a good job, they would recommend me to their teammates.

I could see how the business was and how I could be better. I wanted to make the agent industry better by elevating it to a new standard. Back then, agents spoke to clients only once in a while. It was like an attorney-client type of relationship. It was businesslike, conducted only when necessary. It was an easy job in which agents didn't have to work very hard. There weren't a ton of agents and the competition wasn't as fierce as it is now. Jason and I changed the business for the better as every agent has to work harder and do a better job or their client will be calling me.

While the competition tripped over their own feet, rising fast was (as Jason says all the time) just a matter of two things—working hard and working smart.

That's what I did for Massey. I either talked to him over the phone or visited with him every day. Robert knew that although I lacked experience, I would make up for it with dedication, determination, and drive. He believed in me and I in him.

Robert and I became like brothers. The business would change forever as I turned representing players from a business relationship into more of a family relationship. We were closer to our clients than the competition. It became our way of life to develop close bonds and friendships with our clients as we were each making our dreams a reality.

Shortly after the draft, Massey and I got a lot of recognition as an intriguing duo. I was brash, flashy, energetic, and confident. That made for good TV features and newspaper articles. The locals were shocked that a Duke law student could be an agent at the same time.

I saw that utilizing the media could be a big way for an agent to distinguish his client and himself. We had great results, and I didn't want the exposure to end on draft day. I asked myself what more I could do to promote Robert. He was a cornerback from North Carolina Central who was drafted in the second round by the Saints—that's not very sexy. It was tough enough to get ESPN to do a feature on him. Back then, in 1989, there was ESPN and that was it. There was no Internet or other sports-oriented channels hungry for stories. It was ESPN's market and they were very selective.

What else could I get ESPN to do? How could I take distinguishing ourselves one step further? If you were in my shoes, what could you do? What would you do?

What I did was make an ultra-aggressive move. I went to ESPN and asked them if they would be willing to film, for the first time in NFL history, the actual negotiations. I told them that I wanted to bring an ESPN camera crew in with me when I met with the Saints' powerful general manager, Jim Finks, to negotiate Robert's contract. Now, Finks was a top candidate to replace Pete Rozelle as NFL commissioner. He was almost sixty and was part of the old guard. He had a reputation as a tough, hard-line negotiator. He was as powerful in the NFL as a GM could get, as he was the chairman of the competition committee.

I, on the other hand, was a twenty-two-year-old kid still in law school, trying to negotiate my first contract. ESPN loved the angle of David versus Goliath. They, of course, agreed. The hard part was getting Finks to do something that no other executive had ever done. How could I persuade him to do it?

Well, he was making a push to become the next commissioner. Here was an opportunity for him to promote himself as the stalwart negotiator that he was. I was shocked when he agreed to do it. I guess he couldn't turn down a challenge from a kid agent.

Keep in mind, most second-year law students are nervous taking an exam. There I was, having no training or experience whatsoever, about to walk into the NFL's toughest negotiator's office. To top it off, I was about to do it with an ESPN camera crew filming the whole meeting. If Finks were to rip me apart and crush my arguments, I would be ruined on national TV. Was I scared? No.

The most important thing of all to me was to win for the person who trusted me with his future, who believed in me, who was my true friend—Robert Massey. I was so hungry to succeed for him that I thought Finks was the one who should be scared.

On the big day, I showed up dressed like Sonny Crockett, Don Johnson's character in the 1980s TV show *Miami Vice*. I had the sport coat with T-shirt underneath. I wore black shoes without socks. I was sporting a gold necklace, gold bracelet, and gold ring. And, of course, I had the slicked-back, moussed hairstyle. ESPN ate it up.

There I was, only twenty-two years old, still in law school, mind you, getting ready to walk in the door with an ESPN camera crew and negotiate against Jim Finks, the toughest negotiator in the NFL. The guy was old school and hard-nosed.

The ESPN people stopped me as I was walking in, and filmed me saying, "I'm fired up. My adrenaline is pumping!"

Ever since I started training with Young Soo Do, ever since I wanted to make my dad proud, ever since I decided in high school that I wanted to be a winner, ever since I decided in college to be an agent, and ever since I busted my butt studying insane hours at Duke Law School, I had been training myself for that meeting.

Where other twenty-two-year-olds would have crapped their pants, I was sticking my chest out like Superman. I walked in there without any fear and made my arguments. Finks was very professional and courteous with me, but he made his point clear. We both made our points and, objectively speaking, walked out of there at a friendly impasse. To quote Ron Burgundy, the Will Ferrell character in *Anchorman,* we agreed to disagree.

That, in and of itself, was a victory. That I held my own was a victory. Afterward, Finks said to ESPN, "Drew doesn't lack enthusiasm [and] he's a pretty smooth operator." That was high praise from the most respected NFL negotiator in the business at that time. We made some big waves in the big pond.

Once again I garnered a lot of recognition for my client. Once again I distinguished myself from among my peers as an agent. What I realize, looking back, is that I'd been trying to distinguish myself from high school on. As a kid, I loved the movies *Rocky* and *Conan*

Me with Pro Bowl Tampa Bay Buccaneer defensive tackle Warren Sapp at his January 1998 wedding in Hawaii.

This is me concentrating as I prepare to karate chop ten concrete blocks with my teacher Grand Master Young Soo Do and Jason at my side in 2003.

Here's Jason punching through ten concrete blocks trying to impress Cassandra when they first started dating in 2003. Grand Master Young Soo Do and I are there hoping he doesn't break his knuckles.

Me with New England Patriot linebacker Larry Izzo and Miami Dolphin linebacker Zach Thomas at a 2004 Pro Bowl practice in Hawaii.

Here's Jason, Jeremy Shockey, and me hanging out in South Beach in 2004.

Here's Jason standing in front of a huge poster of his wife, Cassandra, a Miami Heat Dancer, at the American Airlines Arena during the 2006 Heat Championship season.

Me with Pro Bowl Carolina Panther linebacker Dan Morgan at a 2007 event in Charlotte, North Carolina.

Here's Jason and me standing in front of the Crown Plaza Hotel at the 2007 Indianapolis NFL Scouting Combine.

Our Rosenhaus Sports mascots—Chubby, the big English bulldog, and Spanky, the smaller French bulldog.

Jessie Armstead, me, Robert Bailey, and Jason at Robert Bailey's annual golf tournament in Miami, 2008. *Claude Zick Photographer*

Here's the Rosenhaus Sports crew in April 2008 with Jessie Armstead, Danny Martoe, me, Robert Bailey, Hugh Fuller, and Jason. Note the picture of Sean Taylor on the shirts. *Big C Photos*

Me with client Devin Thomas on draft day April 26, 2008, in Miami Beach.

Me with client Kenny Phillips on draft day April 26, 2008, in Miami Beach.

Jason and his wife, Cassandra, with their daughter, Aubrey.
Butch Stark Photography

the Barbarian. My favorite comic-book character was Batman. What they all had in common was that they overcame great adversity to become superheroes. That may sound corny, but having the heart and toughness to distinguish yourself is something I take great pride in. It's something everyone should take pride in.

When I was learning karate, I wasn't the best martial artist, but I earned Young Soo Do's admiration for my effort. When I was in high school, I wasn't the most gifted student, but I got my stuff together and studied harder than everyone else. When I was at the University of Miami, I could have spent my time partying like all the other kids, but instead I was in the library. I developed confidence in myself by being a harder worker than the next guy. When I got to Duke Law School, I was surrounded by some of the brightest legal minds in the country, yet I was the one who found a way to distinguish himself by being an agent who appeared on ESPN in only my second year. And when I got out into the business world, I continued to work hard and smart to find ways to distinguish myself.

The point is not that I am special. The point is that no matter how young or old you are, no matter what you do, there is a way for you to distinguish yourself and take pride in who you are. My parents take great pride in being great parents—is there anything more important than that? My uncle Howard, who works with us by helping entertain the guys, takes great pride in being a ladies' man at sixty-five years old and at being a great uncle. My uncle Richard takes great pride in leasing office space in Manhattan. My uncle Sonny takes great pride in being a renowned heart surgeon. My mom takes great pride in having raised three children who turned out to be like her—a good person with a sense of family and a heart of gold.

My sister, Dana, takes great pride in being an attorney and an outstanding mother. Her husband, Adam Swickle, our brother-in-law, takes pride in working with our clients as their attorney and does an unbelievable job as their legal representative (and also in being a father). Everybody can work hard to be their best at something and that's what distinguishing yourself is all about.

Okay, I broke into the business and negotiated Robert Massey's second round rookie contract in 1989. I gained national recognition and let my competition know that I was a force to reckon with. In the end, as great a person as Massey was, he was one client. I wanted to break one hundred. I wanted to get to the top. In order to do that, I had to come up with a plan to build an empire. I didn't have any money. I didn't even have an office. But I had a plan and that plan was to become the king of Miami.

CHAPTER 7

KNOW WHICH BATTLES TO PICK

WHEN PEOPLE SPEAK OF SOUTH FLORIDA IN A POSITIVE light, they will usually tell you about the warm weather, the South Beach nightclubs and restaurants, the fun in the sun at the beach, the boating, the tennis, and the golf. If you love beaches, nightclubs, water sports, tennis, or golf, you'll love Miami. But there's one other aspect to South Florida that you don't hear about that is unparalleled in the country—football players. If you want to be an NFL agent, there is no better place than South Florida to make your headquarters.

When I first got into the business, between the Miami Hurricanes and the Miami Dolphins, there were football players all around me. Plus, there were dozens of players from South Florida who'd gone to other schools and played in the NFL. South Florida was and still is a pipeline to the NFL. And because I had South Florida in common with all these players, potential clients were everywhere. I wanted to make the University of Miami Hurricanes and the Miami Dolphins my turf. I wanted every agent to know that those two teams were my backyard. I knew that if I could monopolize South Florida, I could build an empire. So I picked the Hurricanes and the Dolphins as my target market. I pitched my tent and made South Florida my battleground.

When I came back to Miami after graduating from Duke in 1990, I went after the University of Miami Hurricanes. Two players from my UM days with whom I had maintained a relationship hired me—linebacker Bernard "Tiger" Clark and defensive lineman Jimmie Jones. Both went in the third round of the 1990 draft. Jason and I were so excited when the players were drafted that we jumped into our backyard canal to celebrate. That year, I also recruited two other players who were both top ten picks and came in second place. Guess what an agent gets for second place? Nothing but heartache! But that failure only made me more determined to succeed.

I swore that the next year I would get a first-round pick from UM. I targeted wide receiver Randal "Thrill" Hill. Randal was super fast and highly rated. He came from a great family and we became friends during the recruitment process. I called him or visited with him every day toward the end of the season. I outworked the competition and was no longer a rookie agent. The previous rookie contracts I'd negotiated fared well with respect to the market. I finally had some experience, and although it wasn't a great deal, I overcompensated for it with hands-on, personal attention. Randal hired me and we were confident he would be a first-round pick. We also signed Jason's friend and UM cornerback Robert Bailey.

The Dolphins at the time had just built Joe Robbie Stadium and were gracious enough to allow us to hold our draft party in one of their sky-box suites. The flagship radio station for the Dolphins, WIOD, had a huge draft party at the stadium as well. Randal also had a big crew. As the middle of the 1991 draft approached, I started to get uptight that Randal might not go in the first round. There were only a few teams that needed a wide receiver and all of them passed on Randal except for one team—the Dolphins. They had the twenty-third pick, and when they were on the clock, we got nervous. They had fifteen minutes to make their pick and each second ticked by as if it were an hour. If they passed on him, then Randal would go in the second round and would lose millions. It would be devastating for him and for me. On the other hand, if the Dolphins, our hometown team, were to draft him it would be our greatest dream come true. After ten minutes had gone by, I was dying. We were either going to be big winners or disappointments. Any second now and we would know which. Then the phone rang and Miami Dolphin head coach Don Shula's voice was on the other end of the line. The room erupted with joy! Jason and I hugged each other, screaming and yelling like we'd won the lottery. It was one of the happiest moments of our lives.

We were ecstatic because not only did we do a great job for our client, but we finally had our first-round-pick rookie, who'd been a Hurricane and was going to be a Miami Dolphin. It was everything we dreamed of. As Dolphin fans, we were thrilled about the idea of Randal catching passes from Dan Marino for the next ten years. From every standpoint, our client's, our business's, and as Dolphin fans, this was amazing. We were the big winners.

I was convinced that having a Hurricane as a first-round pick would allow me to take over and dominate UM. I was convinced that having a Dolphin first-round pick would allow me to take over and dominate the Dolphins. I was convinced that I was going to make it big in this business. The future was bright and everything was there for the taking.

Once again, I wanted to maximize the situation by getting a lot of media exposure for my client. I was very high profile and wanted an outstanding contract. I negotiated through the media and the negotiation became very public. When training camp started, I kept Randal out since I wanted a superb contract. It became a protracted holdout, which pissed the Dolphins off. I became known in South Florida as the holdout agent and people would come up to me and say, "Drew, get 'em signed on time."

In the end, I got the contract that we wanted for my client. We were now on top of the world. My first first-round contract was an outstanding win. I took on the Dolphins and succeeded. I was poised to be the man.

And then one day, just a few weeks after the negotiations, Don Shula called me. He wanted to talk to me and Randal at the same time. He asked us if we were sitting down and then told us that he'd traded Randal to the Phoenix Cardinals.

No way! That was impossible! It had to be some kind of prank. No team trades away their first-round player the same year that they sign him. It was devastating.

Just like that, everything I worked so hard for was gone. I was hurting bad, and to make matters even worse, so was my client. Flying to Phoenix with Randal, while trying to put a positive spin on things, was gut-wrenching. Just a few months after celebrating like madmen, I lost my Dolphin first-round pick.

Randal was upset because he loved the idea of staying in his hometown and playing for the Dolphins. I was upset because the trade came as a consequence of the holdout. Don Shula wanted to teach players and agents the lesson that if you hold a player out and negotiate through the media, he is going to get rid of you. It was extremely humbling.

My local competitor agents loved it! The media and fans crucified me. Everyone in the business predicted that I was ruined. Everyone except for Jim "Mad Dog" Mandich, who was the starting tight end on the undefeated 1972 Miami Dolphin Super Bowl team. Jim, whom I consider a friend to this day, told me that I was going to take a hit and have a tough year, but I'd be back. He had a local TV show on Sunday nights called *Sports Wrap.* He put me on his show so that I could state my case. He was the only guy in the media who was fair with me and was a straight shooter. Everyone else blew with the wind and figured I was done.

There was one great development, though. Shortly after the trade, I went to a Dallas Cowboy game at Tampa. While I was in the stands, my UM friend Michael Irvin, who'd helped me get into this business, came over to me and actually told me that he wanted me to represent him. Since Mel turned out to be a crook, he was looking for a new agent. I jumped all over the opportunity and was ecstatic to sign Michael.

He was just coming off a severe knee injury, but I knew he would make it back in a big way. He'd had an awesome year and his contract was coming up for renewal. He was the kind of client I could build my entire business around. I was back!

And then, a few months later, he fired me to go with a local Dallas agent. It was a real kick in the balls! First the trade and now this. I should have been dead and buried.

Mad Dog was right: I did take a hit. I lost my presence on the Dolphins and I couldn't get any college players to sign with me the next year, in 1992. The 1992 NFL draft came and went without me being heard from. I was forgotten.

Down but not out, I came back swinging. The Dolphins had a Pro Bowl defensive end named Jeff Cross who was a ladies' man. Although very professional and responsible, Jeff liked to go out and have a good time like everybody else. Jeff had watched closely how hard I fought for Randal to get the contract we wanted. He saw how I wasn't intimidated by Shula. He also saw how determined I was to succeed. He wanted an agent who was hungry to succeed for him. He saw how pissed off I was. He saw how much I wanted to show everyone that I wasn't finished. He told me that he was interested in me and so I went out with him every weekend until he hired me. Not only was he a great guy, but he was also a heck of a football player. His contract was coming up and he was the big upcoming negotiation for the Dolphins.

When Jeff signed with me, he recommended me to a lot of his teammates. Before long, I represented several other Dolphin players like Pro Bowl kicker Pete Stoyanovich, running back Mark Higgs, and cornerback J. B. Brown. And you know what, I got their deals done on time without a holdout. I thought Coach Shula would harbor animosity toward me over what had happened with Randal. But I was wrong. Coach Shula was a class act toward me. I never met a more principled man. I have an incredible amount of respect for Coach Shula because not only was he the winningest coach in the history of the NFL, but he did things the right way. He never lied, cheated, or was unethical. You always knew where he stood and that was for what was right. Nowadays, coaches are like politicians in that they will say and do anything to get what they want. Coach Shula never compromised his principles and was one of a kind. And he was an outstanding family man as well.

Okay, I was back with the Dolphins, having several players and expanding my roster. I also signed several veterans who used to be with Mel Levine—wide receiver Brett Perriman, wide receiver Brian Blades, and a couple of others. I was on the rise again, but I had to get back on track with the rookies.

I targeted the best college linebacker I had ever seen up to that time—FSU stud Marvin Jones. Marvin grew up in Coral Gables right across from UM, but somehow went to FSU. His brother Fred, a tough, hard-nosed cop, handled his agent selection process. Fred's a good guy, don't get me wrong, but he was hard to win over. Jason and I worked our butts off to impress him. We wanted him to see we were hard workers who were hungrier and more determined than the competition. We would go jogging with him even if we were in jeans and boots (back then we actually wore cowboy boots all the time—don't ask why). We put out an unbelievable effort and signed Marvin, along with two other Hurricanes that year—wide receiver Kevin Williams, who went in the second round to the Cowboys, and linebacker Jessie Armstead, who went to the New York Giants.

Jessie would go on to become a perennial Pro Bowl player for the Giants who had an outstanding career. He's an exceptionally bright, talented young man with an equally bright future after football.

It turned out that Marvin was the fourth overall pick in the first round of the 1993 draft. He was taken by the New York Jets. Since we had family in New York (our cousin Jordan was a huge Jet fan), we were excited to represent a Jet and a Giant.

When we first signed Marv, the agent community was shocked.

They thought we had come and gone. They thought wrong. The problem for us was that I was fresh out of school with limited funds.

As a top five pick, Marvin expected us to treat him like every other agent would—after he signed, to provide him with housing, a stipend, and transportation for him to train. We had to lend him our car, move him into our apartment, and borrow money to give to him. Jason and I moved into our parents' house, shared one car, slept on the floor of our parents' living room, and worked out of our mother's interior-decorator office. It wasn't easy, but we stretched every dollar to the max and got the job done.

Signing Marvin, Kevin, and Jessie was monumental. We got back all the momentum we had lost and became hot.

Over the next couple of years I continued my campaign to sign Hurricanes and Dolphins. From UM, I signed fullback Donnell Bennett, who was the 1994 second-round pick of the Kansas City Chiefs. From the Dolphins, I signed Pro Bowl safety Louis Oliver and several other good veterans like defensive lineman Chuck Klingbeil. We also started to branch out around the league and signed Pro Bowl defensive end Hugh Douglas with the New York Jets as a consequence of Marvin's recommendation.

The other big catch for me that year was Dolphins rookie first-round pick Tim "Timbo" Bowens. Tim was a defensive tackle out of Ole Miss. I signed him shortly after he was drafted. His agent at the time was charging him more than the industry-standard commission, and he was looking for new representation. Being from a small town—Okolona, Mississippi—Timbo wanted someone in Miami to help him out. He asked around and the most respected veteran on the team, Jeff Cross, recommended me. Next thing I knew, I was calling Jason to tell him, "And so shines a good deed in a weary world."

You might recognize that phrase; it's from the Gene Wilder *Willy Wonka* movie. Jason and I loved that movie as kids. The scene is where Willy Wonka chastises young Charlie and his grandpa Joe, telling them that they lost a contest because they broke the rules. Charlie, a great kid, made a promise to Mr. Wonka that he would not take an Everlasting Gobstopper candy. Wonka's competitor, Mr. Slugworth, promised Charlie big money if he would steal an Everlasting Gobstopper and give it to him. In the big scene, Charlie keeps his word and returns the Gobstopper to Mr. Wonka.

Clutching the Gobstopper with his left hand, Mr. Wonka says to himself, "And so shines a good deed in a weary world." He then turns around and says, "Charlie…Charlie, my boy, you won! You did it!"

By being a good kid, Charlie proves he has a pure heart and wins the contest. He wins everything he ever dreamed of. It's the ultimate happy ending. So every time I sign a player, if Jason is not there, I either call to say or text him, "And so shines a good deed in a weary world."

Every time we hear that phrase, it is music to my ears. And we heard a lot of it as we were signing players left and right. We represented more Hurricanes and Dolphin players than other agents by far. We dominated the competition. That meant stepping on a lot of toes and making enemies. But as Conan the Barbarian, when asked "What is best in life?," answered, "To crush your enemies, see them driven before you, and to hear the lamentation of the women."

Well, every time a competitor bad-mouthed us behind our backs, we loved it because we knew the insults were nothing more than the lamentations of losers. We soon had thirty clients in the NFL, a dozen of them Hurricanes and another dozen Dolphins. We ascended to the upper echelon of agents.

Timbo went on to become a Pro Bowl player and had an outstanding eleven-year career with the Dolphins. He was a centerpiece client who recommended many players to us over the years. I had targeted my market of the 'Canes and Fins, and they became mine. But now there was a new target that I wanted—a client who could take me to the next level—the superstar!

That superstar's name was Warren Sapp, All-American defensive tackle from the University of Miami. In late December 1994, right before Sapp was getting ready to play the Nebraska Cornhuskers in the Orange Bowl for the national championship, my client and Dolphin kicker Pete Stoyanovich went to Sylvester Stallone's Christmas party in Miami. The party was at Stallone's house.

It was something special for Jason and me to go to Stallone's house. We grew up on the *Rocky* and *Rambo* movies. The first *Rocky* movie was our all-time favorite. We were inspired by the main character's heart, toughness, and determination to become a winner. We viewed Sly as the same person as Rocky Balboa. If we ever had an idol, it was Rocky.

We walked around the waterfront property, got a tour of the house, saw Stallone's impressive art collection, and couldn't wait to converse with him. He was an absolute gentleman, but do you know what he asked us: "Are you going to sign Warren Sapp [to be your client] or what?"

Being THE badass Hurricane, Sapp was the man in Miami. He was as fearless, aggressive, and ruthless as Mr. T's character Clubber Lang in *Rocky III*. A few nights before the big game against the 'Canes, the Cornhusker team went to the Dolphin game together for entertainment. When they were acknowledged at the game by the announcer, the crowd booed them and started taunting them, chanting, "War-ren Sapp! War-ren Sapp! War-ren Sapp!"

We had never before seen a college player take over this town. And for a defensive lineman to do it, rather than an offensive player like a quarterback or running back, was remarkable. He was the best defensive tackle we'd ever seen and was a one-of-a-kind player that we had to have.

The thing about Sapp is that he is not only brutal and ruthless on the field, but he is equally abrasive, offensive, and intimidating off it. At the same time, to his friends and family, he is the best. As rough and tough as he is, he can also be a charming, likable teddy bear. To see him with his kids, Mercedes and Warren "Deuce" Jr., is something special.

Unfortunately for us, when we recruited him, he didn't consider us to be either friends or family. He didn't care that we represented his friends and Hurricane teammates in the NFL. We got no special treatment other than being cussed out and insulted. He found fault with any little thing and was verbally confrontational. I guarantee you that he sent a lot of agents home in tears and caused them to quit being or trying to be an agent. Sapp knew the term *scrutiny* very well and applied it to agents better than any recruit I had ever seen.

Pro Bowl Giant linebacker Jessie Armstead and Cowboy cornerback Robert Bailey, two of Jason's closest guys, were also very close to Sapp. Robert told him, "Hey, if I was standing in a sinking boat, I wouldn't tell you to jump in. I'm telling you these guys are like family to me. They are the best. You'll love 'em like I do."

One night we were at a nightclub where Sapp was. Jessie was also there and told Sapp that we were "good people," and recommended us. Sapp's close friend Mark Caesar, a Miami Dolphin defensive tackle from UM who was also our client, put in a good word for us as well. Even Timbo got in on the act and recommended us. Eventually, Sapp wore down and gave us a chance.

Whether it was at Duke Law School or the UM Law School, Jason and I were grilled by top law professors, masters of the Socratic method of teaching. Sapp was as good as any of them in breaking down your response and making you explain what you'd just said. In my opinion, after Sapp retires and gets into broadcasting, he will amaze you and be one of the best in the business.

The worst part of recruiting college players is that too often they go with someone who bought them off or developed a friendship with them. With Sapp, you couldn't buy him or befriend him. You had to earn his respect with your knowledge of the NFL. He was a real student of the game and expected you to be the same.

Fortunately for me, I can name every defensive lineman (and every other position) on every team. I can tell you who the starters are and their backups. I can tell you what college they went to and in what round they were drafted. Jason and I can tell you what they're making as well.

Where Sapp brought other agents to their knees, Jason and I stood tall. In January 1995, we prevailed and signed him.

After we signed Sapp and negotiated his contract with the Buccaneers, there was a new challenge for us. We'd signed the Hurricane superstar; now we wanted the Miami Dolphin superstar.

We hoped Pittsburgh Steeler tight end Eric Green could step up to be that guy. The Dolphins wanted to sign Eric in free agency. In March of 1995, Don Shula targeted Eric and we got the deal done, making Eric the highest-paid tight end in the history of the NFL at the time. The fan in me was thrilled. After losing Randal in the trade, it felt great to have Eric as a Miami Dolphin.

The problem was that the next day the *Miami Herald* came out with an article that said I'd manipulated the Dolphins into thinking there was another team out there that wanted Eric and I artificially drove up the price. In getting the Dolphins to pay top dollar for my client, I did my job. But it was a mistake to tell the paper I got the Dolphins to pay more than they had to. It was not my intent to make the Dolphins look bad, I just wanted to promote the quality of Eric's deal.

The article made Eric's contract look great, but it also embarrassed the Dolphins' negotiator, and that is something I regret. It was unnecessary and counterproductive. I have since learned to promote contracts as beneficial to both sides.

It's a good thing I got Eric a record-breaking $3.5 million up-front bonus because only one year later, Coach Jimmy Johnson came in and shipped him out. Eric was released during Jimmy's first year with the Dolphins in 1996.

Jimmy brought me into his office and told me, "Drew, we're not going to win on this one, but there will be others."

Jimmy was right. There would be others. After dominating the Hurricanes by representing Sapp, what I wanted next was to represent a great player in my hometown. A guy I would enjoy watching play and working with. I thought that wide receiver Yatil Green, from the University of Miami, would be that player. When Yatil was drafted by the Dolphins, I hoped he would become a great player for many years in Miami. Unfortunately, at the start of training camp, he suffered a career-ending knee injury. He never got the chance to show what he could do. At least Yatil received an outstanding contract and was paid millions of dollars. As for us, once again we thought we had an exciting Dolphin client who would become a great player like Jeff Cross, Pete Stoyanovich, and Tim Bowens did. Once again, it didn't work out. That's the nature of the NFL; only the strongest of the strong play a long time and beat the system.

That's the toughest part of this business—seeing your guys get hurt. Getting fired by your players, guys you are close with, is brutal, too. Right around the time that Yatil went down with the injury, we were fired by Baltimore Raven linebacker Ray Lewis.

Ray's termination letter caught me completely off guard. I thought we were extremely close. He and I were in a *Sports Illustrated* photo celebrating on draft day. What were the odds of that happening? He told me that he wanted to go in a different direction because I didn't have any superstars but went and hired an agent who had only one client. That client, Kenard Lang, an all-time great guy, later fired him to hire me. Ray ended up firing the guy, too (along with several other agents).

When I got the letter firing me, I tracked Ray down, flew into Baltimore, and drove to his house. When I talked to him face-to-face, he re-signed with me and all was well. As soon as I got back into town, there was another termination letter from Ray waiting for me. The next year, after Ray fired the guy, Jason and I met with him again. He promised us he was going to sign with us just as soon as he talked it over with his family in Orlando. To maximize our chances, Jason drove with him from Miami to Orlando. When the time came, Ray went with a different agent again.

Don't get me wrong. I like Ray and am happy for his success, but I wish I could have been a part of it. I negotiated his rookie contract, one of the best rookie contracts I ever negotiated. It was special because it had a voidable year and allowed Ray to get out of his contract a year early and sign a huge second contract faster. When it turned out that someone other than me negotiated that second contract I felt it a little (maybe a little more than that), but in this business, you won't win them all. You will lose again and again. The question is, will you win more and more?

That 1997 season started rough for me. Yatil suffered a career-ruining injury. I was fired by Ray and another player I was close to—Tampa Bay Buccaneer running back Errict Rhett. Those were hard losses for me. I thought a lot about what Jimmy Johnson had said to me earlier: that although it hadn't worked out with Eric Green (and now Yatil), there would be others. One of the great things about the NFL is that there are always new opportunities. Jimmy Johnson had another saying he liked to repeat: that luck is when preparation meets opportunity. I believe that 100 percent. Any agent who works hard to put himself in a position for opportunity to come along will get that chance.

I wanted the chance to represent the best player on the Dolphins. Through hard work, I got it.

The very first year of Jimmy Johnson's regime, 1996, he drafted linebacker Zach Thomas out of Texas Tech in the fifth round. Wearing the number 54 jersey, Zach was the 154th player to be picked. He was an instant sensation and budding superstar. He was a cool Texas guy out of Pampa, who'd never gotten soft just because his dad made it big in the oil industry. A natural-born football player, Zach was a throwback. Whether he got paid $30,000 a year or $6 million, he would love the game just as much.

Zach had another agent when he first came to the team. He was drafted in 1996 along with several other rookies, including safety

Shawn Wooden, defensive lineman Shane Burton, running back Jerris McPhail, and fullback Stanley Pritchett. All of these rookies from Zach's draft class signed with us. Even though Jimmy cleaned house and got rid of a lot of Shula guys, we still represented well over a dozen Dolphins by the start of the 1997 season.

Since the Dolphins were a close-knit group, they hung out together at the same places. So when one client invited us to join them, a lot of other clients were there. Other players who were not our clients saw us always around. They witnessed firsthand how hard we worked to develop a good relationship with our clients. Guys talk in the locker room.

Hearing over a dozen of his teammates brag about how they could get us on the phone faster than other players could get their agents on the phone, Zach became very familiar with us. He saw us around all the time. Because he had an agent, we didn't talk much and I respected that. I don't pursue players unless they approach me and say they are unhappy with their agent.

Zach came out of nowhere to be a rookie sensation for the Dolphins. He was an instant fan favorite. One night he was on Jim Mandich's show, *Sunday Night Sports Rap*. I was, too. Zach was a gentleman and complimented me on the way I represented several of his teammates. From then on, we were cordial whenever we bumped into each other.

It turned out that Zach's roommate was an undrafted, unknown linebacker named Larry Izzo. Larry was from Rice University, another Texas guy. I didn't know him but had a lot of respect for him because he was an absolute warrior on special teams. He and Zach were both undersized and overlooked. Yet both would become Pro Bowl players and the best at what they did. They were two winners on and off the field.

Always looking to make preparation and opportunity meet, we went to a Dolphin party at a South Beach nightclub. Zach was there. When he came up to me and said that he'd had a falling-out with his agent, that he liked the way I represented his teammates and wanted me to be his agent, I felt like he'd just given me a winning lotto ticket. Zach told me that all I had to do was meet with his dad and get his dad's approval.

Jason and I hugged him, thanked him, and raced out of there. We got on the phone with the airlines and caught an early-morning flight to Zach's hometown in Texas. I couldn't wait to meet his dad and assure him that I would work extremely hard to successfully represent his son.

Zach's dad, Steve Thomas, a very successful businessman in the local oil industry, gave us directions to his house. Along the way, we came across a huge monument in the shape of a cross. It looked like one of the Seven Wonders of the World. I thought I was lost and called his dad. It turned out that his dad had actually had the cross built. Steve Thomas didn't like all the new advertisements in town for strip clubs or XXX stuff that he was seeing. So to hold the fort, he took it upon himself to design, finance, and build these truly astonishing artistic crosses—gigantic ones. When he told me that, I couldn't help but like and admire the guy.

When we got to the Thomases', Jason and I put on our jackets because it was below freezing outside and we had to ascend a small hill to reach the door of the impressive house in which they lived. It had taken all day to get there because we had to make plane connections, deal with delays, and then drive for several hours. About halfway up the hill, Zach's dad walks out to greet us in a T-shirt and a pair of shorts. Despite the cold, he looked totally comfortable in that outfit, while Jason and I were freezing in our pants and jackets. Once we got inside the house, he told us a great story about Zach as an infant. Don't get scared, but when Zach was little, somehow a truck backed up on top of his head for an instant. Miraculously, he didn't get hurt.

His dad said with pride and a smile, "Since then, Zach's always had a high threshold for pain."

I told him, "I knew Zach had a hard head, but I didn't know it was that hard!"

Zach's mom and dad gave us their blessing and we promised to do right by Zach. Over $50 million later, I believe we kept our promise. It was a gigantic win to get Zach! We finally landed our local superstar Dolphin client. We felt like we won the Super Bowl.

So it meant a lot to us when Zach said to the *Buffalo News* in October 2003, "Drew is the man...If he says he's going to do something he gets it done. He's the best."

Once we signed Zach, we signed his roommate, Larry Izzo, as well.

I've got to take a moment to tell you a thing or two about Izzo. He is an absolute legend among the guys he's played with. Larry is a kamikaze on the field and the funniest guy off the field. As an undrafted free agent, he beat all the odds to play in the league for so many years. He is entering his thirteenth year. No one plays thirteen years as a special-teams guy—no one, that is, but Izzo. He's won three Super Bowl championships with the Patriots and is an icon among his peers. Larry is not a great athlete, but he has the gift to be able to think intelligently, clearly, and calmly amid the chaos. And it's that gift, coupled with courage, that has allowed him to be one of the all-time greatest special-teams players. I suppose he gets that from his dad, who was a war hero in Vietnam. Sadly, Larry's father passed away a few years ago from liver cancer. I saw Larry play through losing his dad and I know how much he loved him. Larry's heart is that of a champion and everyone respects him.

And then Larry will do something like have an annual charitable fund-raising event to salute the troops and grab Jason, bring him on the stage and sing together the karaoke version of Joan Jett's "I Love Rock and Roll"! Larry will say anything to anyone and one thing is guaranteed—it will be entertaining. Playing tennis with the guy is hilarious, as he uses old-school techniques and loses his temper.

I can't tell you how great it felt (still being that same little kid who loved his team) after all the ups and downs early in my career to go on to represent Zach, Izzo, Tim Bowens, Jeff Cross, Pete Stoyanovich, J. B. Brown, Mark Higgs, Chuck Klingbeil, Shane Burton, Shawn Wooden, Olindo Mare, and so many other great guys who were tremendous Dolphins players.

The next year, we signed Hurricane cornerback Duane Starks, who was the tenth pick of the 1998 draft. He was taken by the Ravens. By that year, we represented approximately twenty Hurricane players and almost as many Dolphins.

That was not by coincidence but by design. We knew which battles to pick. We specifically targeted markets where we were at our strongest and where our competitors were at a disadvantage. We found our advantage, which was working with local players to provide hands-on and proactive representation. We spent a lot of time with our clients building a close rapport. As a result, other NFL players saw how hard we worked to produce for our clients. Because we spent so much time with them, they went out of their way to recommend us when asked by their teammates. Being based in Miami, we couldn't have become dominant agents with the USC Trojans, the Texas Longhorns, or the Green Bay Packers. We had a great game plan to create mismatches against our opponents and we executed that plan as designed.

We knew which battles to pick. The next chapter is about how to win those battles.

CHAPTER 8

THE BIG IDEA

I REALLY BELIEVE THAT IF YOU WORK HARD TO ACHIEVE your goal, hard work alone won't get you there. It's the hard work that puts you in a position to have a chance at getting what you want. But the difference between success and failure is so often a single idea. There is one idea out there that can change your life ... or screw it up. So when you find yourself in a difficult situation, remember that it takes more than hard work, it takes smart work, too.

Such being the case, I'd like to create a couple of scenarios and ask how you would handle yourself in each of them.

Imagine you are seventeen years old and at a high school party. Someone you know and don't like throws a glass bottle at you when you're not looking and it hits you in the head. You have a bloodied forehead from the broken glass and the guy is coming after you from a distance. Here's the question: Do you get out of there or take him on? Would it make a difference in your answer if you happened to be the same size as the other guy, about six foot two, 210 pounds, but you are as fast as a cat and as strong as a lion? How about if the guy coming after you had seventeen of his friends charging you and the two friends with you? Being outnumbered seventeen to three, would you run like hell or rumble?

As for what I would do, well, my ego isn't too big to admit that I would get me and my friends out of there immediately. As for the teenage Jeremy Shockey, well, he fought the whole group with his two smaller friends. Jeremy had the guy who threw the bottle hospitalized. He broke the guy's cheekbone and managed to fight his way through the rumble.

Okay, now let me ask you another question. Imagine that you are in high school, and toward the end of the day, there is a minor fire. Everyone vacates the building and the firemen arrive on the scene. It takes a while to handle the situation, and so when the school day should be over, your car and several others are still blocked in by the fire truck. You are tired and want to get home. The firemen all seem busy and aren't going to be leaving for a while. What do you do? What do you do if you are the same Jeremy Shockey character? Well, Jeremy jumped in the fire truck, started it up, took it for a spin around the neighborhood, and parked it somewhere else.

Here's another one. Suppose a mean, rough, and tough guy from a rival high school shows up looking for you. He's heard you are the toughest kid in the school and wants to fight you for the title. He is a lot bigger than you, but no weapons are involved. It's an honest fight. What would you do? You would do what I would do. But Jeremy...well, he punched him in the face and kicked his ass.

How about if you are the New York Giants' first-round draft pick and you stayed up all night because you caught a late flight into town and then had to drive several hours to reach the training camp. With no time to check into a hotel, you sleep in the car for an hour and then go to the facility to sign your contract. After you get the contract signed and step onto the practice field, you bust your butt to show your teammates and coaches that you have what it takes to play in the NFL. Exhausted after the morning practice, you take a break and eat lunch in the cafeteria. While you are trying to rest and relax during lunch, a veteran linebacker tells you that you must get up and sing a song in front of everyone. The reason he tells you this is that all rookie Giants are hazed in that fashion. He is a big dude and means business. Do you do what all the other rookies do and sing whatever song you want, or do you tell him you don't feel like it right now? Well, Jeremy told him politely that he would sing later. The veteran insisted in a threatening manner. Do you sing now or tell him to get out of your face? I think you can figure out what Jeremy did. He told the guy to get out of his face. The guy responded by throwing a punch; Jeremy grabbed him and slammed him onto the table.

Last question. How about if you are hanging out at the most happening restaurant in town with your client, New York Giant tight end Jeremy Shockey. He has been harassed all night by an overzealous fan. You politely tell the fan that Jeremy has been a gentleman and request that he behave likewise and stop coming over to the table. The guy responds by getting in your face like he wants to fight you. He insults you in front of your client and then goes back to Jeremy and is obnoxious. Do you smack the guy or keep your composure? My brother Jason was out with Jeremy and he did what most professionals would do: he kept his cool. How about if the guy comes back over to the table and in front of your client says, "Fuck You!" Do you stand up and kick his ass or do you keep your client from getting into a bad situation and keep the situation under control? Well, Jason kept it under control to keep Jeremy out of trouble. To calm down, he went to the bathroom to wash his face and take a couple of deep breaths. Now imagine that while you are washing your face to relax, another client, Pro Bowl Miami Dolphin linebacker Zach Thomas, calls you. As you talk to him and walk out of the bathroom, you see that same overzealous fan waiting for you with blatantly bad intentions. There are no waiters around to separate you two or keep the guy away. Jeremy is in the other side of the restaurant and out of sight. You are on your own. Just him versus you. He gets in your face and you know he's going to take a shot at you. You tell him, "Go ahead, say it to my face!" He says it again, "Fuck you!" and moves like he's going to grab you. What do you do this time? I'd do what Jason did and punch the guy out.

I got a call late that night from Jason and he said to me, "Drew, I'm okay, but I just punched some guy in the face. The waiters grabbed me and ushered me outside. I'm in the alley by myself. He's got ten friends with him! I'm in trouble. Call Jeremy, tell him I'm in the alley."

In a rare state of panic since I was in another city, I called Jeremy and told him what had happened. Jason was standing alone in the alley. I told him Jason was in trouble. Now, at this moment, Jason was staring at the door to see who was coming outside. Was it going to be the guy with his ten friends or was it going to be Jeremy? When the door was kicked open and Shockey came running out, Jason smiled. He didn't care how many buddies the other guy had, he had Shockey!

How we got Shockey to sign with us is a whole new adventure. Jeremy left UM as a true junior to enter the 2002 NFL draft. He was our number one target. Ever since he made the game-winning touchdown catch to beat Florida State, Jason was convinced this guy was going to become a superstar. When he first made the decision to enter the NFL draft, Jeremy interviewed numerous agents and involved his mother Lucinda in the process, but was in no hurry. We met with Jeremy in early January at Joe's Stone Crab restaurant in Miami Beach. The meeting went well, but after a couple of weeks of Jeremy's interviewing other agents, we felt he was slipping away.

The year before, we'd represented two of his teammates who were first-round picks from the University of Miami. We signed wide receiver Santana Moss, who was drafted by the New York Jets, and defensive tackle Damione Lewis, who went to the St. Louis Rams. That year, 2001, we also represented another first-round pick, cornerback Willie Middlebrooks, who went to the Denver Broncos. All three contracts were very strong in relation to those of the players around them.

We thought because we represented so many Hurricanes in the NFL, guys Jeremy knew, respected, and trusted, we were the natural fit for him. But after a couple of weeks went by, we were losing the momentum and other agents who represented Pro Bowl tight ends were getting hot.

By the time of the 2002 Super Bowl in New Orleans, we were very concerned that Jeremy was going in another direction. Since he'd told me he was going to be hanging out at the Super Bowl festivities that weekend and Jason and I were already there setting up appearances for our clients, we were looking to catch up with him.

On Friday night, February 1, right before the Super Bowl Sunday showdown between the New England Patriots and the St. Louis Rams, Jason and I were cruising up and down Bourbon Street, going into the various establishments. The scene was super crowded and festive and it seemed like everyone associated with the NFL was there.

Each year, hundreds of NFL players fly in on a Wednesday to do some appearances and partying before the big game and then typically leave town Sunday morning before the game.

Around midnight, Jason and I were with a bunch of clients at a party in a nightclub. It was jam-packed. The music was loud and the people were partying it up New Orleans style in a big way. I was in the VIP area waiting for some more of my clients to show up. I was also there because I'd invited Jeremy and hoped he would show.

Every year it is imperative for agents to have success signing rookies coming out of college. Jeremy was the guy I'd targeted as the one player in the draft I had to get. It was a matter of life and death to me.

Soon Jason spotted Jeremy walking in with a few friends. We immediately went over to him. Jeremy was a gentleman and friendly, but he was still distant. I wanted to break through the barrier, get him to stop looking at me as an agent and instead look at me more like one of his friends.

I was frustrated and looked for an opportunity to get in with him. Finally something happened to help turn the momentum in my direction. Five St. Louis Ram cheerleaders walked through the door. I recognized them from an appearance they'd made at an event earlier in the day. Jason and I looked at each other and thought the same thing.

Now, Jeremy, being a handsome guy at six foot five inches and 250 pounds of ripped muscle, didn't need any help with women. It didn't take a rocket scientist to deduce that the guy was a big-time ladies' man. However, his four friends from Oklahoma needed all the help they could get. On his own, Jeremy was going to have a good time; however, his friends, who had never been out of Ada, Oklahoma, were a different story. Jeremy had his work cut out for him if he was going to entertain his friends.

Jason and I knew we could be of some big-time assistance, so we approached the cheerleaders.

"You're the agent guy, right?" the prettiest of the girls asked as I walked toward her. Luckily, I'd been at the same event she attended earlier in the day. Dressed in the same suit, I not only stood out at that event, but also at the nightclub.

"That's right. I'm Drew and this is my brother Jason."

Having had more than a night or two's experience with the South Beach club scene, I knew exactly what all single women in clubs want to hear.

"Do you ladies want to come into the VIP with us? I have a table."

All five girls started smiling and almost simultaneously cheered, "Sure!"

Next thing I knew, I was introducing Jeremy and his boys to five hot cheerleaders. After a few drinks, everybody was having a fun time and all of a sudden Jeremy and I were like lifelong buddies.

Before I left, I told him that I was throwing a big party the next night and that my clients were going to be there. I encouraged him to drop by and promised that it would be an awesome party. It turned out that I was right. The party was packed and my clients had a great time. The only problem was that Jeremy didn't make it—another agent took him to the Playboy party instead. The competition can be crafty as well.

Despite Friday night's success, we lost touch with Jeremy. He didn't answer or return our calls. Things were not going our way again. I kept calling him and finally, about a week after the Super Bowl, I got him on the phone in Miami. He agreed to allow Jason and me to come over to his place off campus.

Jeremy shared a house with three roommates. One of them was a highly respected fifth-year-senior player; the other roommates weren't on the team. Jeremy was only a third-year junior entering the draft and he respected his older roommate's advice. In fact, they were close friends. We had previously recruited the roommate and he'd strongly considered hiring us, but his mother preferred another agent and he went in that direction.

The moment we walked in the door, Jason and I wasted no time and got after Jeremy with a hard-core sales pitch. We hit him with point after point as to why we were the best choice for him. Jeremy seemed ready to go with us and then his roommate walked into the living room, where we were meeting. He told Jeremy to hold up and got his agent on speakerphone. One thing led to another and I was going back and forth with the other agent, exchanging insults. Even though I felt I got the better of the exchange, in the process, I lost the momentum I had with Jeremy. The roommate asked Jeremy not to sign with us until his agent came to town on Monday. It was a Friday and the roommate was getting ready to travel back to his hometown for the weekend. He would be back on Monday with his agent.

Jason and I walked out of that house knowing that come Monday, we would be at a huge disadvantage since the roommate would do everything he could to get Jeremy to sign with his agent. I knew that the roommate was insecure about the decision he'd made to hire that agent since the agent did not have any experience representing UM players. Thus the roommate would feel better about his decision to hire that agent if Jeremy hired him, too. With the roommate being Jeremy's friend and teammate, I knew we had our hands full.

If you were in our shoes, what would you do? It was Friday, you just left Jeremy's house, and on Monday his roommate was going to bring in his agent. There was an idea out there that could allow us to pull it off. I believe there is always that one big idea that can change everything. You just have to find it.

On the drive back to our place, that idea came to Jason. We had to get Jeremy to meet with us again before Monday when the roommate came back to town with his agent. The agent was competent and experienced despite his lack of UM players. The combination of the roommate and the agent was formidable. Since Jeremy barely knew us but was very close with his roommate, we knew we were in trouble. But although Jeremy hardly knew us, he had told us that he liked us the best among the agents he had met. Had it not been for his roommate's interference, he'd have been ready to go with us. Our problem was the roommate. The key for us would be to get another meeting with Jeremy before Monday. That's what it came down to.

How? How could we get that meeting? That one idea would make us or break us. From here on out, it was going to be a battle of wits. In that arena, I'll match Jason up against anyone. You see, Jason had some unique training. When I went off to Duke Law School, I spent every night on the phone with him brainwashing him into studying like a fanatic. Having already learned discipline and mental toughness from Young Soo Do, Jason was able to make himself study more than anyone else on campus. He became a numbers guy—a CPA—despite his interest being literature and history. But when he got to law school, it was fun. Since he'd already worked with me around the clock after I returned from Duke, law school seemed like a vacation.

Jason was already in the real world, was already an agent, at this time; he knew what pressure was. Most law students are scared because they take one exam, which is 100 percent of their grade in a given class. Jason would look at the other law students before taking exams. He'd see them sitting in a group discussing a particular topic. They'd be dressed sloppy and look like they hadn't slept, showered, brushed their teeth or hair in the past twenty-four hours. Throw in their coffee breath and stink from cigarettes and you get a good picture of what Jason—who was himself neatly dressed and looked like he was getting ready for a hot date—saw. Now you know why Jason laughed at the sight of the other law students wilting under the stress of the final exam. Sure, there was pressure to do well; if you failed that exam, you would be ruined. That's real pressure. But for Jason, who had been involved with me in everything I'd gone through with Massey, Randal Hill, Michael Irvin, Jeff Cross, and Marvin Jones, law school exams were easy. To him, school was fair in the sense that if you worked hard, you would get good results. In the business world, you can work hard to recruit a player and then lose him at the last minute because the competition cheated and paid the guy off. That's not fair, but it's reality. School is not reality; it's fair. On a test, you will perform as well as your preparation. So Jason ate law school up.

So being on campus and studying was peaceful for him compared to the roller-coaster ride of being an agent. Law school was also fun for Jason because after studying accounting, almost anything is a pleasure. CPA training made Jason think quantitatively. His interest in literature and law school honed his qualitative thinking skills. Thus, intellectually speaking, he became very balanced. Additionally, by 2002, he had the experience of working with me and negotiating with truly brilliant executives like Rich McKay, who was incredible at building the Tampa Bay Buccaneers, the biggest joke in the NFL, into Super Bowl champions. I don't know why things went so wrong for Rich in Atlanta, but I guarantee you this guy is as sharp as anyone anywhere in any field.

Seeing how extremely talented NFL coaches like Don Shula and Jimmy Johnson, as well as top NFL executives, handled difficult situations, Jason learned a great deal. When he was in college and I was breaking into the agent business during breaks from law school, he went through everything I went through. Every lesson I learned, he learned. He saw how being proactive creates opportunities. He saw how a single idea could be the difference. He quickly realized how he could best contribute as my partner.

I think it's ironic that one of the most lasting impressions on Jason was probably made by Dolphin coach Don Shula, who emphasized above all else winning within the rules. This is ironic because I can only think of one time when Jason ignored the rules. He was smitten with a girl from Texas named Cassandra who became a Dolphin cheerleader—this is the "Casie" I alluded to in an earlier chapter. To make a long story short, because I dated a Dolphin cheerleader or two, the Dolphin cheerleader director instituted a rule that the cheerleaders could not date agents. Of course our names were not specifically cited in the rules, but what other agents were they going to date?

In any event, Jason would look for Casie after every game and covertly talk with her. Eventually they started dating despite the rule and now they are married. So much for that rule!

I guess we can overlook a minor rule infraction here and there.

Personal life aside, Jason evolved into a strategist and behind-the-scenes operator, which worked well with me being so vocal, demonstrative, and high profile. While I talked in meetings and made my points, he read the reactions and would search for weakness and opportunity. He became a strategist.

For some reason, being around me, Jason doesn't get the chance to talk a lot. I use the machine-gun approach, firing a lot of bullets until I hit my mark. Jason adapted to be the sniper who would hit with a single shot whatever marks were left.

With negotiations, early on, he became a detail guy, handling the legalese and the numbers while I did the communicating. These days, with certain contracts, such as rookie contracts, which are all about numbers in relation to the salary cap, Jason is just as involved with the negotiations as I am.

So when we were in a tough spot with Jeremy, needing the big idea to get Jeremy to meet with us again before Monday, Jason came through as the man with the plan.

He suggested that I try to persuade Jeremy's mother Lucinda to come to town on Saturday. Then we would be able to meet with both her and Jeremy that day. He was convinced that Jeremy wanted to go with us, but there was a lot of outside pressure for him to go with other agents. We were both confident that if we could remove the outside influence, Jeremy would go with his gut and pick us. So Jason came up with the plan and I made it happen. I got Lucinda on the phone and persuaded her to visit sunny Miami.

Twenty-four hours later, we picked her up at the airport. Once she was with us, she called Jeremy and we all went to lunch at the Bal Harbor restaurant Carpaccio's. At lunch, we laid it all on the line and talked it through.

Jeremy told us that he had already done all his homework regarding the interview process. He attended numerous meetings with other agents and had extensive follow-up conversations with those agents. After weeks of the process, he had heard sufficient bashing of agents by other agents to last a lifetime. He told us that he liked two things about us, which separated us from the competition.

First, we only talked about ourselves and what we could do. At no time were we critical of other agents. Everything we said was positive and confident. Jeremy liked that.

Second, UM was our bread and butter. He knew it was extremely important to us to continue representing Hurricanes year in and year out. He saw that this was a kind of insurance policy for him, that if we didn't do a great job for him, he wouldn't recommend us, and then we would lose our reputation at UM. He knew we would never let that happen. We were the smart move and he knew it.

Feeling good about the situation and wanting to put an end to all the drama, Jeremy pulled the trigger and signed with us on the spot.

Jason and I were thrilled. We believed Jeremy would be a true NFL superstar. He signed the contract and the battle was over, right?

Wrong.

Just as we were taking Lucinda to the airport the next day, she called Jeremy to check on him about nothing important. Next thing I know, there are screeching brakes and I am telling Jason to make a U-turn back toward Jeremy's house. It turned out that another agent had told Jeremy that the New York Giants general manager, Ernie Accorsi, did not like dealing with us. Jeremy wanted to be drafted by the Giants, who had the fifteenth pick in the first round of the upcoming NFL draft. The agent just recently became an agent, was desperate to sign Jeremy, and told him that the Giants wouldn't draft him because he'd hired me.

We raced back to Jeremy's place, pulled into the driveway, and dropped Lucinda off. She went inside while Jason and I were waiting in the car. We waited in the car so we could make productive use of the time calling our clients. Moments later, a Cadillac pulled up with four agents inside. Jason and I jumped out of our Hummer and approached them. Knowing Jeremy wasn't there yet, they stayed in the car. The main agent was driving and lowered his window.

Jason leaned in and immediately made him aware of the fact that they were in violation of the NFLPA rules governing agents since Jeremy had already signed a contract with us, and they were communicating with him about representation. In a professional manner, he went into great detail explaining how their conduct was inappropriate and advised them to govern themselves in accordance with the rules and vacate the premises.

They refused, saying that Jeremy had called them and invited them to come over. We knew they were full of it. We had handled ourselves in a professional manner and they refused to leave.

On to plan B. I let them know they were making a big mistake in interfering with our client. At that point, the agent's forehead was accumulating sweat and his eye began twitching.

Jason and I had fought hard to sign Jeremy, we were furious that those guys were trying to manipulate him under false pretenses. They wanted to take Jeremy away from us and we were not going to let that happen. We gave them the opportunity to do the right thing and leave; they refused. In doing so, they had crossed the line and now the situation couldn't be resolved amicably.

Our patience had run out. No more legal talk. Jason leaned in through the open window and said, "You keep twitching your eye." The other agent was stifled. Jason smiled at the agent in an eerie manner and, moving in closer, literally an inch from his face, said as the guy's eye twitched, "Are you flirting with me? If I didn't know better, I'd say you wanted to kiss me. Do you want to kiss me?"

Again the agent didn't say or do anything. He was frozen. Jason's smile turned into a snarl. We were ready for anything. Wouldn't you do the same to protect your client?

"Fine!" the agent exclaimed, put the car into reverse, and peeled out of the driveway.

As he pulled out, Shockey pulled in. He could tell that we had run them off and got a huge kick out of it. We all went to lunch with his mom at Benihana restaurant. At lunch, Jeremy told us that the agent had claimed that Giants general manager Ernie Accorsi wouldn't draft him because he signed with us. Knowing this was total crap, I took action and immediately got Ernie on the phone.

A gentleman, Ernie made a point of telling Jeremy the truth, that what the agent said was nothing more than a backhanded, cowardly lie to try to get Jeremy's business. Ernie told Jeremy that he had a lot of respect for me and that Jeremy had made a smart decision in hiring me. Ernie was clearly annoyed by the underhandedness of the other agent.

The next day, Monday, we dropped Lucinda off at the airport. Wouldn't you know it, as she departed Miami, the agent for Jeremy's roommate arrived with a briefcase-size presentation for Jeremy. Like the previous agent we'd dealt with, he, too, left town empty-handed.

When Jeremy signed with us, I told him and his mom that he would be a first-round pick. That wasn't too bold a prediction because we knew how great a player he was going to be. But believe it or not, shortly after we signed Jeremy, a GM on an NFL team told me that he wouldn't go in the first round. He and I disagreed and actually bet lunch at Joe's Stone Crab restaurant over it. When Jeremy held his big workout in March, running his forty-yard dash and showing off his receiving skills, the GM walked up to me and jokingly said, "The bet is off!"

He knew what I knew and Jeremy became the fourteenth pick

in the first round by Ernie Accorsi of the New York Giants. We were thrilled because not only was he going to a great organization, but there would be huge marketing deals for him in New York. Just six days after we completed his contract, Jeremy suited up for his first game. That game happened to be the first preseason *Monday Night Football* game of the year and Jeremy became an overnight sensation. With his first catch, he ran by one defender and over another. He was awesome and the Shockey legend among Giant fans was born.

I could write a whole book just on the adventures Jason and I had gotten into because of Jeremy. Hanging with the guy is always action-packed!

But just think, what if Jason hadn't come up with the idea of bringing Jeremy's mom into town that Saturday? If we didn't get the meeting with him before Monday, who knows what would have happened once Jeremy's roommate and that agent came to town.

That was a perfect example of one big idea that not only allowed us to outwork the competition but to outsmart them as well.

CHAPTER 9

KNOWING WHEN TO
PULL THE TRIGGER

JEREMY WAS A PRO BOWL ROOKIE SENSATION. AS A NEW Yorker, he became a household name nationwide. That same year, Warren Sapp, the Tampa Bay Buccaneer defensive tackle, had become an icon in the NFL. Leading the Bucs to a Super Bowl, Sapp was the man. Not only was he the NFL's 1999 Defensive Player of the Year, but he was also the most publicized defensive player in the game. Never before had a player at his position ascended to such unprecedented heights of popularity on TV, in magazines, and in commercials. Shockey and Sapp were two of the most popular players in the league. Along with Willis McGahee, who received a tremendous amount of publicity after his draft success, they were promoted as well as anyone in the business. Our partner Robert Bailey very quickly emerged as a marketing mogul in NFL endorsement circles.

To capitalize on Sapp's success, Robert secured a six-figure appearance for him to appear live on ABC's *Jimmy Kimmel Show* after the Super Bowl. It was the big debut of the show, and to hype it up, they went all out to get Sapp. The problem was that the game was in San Diego and the show was in Los Angeles. So right after the game, they arranged to take us via helicopter to the show.

When the game was over, Robert and I went down to the field and joined Sapp in the locker room. He did his postgame interview with the media, hopped into the shower, and then the three of us jumped into the helicopter.

The helicopter had five seats. Sapp sat in the middle of the back-seat flanked by me and Robert. It was our first helicopter ride and we requested that the pilot go easy on us. But the pilot had orders to get us there in record time. The chopper raced from the start to finish. At first, we started low and fast. Then, as we approached downtown L.A., the pilot went crazy. He flew us up and down over buildings. He tilted right, then tilted left, flying between close buildings. It was like noth-ing I'd ever experienced. We were so happy to get out of that copter that if the pilot hadn't profusely apologized for flying like he was back in Vietnam, Sapp would have smacked him around when we landed.

The flight notwithstanding, the show's debut with Sapp was a big success. I knew that with Sapp, Shockey, and Willis garnering so much exposure, big things would follow for us. And they did.

After the hoopla surrounding Willis in the April 2003 draft, we were visiting Shockey at the University of Miami. Jeremy decided to train there in the off-season rather than at the team facility in New Jersey. He liked to work out at the University of Miami campus. Most of the Hurricane alumni opt to do their training and conditioning there. UM has a renowned conditioning coach, Andrew Swayze, and the players all swear by his training regimen. On any given day, you will find NFL Pro Bowlers such as running backs Edgerrin James,

Frank Gore, Willis McGahee, and wide receivers Santana Moss, Reggie Wayne, Andre Johnson, and defensive players such as cornerback Antrel Rolle, Nate Webster, William Joseph, and safety Ed Reed. These former teammates share a sense of camaraderie with each player pushing the others to the limit. It is great for the young players still in college to see the work ethic and discipline of the successful NFL veterans. The guys who come back to UM to train feel a lot of pride, and no one more than Shockey.

While we were waiting for him to finish training and meet us for lunch, Clinton "CP" Portis walked out—the only player who arguably had a better rookie year than Jeremy.

Now, the guy had just finished working out all morning long and you would think he'd be walking out in shorts and a tank top. Not exactly. He was wearing shorts, but they didn't look like shorts. They were long and looked almost like stylish, dark blue jeans. He had on a designer shirt, was sporting a matching hat, and had cool shades. He was color-coordinated from head to toe like he was about to model in a *GQ* photo shoot. To top it off, he had a huge studded belt buckle that perfectly matched his necklace, bracelet, and earring. He looked immaculate and very masculine.

Clinton was one of the UM players who got away—we didn't sign him. He was voted the 2002 NFL Rookie of the Year and ran for over 1,500 yards. After his exceptional rookie season with the Denver Broncos, guess how much incentive money CP got? Not one cent.

Clinton's contract called for him to make the minimum in salary all four years of his contract. He was paid an up-front signing bonus of $1.290 million and his four-year salaries ranged from $225,000 in 2002, $300,000 in 2003, $380,000 in 2004, to $455,000 in 2005. To put this in perspective, compare the rookie contract we negotiated for wide receiver Jabar Gaffney with the Houston Texans, who was also a second-round pick in the same draft as CP. Like Clinton, Jabar signed a four-year contract with similar salaries. However, Jabar had incentives worth $1 million in his rookie year alone. Over the four years, he had the ability to earn almost $4 million extra in incentives. If CP had a contract similar in structure to Jabar's, he could have more than doubled his salary that first year. Why did Jabar have incentives and CP none? That's something CP wanted to know.

I can say this much: the Houston Texans had another second-round pick in addition to Jabar. The Texans drafted offensive lineman Chester Pitts. Chester had no incentives in his four-year contract. His contract was structured similarly to CP's. Why didn't Chester have incentives? That's a question more appropriate for Chester's agent to answer. However, I do believe if I had been Chester's agent, he would have had incentives in his contract like Jabar did.

Nothing is given to you in the NFL; you have to fight for everything. If the agent doesn't fight for something, his client isn't going to get it. And just because you fight for it doesn't mean you'll get it. Just like anything else, it requires an intelligent strategic approach to persuade the other side to do more than the average deal.

Other agents repeatedly negotiated subpar-to-average deals. They assumed that signing the player was the hard part and negotiating their contract the easy part. Jason and I instantly recognized that showing a player how our contracts matched up against our competitors' when the opportunity came to meet with him would be a huge competitive advantage.

So when Clinton approached Jason and me while we were waiting for Shockey at UM, we were very excited. The players all talk in the locker room. I am sure that our numerous clients who were training at UM that summer probably said something that made CP think about us. You can call it luck that we just happened to bump into him, but I won't. Jason and I could have been eating lunch like the rest of the agents, but instead we were putting ourselves in a position for opportunity to come our way.

CP told us that he would like to sit down face-to-face with us in a couple of months after he got through training camp and the preseason. We were crossing our fingers that he would still want to meet with us once the season started.

When the time came, CP was a man of his word and invited us to have a sit-down. We showed him Jabar's contract and he was impressed. We also showed him Shockey's contract as well as others. He was particularly interested in the work our partner Robert Bailey was doing.

Since Robert had been a Hurricane, CP was familiar with him. Clinton had two mandates for us: first and foremost, get him a new contract; and second, get his name out there. The first assignment was for Jason and me to accomplish. The second was Robert's.

This occurred at the start of the 2003 season, the beginning of CP's second season. He told us that he did not want to be playing for the minimum in 2004. He told us that he wanted an agent who would fight for him to get a new contract after the current season. He asked us if we were that agent.

I said no thanks and walked out. Just kidding! I nearly jumped through the roof and promised him that I would do everything humanly possible to get him a new contract. It was understood that I had one year to get the job done. And not just any new contract, but a contract that would make him the highest-paid running back in the

NFL. Knowing that if there was no new contract by 2004 he would be looking for a new agent, I assured him we were the guys for the job.

After word broke about CP's hiring us, he told the *Rocky Mountain News* on September 12, 2003:

> I just needed to go with a big hitter...Sooner or later, I'll be coming up with my contract, and I need some power punches behind me, and I think the Rosenhauses are exactly what I need. They're visible, with Shockey and Sapp. That's who's getting all the marketing and the TV. I hope to slide up there to that...
>
> I think just teaming up with them gives me a lot more power.

No pressure, right? Wrong. Clinton went on to have a Pro Bowl season, rushing again for over 1,500 yards. He had unprecedented success for a second-year running back. He did everything the Broncos could have asked of him and then some. He completely outperformed his contract.

Clinton had done his part, Robert got him the hype he was looking for, and now it was my turn to deliver the contract. The clock was ticking.

I had visited CP a couple of times during the season because I wanted to improve my relationship with him. I had to do this because he and I did not have much of a rapport. As far as he was concerned, I was a gun for hire and we would not become friends until after I had gotten the job done.

Nevertheless, Jason, Robert, and I tried to bond with him. When CP went to the February 2004 Pro Bowl in Hawaii, I thought that could be the opportunity I was looking for to soften him up.

Jason and Casie, his fiancée at that time, took Clinton, Clinton's mom, Clinton's girlfriend, and twelve of Clinton's family and friends on a boat off Honolulu's shore. It was one of those whale-watching boats. They got lucky and saw a mother whale and her baby jump very close to the boat several times. Overly excited (he is my brother after all), Jason couldn't resist the chance to swim with a whale, so he dove into the water, hoping to get a close-up look with his mask. To Jason's surprise, there was a big splash next to him. Jason suddenly remembered that tiger sharks often swim near whales. When the bubbles cleared, he saw CP snorkeling right beside him. That was pretty impressive; CP was not only fearless toward linebackers but toward tiger sharks as well.

Although it was a fun time in Hawaii, CP still would not open up to us. He kept the pressure on. We had to produce or else. To make matters worse, when I called the Broncos in February 2004, they refused to renegotiate his deal. They had a team policy of not renegotiating a contract until the player was in his final year. And since Clinton had two years remaining on his contract (2004 and 2005), the Broncos took the position that he would have to play the 2004 season at the minimum salary of $380,000. The Broncos told me they wanted him to play out the third year of the deal and that he would get the big contract at the start of his fourth.

That was not the answer I was looking for. After I hung up the phone, I immediately called CP. He took the news better than I'd anticipated. He was not surprised. CP was very astute as to what was going on with the organization. Other teammates and agents told him there was no way he was going to get a new deal after playing just two years of a four-year contract. I thought I might be in some trouble, but instead of being difficult, he showed a lot of class. CP was very supportive and told me he had faith that I would find a way to get the job done. I really appreciated this first gesture of friendship.

However, as cool as he was, I knew I had to meet his expectations or else. And I had no problem with that; we all knew what we were getting into from the start. But with the team taking a hard-line approach, I was in a tough spot.

Over the years, the Broncos had acquired a reputation for being able to replace one great running back with another, so I knew that if we held out and played hardball, they would just plug in another running back to take CP's place.

At the same time, I knew they did not want a public standoff with their best player. If they were not going to give him a new contract and CP would not play under his existing contract, there seemed to be only one solution—a trade.

I spoke to the Broncos' negotiator Ted Sundquist about the idea and it was so remote that he agreed to allow me to call other teams and see if I could put together a trade. Neither Ted nor I thought there was any chance of that happening, but it was the only way I could keep moving forward.

I made the calls to the general managers and, as expected, got no bites. At that time, it was very rare to trade a superstar. Teams just aren't in the business of trading away their best players. The reason why trades are so hard to pull off is that GMs don't want to get fired. Trades are extremely risky. If you are the Broncos, it is a huge risk to trade away your team MVP because what if the player you trade for doesn't play up to expectations or gets hurt? If you already have a great player whom the fans love, why take that chance of trading him away? Trading away good players is how GMs get fired in this league.

On the flip side, if you are the team who is considering trading for

Clinton, you would have to give away a lot, and if he got hurt, you'd be screwed. Trading away good players or high draft picks in exchange for one player who may get hurt is also a great way to get fired as a GM.

Moreover, trades cause financial complications. If a team trades away a player, it can have a very negative effect on their salary cap. Additionally, if you trade for someone like CP, you have to pay him a lot of money. The thing about trading away draft picks is you are trading away good young players who are inexpensive. So not only are you giving up your cheap labor, but you have the double whammy of paying big money to someone like CP. Trading away good inexpensive players for one superexpensive player is not a moneymaking move.

In effect, my problem was to persuade a GM to take the chance of getting fired. It seemed impossible. No wonder Ted wasn't surprised when I called him a few days later to say that there hadn't been any bites. Nevertheless, I told him that I was confident that something would develop.

What I was banking on was that the Indianapolis Combine was coming up and all the team general managers would be there. As you'll recall, the Indy Combine is where all the top college players entering the draft gather to work out and interview the teams. The Combine typically occurs at the end of February. The start of free agency occurs the first week of March. Free agency is when players whose contracts have expired after four years of playing in the NFL get the chance to go play for whatever team they want. However, teams are not allowed to talk to players on other teams until free agency begins. Now, even though talks at the Combine take place prior to the start of free agency, theoretical conversations happen... wink, wink.

Agents and GMs also meet at the Combine and contract extensions are often renegotiated and extended at the midnight hour to keep the player on the team before free agency. Additionally, agents attend to promote their rookies to the teams.

With all that action going on, I was hopeful that something would break our way. The night before leaving town, Jason, the man with the plan, had a big idea. It was not exactly a secret that the Washington Redskins were having difficulty re-signing their top defensive player, Pro Bowl cornerback Champ Bailey.

Roland "Champ" Bailey was the first-round pick of the Washington Redskins in 1999. He signed a five-year deal and, after playing all five years of the contract, had established himself as the best young cornerback in the NFL.

Since the Redskins and Champ could not agree on a contract extension, Champ was set to be a free agent when his contract expired after the 2003 season. If the Redskins weren't willing to pay him what he thought he was worth, he wanted to see if there were other teams who were willing to do so. There was an obvious disagreement between the Redskins and Champ's agent as to what Champ's value was. The situation had become unpleasant for both sides and neither party was happy.

Instead of losing Champ to free agency and getting nothing in return, the Redskins placed the franchise tag on him. By making Champ a one-year offer of $6.8 million, the Redskins were able to keep his rights for the 2004 season and prevent him from being a free agent.

Now, that may seem like a lot of money, and it is, but Champ's worth was several times that amount. Jason recognized that the situation was bad and only going to get worse since Champ would not want to play out that one-year deal. An ugly holdout was inevitable.

As if we were playing fantasy football—because it seemed like a crazy fantasy—Jason proposed his idea, asking, "Hey, Drew, what are the odds of you persuading [Washington Redskins owner] Dan Snyder to trade Champ Bailey for CP?"

I thought it was an amusing idea, and then before I could smile, it hit me. Jason said Snyder—the owner of the Redskins, not the GM. By going straight to the owner, we would remove the biggest obstacle to the trade, since the decision would come straight from the top. I knew Dan Snyder well. He is a self-made big-time millionaire. He didn't inherit old money. He made it off his brains and balls. The guy is the ultimate NFL owner. He is nothing but great for the NFL. Every fan should be so lucky to have their team owned by Snyder.

As an owner, he will do whatever it takes and pay whatever price is necessary to win. As a fan you can't ask for anything more than that. With an owner as hungry to win as Snyder, I knew if I could get in front of him, we had a chance of making Jason's idea happen. Bringing in Clinton Portis would cause an excitement craze among the fans. It would be the biggest trade since Herschel Walker went from the Cowboys to the Vikings in 1989. That trade was disastrous for the Vikings and got the GM fired, by the way.

But Dan wasn't scared about being fired since he was the owner. It would be huge news and Snyder would be viewed as a super-high-profile, hands-on, major power broker in the NFL. Portis would be a great sell for Snyder to his sponsors. Portis was also young and entering his prime.

As for the Broncos, with Champ Bailey, the best cornerback in the league, and with their ability to replace one stud running back for another, I thought I could make it happen.

Jason had a great idea and I knew it was up to me to make it happen.

We flew out to Indianapolis and hunted Dan Snyder down. We were men on a mission. I knew I had one chance at this and arranged the meeting in the lobby of the Marriott Hotel. I told Snyder that I had something big to discuss in person and his curiosity was piqued. At the meeting, Dan brought his head coach, Joe Gibbs, and his right-hand man, Vinny Cerrato.

As soon as Dan sat down, he asked me what the big secret was. As soon as I pitched it, his eyes opened wide. With his extraordinary business acumen, he could see all the angles and jumped all over it.

Within minutes, he was working on the deal with the Broncos. The ball was out of my hands and it was now up to the two teams to agree on the trade. Throughout the night, Dan was calling me with updates. Of course Jason and I, as well as Robert, were awake. CP was traveling and having a good time while we were sweating it out, and we tried to reach him by phone for hours.

When Dan called us at two in the morning, he said that he and the Broncos had agreed on the trade, but it was conditional upon one thing—CP playing for the minimum $380,000 salary with some added incentives that year. The negotiator for the Redskins got on the phone and said that if CP had a big year for the Redskins, he would get the contract he'd wanted the following year.

I told Dan that I would talk it over with Clinton.

Shortly thereafter CP called back. He was initially excited and desperately wanted the trade. He liked Denver, the fans, his teammates and coaches, but this trade would make him huge news in the NFL and get him the type of endorsement deals he was looking for. If he had to play out the one year at $380,000, it would be much better to do it with the hype of the trade to the Redskins. Plus, Snyder would throw in some incentives this year with the promise of redoing the deal the following year. We couldn't lose by accepting the trade.

Then again, maybe we could lose. What if we took the one year at

$380,000 plus incentives and CP got hurt? Perhaps we were losing out on the opportunity to get the huge bonus.

The time had come to make the decision to take the deal or not. This is where an agent's experience, intuition, and command of the situation should take over. We could play it safe and take the deal or turn it down.

When Clinton asked me whether we should do the deal, I told him that it was his call but that if I were him, I would turn it down. As tempting as it was to do the trade and make the extra money with incentives and endorsements, we had to have the big deal.

I told him that if I were Dan, I would say the same thing and try to delay doing the big contract until the next year. Remember, no one in the NFL gets a new contract after just two years of playing a four-year rookie deal. Then again, trades like the one we had been proposing never happened anymore. I figured that Snyder had to at least try to get us to do it without the big contract.

I told CP that we had to gamble and turn it down. The hope was that the Redskins would be so excited about making the big move that they would be willing to pay the big contract. Clinton was a young Pro Bowl running back. It is impossible to get a young stud at running back, a proven commodity, by trade anymore. By the time they hit free agency, they're already beaten up and damaged goods. The Redskins were poised to lose Champ Bailey after one more year, so it was the smart move for them to pay CP the big money and do the trade.

I told CP we had to stick to our guns and go for it. He followed my lead. Now, take a step back and think about it for a moment. This was my only chance to get a deal. If the Redskins walked, the deal would be lost and CP would be nowhere. If we had taken the deal and played for the minimum with incentives, CP would have been happy enough because the new team would be exciting, it would be great for endorsements and recognition, plus he would make more money off incentives. That could have been good enough and we could have played it safe and said yes.

I instinctively knew the Redskins were going to make the trade and we were going to get the big contract. I told him we had to fight for the big contract and let me do the job he hired me to do. He trusted me and backed my play. CP could have warned me and threatened that if I made a mistake, he'd fire me. CP could have been very negative. But he was smart and supported me all the way, which allowed me to be at my best.

I called the Redskins back and told Dan that in order for the deal to work, CP had to get a new contract...and not just any contract, but the richest contract in the history of the NFL for a running back. After going back and forth awhile, the Redskins agreed and CP was thrilled to pull the trigger.

We had done it. We gambled and won. So did the Redskins and Broncos. It was a win for everybody. Even Champ Bailey won by getting a new deal (you would think I would have at least gotten a thank you from Champ or his agent). As for my client, CP received an eight-year $50 million contract with $17 million in bonuses—that's a lot better than $380,000. CP was overjoyed, and the moment I told him we had the deal, he gave me a big hug. We were no longer just an agent and a client, we were now friends. The trade was the biggest transaction of the year and the contract was a landmark deal for me. You have to know when to pull the trigger.

CHAPTER 10

KNOW WHEN TO STAND YOUR GROUND

IMAGINE THIS: YOU ARE SIX FOOT FOUR, 260 POUNDS, exceptionally handsome, and women of all nationalities, races, and religions go crazy over you. You are a prince in your native country and your name actually means "Iron God." You attend Indiana University and the farmers' daughters there are infatuated with you.

At twenty-one years old, you are an unbelievable college football player entering your senior year. You are rated in the top two in the country at your defensive-end position and are projected to be a first-round pick. Bright, refined, and polished, you are the big man on campus, you are excelling academically, and all the girls on campus want you. Does it get any better than that?

Now imagine that in the middle of the season you blow your knee out and your football career looks to be over. You are on crutches for months following a very painful surgery and rehabilitation. Your body atrophies. When the NFL draft comes in April, no team is willing to

173

draft you. Because of the injury, you lose millions of dollars and so much more.

A few months earlier, the other player in the top two at your position, Courtney Brown, goes on to become the first pick of the 2000 NFL draft and gets bonuses worth $13 million. As an undrafted player who won't be healthy enough to play the entire season, you are signed by the Dolphins to a contract offering a $7,500 bonus.

That's enough bad luck to make you cry in your beer and give up. That's what happened to Adewale "Wale" (pronounced "WAH-lay") Ogunleye (pronounced "Oh-goon-LAY-yeh"). But Wale didn't give up. He worked hard every day that first year to get healthy. Although it hurt him to watch every game on the sidelines, he became even more motivated to make it back the next year.

Although he never played that first year, Wale earned the respect of his teammates as a hard worker. Running full speed by the start of the 2001 off-season, he developed a reputation as a guy who had a chance to return to his old form and become a talented player. At the same time, there was always that specter hanging over his head of reinjuring his knee and ending his comeback.

It turns out that Wale was friends with a couple of our clients on the Dolphins, primarily Pro Bowl linebacker Zach Thomas and Pro Bowl defensive tackle Tim Bowens. Wale was looking for a new agent. He had seen me around and asked my clients about me. Zach and Tim recommended me. Consequently, Wale approached me about becoming his agent.

We didn't know much about him, but Zach and Tim spoke well of him. We made a few calls and learned the Dolphins viewed him as a guy who had upside and was inexpensive. Jason and I met with him to see for ourselves.

Wale was still under contract with the Dolphins during the 2001 season. Since his previous agent negotiated the initial two-year contract, we would not be entitled to a fee. Wale was a minimum-salary guy. There wasn't any money in it for us in the short run. But we never make a business decision based on the short term.

The key factor for us in evaluating Wale as a potential client was that he had a presence about him—the presence of a winner. Every player has a presence—some more confident and pronounced than others. Wale was a guy no one ever heard of and yet he had the air of a star. He looked the part physically and had that charisma that the studs in this league have even though he was on the bottom of the depth chart. Thinking that Wale had a chance to become a good player, we decided to sign him during the 2001 off-season. Plus, the guy was a world-class ladies' man. I figured if he wasn't a good defensive end, at least he would make a good wingman for me on the South Beach scene.

Initially, Wale looked good during the 2001 training camp and preseason. But even though he displayed a lot of potential, the Dolphins didn't play him much that year. Wale was played sparingly in seven games, recording a total of three tackles with a half sack. Statistically speaking, he was unimpressive.

On paper, Wale looked like he was "just a guy," as they say in the NFL, not special. But after watching him play, Jason saw a natural pass rusher and believed in him. Since Wale didn't play in 2000, 2001 counted as his rookie season. That season was not productive enough to give us leverage for a 2002 contract, so I negotiated a one-year deal for him at the minimum amount for a second-year player—$300,000.

In 2002, Wale's second credited season, he emerged as a good young starting defensive end with a lot of potential. Wale became a starter at left-defensive-end position, recording forty-five tackles and a very impressive 9.5 sack total. At $300,000, the Dolphins got excellent productivity out of him while paying only the minimum salary.

For the 2003 season, the Dolphins offered and we accepted the minimum salary—$375,000. Even though Wale was a starter and had played very well, the Dolphins still had his rights and our options were to accept the minimum or not play. The Dolphins did offer Wale a long-term contract, but it was far below what we thought his market value was, so we accepted the one-year deal at $375,000.

In the real world, that is a lot of money, but for an NFL player, it's not much. Remember, these athletes have to completely devote themselves to their NFL career year-round. They have to spend numerous hours every day while they are in school practicing, lifting weights, running, meeting with coaches, traveling, studying film, etc. They are strategically programmed not to be students but to be athletes. The schools with successful football programs make many millions of dollars directly and indirectly as a result of these programs. The more successful the players are at football, the earlier they should leave school to enter the NFL. The best college players often enter after just three years. The NFL opportunity is too great to turn down and risk injury, so players often leave college before they get their degrees.

Once they are in the NFL, they are required to participate with the team in the off-season. The player has to devote so much time to the team year-round that it is extremely difficult to go back to school or pursue a second career. Too often, the player has to make his NFL career work or else. That is why when the player has the chance to get the big contract, he has to go for it.

My point is that $375,000 would be very significant if it were the annual salary for a professional who had a long career. If Wale were making $375,000 and had a good chance of earning that salary for the next twenty to fifty years, that salary would be outstanding. But Wale's career could last only one play if he took a hit on his surgically repaired knee. An NFL player's career is so short—the average is three years—that he must maximize his earnings.

The way the NFL works is that after three seasons, a player becomes a restricted free agent when his contract expires. That means there was an opportunity for another team to make Wale an offer and sign him in exchange for giving the Dolphins a high draft pick.

Since Wale's 2002 season had been good but not great, he could not command a monster contract in 2003. We had very little leverage, so the strategy was to play out the 2003 season, have a great year, and then go for the big contract.

As we hoped, Wale went on to have a sensational 2003, winning the team MVP award. He had fifteen sacks, which led his conference (AFC), and was elected to the Pro Bowl. In three seasons this guy went from someone who didn't get drafted to a Pro Bowl defensive end. That just doesn't happen every day in the NFL. Wale defied all the odds in coming back from an injury so severe that no team would even draft him. Now he was a Pro Bowler and considered a better player than the number one overall pick of the 2000 draft, Courtney Brown.

Wale had proven he was an outstanding player and done everything the Dolphins could have asked of him. He was a very popular person in the community and very active in promoting charitable causes.

Wale believed that after contributing as much as he had the last two seasons and after being the lowest-paid starter on the team during those two seasons, he deserved to be rewarded with a long-term contract that had a big bonus.

Come March, the Dolphins had basically three options since Wale was a restricted free agent. First, they could sign him to a long-term deal and keep the player they developed as a key component to a winning defense.

Second, they could make Wale a one-year offer for $1.824 million. If they did, then another team would have to give up a first- and third-round draft choice in the April 2004 draft if they signed him. Again, the Dolphins would have the right to match the offer or, if the offer was too rich, take the first- and third-round picks as compensation for letting Wale go to that team.

The third option was to offer Wale a one-year deal for $412,000. Since Wale had not been drafted by the Dolphins at that offer amount, a team would not have to give up a draft pick to sign him, but the Dolphins would have the right to match the team's offer and keep Wale.

The Dolphins decided at the start of March, the beginning of the 2004 league year, to make Wale the one-year $1.824 million offer and force a team to give up a first- and third-round pick. That was extremely prohibitive as the price was too high.

That left us with two options: either accept the one-year deal at $1.824 million and play the season out, becoming an unrestricted free agent in 2005, or hold out. Neither option was appealing to us. (Technically, it would not be a holdout because Wale would not be under contract.)

Remember, when Wale was entering his senior year of college, he could have entered the NFL draft and possibly gone as high as the late first round, or he could have stayed in school, played his senior year, and gone very high in the first round. The downside to staying was the risk of injury. Wale made the conservative decision to stay in school, but unfortunately got injured and lost $13 million.

He wasn't about to let the same misfortune strike him again. He'd earned the right to be paid like a Pro Bowl player and did not want to play for the $1.824 million. The reason the $1.8 million was unacceptable to Wale was a contract we negotiated the very day after the Dolphins made their offer to him. This contract was for unrestricted free-agent defensive end Jevon Kearse. Like Wale, Jevon was a Pro Bowl defensive end, but he received a contract with $20 million in bonuses that was worth $62.6 million over eight years. Jevon would earn close to $24 million in the first three years of the deal. And Wale's 2003 season was very comparable to Jevon's.

We understood that if Wale were an unrestricted free agent like Jevon, his market value would be similar. We also understood that since Wale was not an unrestricted free agent, he was, in fact, a restricted free agent, his market value was not as high as Jevon's, but it was certainly a lot more than $1.8 million.

The Dolphins had a very firm position that Wale had to do what Pro Bowl defensive end Jason "JT" Taylor did. A few years earlier, JT had been in the same position as Wale. He played out his fourth year on a one-year deal and then got the big contract from the Dolphins. Both JT and the Dolphins felt Wale should play out the fourth year like JT did.

I understood that the Dolphins were trying to follow the precedent set by JT. Their position was not unreasonable. Most restricted free agents do play out that fourth year and then get the big contract.

But Wale did not want to do what other players did. As his agent, I didn't want to follow what those players' agents did. Wale did not want to risk blowing his knee out again and losing his shot at the big payday. This could be his one shot at lifetime security; he wasn't going to let it get away from him again.

Thus a line was drawn in the sand by both sides and each side dug in. There was no clear right and wrong. My job was not to mediate and find a compromise. Nor was it to determine who was right. My job was to do everything within my power to get Wale a monster signing bonus.

The situation was basically mission impossible and the media was having a field day with the drama. Wale made it clear that he wanted a long term deal and the Dolphins made it clear that it wasn't going to happen. Somebody had to give and the media couldn't wait to see who it would be.

It all began on March 2 when the Dolphins officially made Wale the one year offer at $1.8 million. That meant I had until the April draft to persuade another team to give up a first- and third-round pick in order to sign Wale away from the Dolphins. I knew that was not going to happen. There was no way a team was going to give up two high draft picks and then pay a big contract. The value of the draft is that teams get players who are young and cheap. They get to have a player's rights for four years at a relatively cheap value. Most players make the minimum salary during those four years (except for their signing bonus).

Although the situation was bleak, I knew I had to try to get a team involved. On March 26, 2004, *Pro Football Weekly* reported: "Dolphins DE Adewale Ogunleye's agent, Drew Rosenhaus, said he met with the Bears earlier this week to discuss putting together a contract for the restricted free agent."

When I talked to the Bears, they expressed interest in Wale, but not at the price of giving up a first and third pick. I hoped that I could get the Dolphins to consider trading him for a good player or for a first-round pick. The problem was that the Dolphins head coach, Dave Wannstedt, was on the hot seat to keep his job. There was tremendous pressure on him to win that season. Trading their Pro Bowl starting defensive end for a draft pick was not going to make the Dolphins better that season. Losing Wale would hurt them and they were not interested in letting him go.

About a week before the draft, on April 17, 2004, the *Miami Herald* reported: "Agent Drew Rosenhaus has said repeatedly he hopes the Dolphins get a deal done or can complete a trade . . . Multiple Dolphins officials, including coach Dave Wannstedt, have said the team has no plans to deal Ogunleye."

Our hope was that on draft day the Dolphins would trade Wale for a high draft pick and they could use that pick to draft a defensive end to replace Wale. We figured that since Wale was only going to be there for that one season and then leave via free agency, the Dolphins would rather have a young player who could play for them for the next four or five years. That made sense from a long-term perspective, but the Dolphins priority under Wannstedt was to win now, not down the road.

When the draft came and went without a trade, the situation looked very bleak. There were two other teams that wanted to trade for Wale and give him the kind of contract he was looking for, but the Dolphins would not trade him. Wale was angry that the Dolphins would not either pay him the big contract or trade him to another team that would. He was dead set against taking the risk of getting injured again. He'd paid his dues and wanted what he deserved.

Our options were very limited. The Dolphins wanted Wale

to play the season out at the $1.8 million. If we had no choice other than to play the season out, Wale could wait to sign until the eleventh game and then become a free agent. We considered this option because with Wale playing in only the last six games of the season, he would minimize the injury risk. The problem was that he would miss ten game checks. The key was that if Wale played only in six games, it would provide the Dolphins with the incentive to make the trade and get something of value in return for him.

On April 28, 2004, the Associated Press reported: "If necessary, Ogunleye said, he'll sit out the first 10 games this year, then make himself available for the final six games so he can become a free agent after the season. While Wannstedt said earlier in the day that Ogunleye would be a Dolphin this season, Rosenhaus cautioned that there is still no guarantee of that."

The next day, on April 29, 2004, the *Miami Herald* wrote:

"We want Wale to sign a contract, but he will not play for the tender," agent Drew Rosenhaus said. Ogunleye wants a five- to seven-year deal that will include a signing bonus in the $14 million–16 million range. That would match the type of contracts signed by unrestricted free agents Jevon Kearse and Grant Wistrom earlier this offseason...the Dolphins privately maintain that Ogunleye was a restricted free agent this year, not unrestricted like Kearse and Wistrom, so the system prevents him from getting a similar payday.

Wale was determined to get the long-term contract and at this point was looking to pressure the Dolphins into trading him to a team that would give it to him. The Dolphins flat-out refused to trade him.

On May 13, the Dolphins made Wale a long-term offer. Unfortunately, it was for half of what other teams were willing to pay. We were not close at all. I am all about making the deal happen if the offer is good at the midnight hour, but their offer was not a good deal and it was not yet the midnight hour. I saw no other solution but to force a trade.

On May 19, 2004, the *Miami Herald* reported:

Dolphins owner Wayne Huizenga said he expects Pro Bowl defensive end Adewale Ogunleye to re-sign with the team... "We would do everything we can to keep Wale... If I [can] borrow a phrase from Jimmy Johnson... Jimmy always had a saying that you pay a good player a good salary and you pay a great player a great salary.

"Now, the problem comes in when you pay a great salary to a good player. And that's kind of where it's at..."

Once the owner made that statement, I knew they had no intention of trading Wale. Mr. Huizenga is a man of his word and I respect him. However, although it was clear that the Dolphins would not trade Wale, that did not mean we should just fold up our tents and go home. Wale, Jason, and I met to debate our options and unanimously decided to stay the course and have confidence that we could find a solution.

The problem with staying the course was that if we did not accept the one-year offer of $1.8 million by the deadline of June 15, the Dolphins would have the right to lower Wale's offer to $412,000 and still keep his rights.

As June 15 approached, the Dolphins told us they would lower the tender if Wale did not accept. Once more the three of us huddled up and again decided to keep our options open and continue to hang in there in case an opportunity came our way.

On June 15, 2004, the *Miami Herald* wrote: "The Dolphins today are expected to lower Adewale Ogunleye's one-year contract tender from $1.8 million to about $412,000 in a move to protect their interests in case the team's 2003 MVP sits out training camp and most of the regular season."

The next day, June 16, I responded and the *Miami Herald* quoted me: "'We really don't want to hold out, or miss one game, much less seven or ten games,' said agent Drew Rosenhaus, who represents the defensive end. '...But we may have to sit out. It may come to that.'"

The Dolphins training camp started on July 28. As we got close to that date, we considered just playing the one year and becoming a free agent the next season. We had fought and fought to no avail. It would have been easy to give up and hope Wale would stay healthy and have a great 2004 season. We fought the good fight and did everything we could, but now we were running out of time. Maybe, we thought, we should give in. Maybe we should come in with our tail between our legs. Maybe Wale wouldn't reinjure his knee and lose another $13 million. And maybe we're not the best agents in the business!

To hell with maybe not! We weren't going to give in. We weren't going to come in with our tail between our legs. We weren't going to risk Wale injuring his knee and losing his shot at a $13 million bonus all over again. And we *are* the best agents in the business!

We all agreed to hold firm until we could catch a break. When training camp opened in July, Wale did not show up. This caused a media distraction the team did not want. However, someone else also did not show up—Pro Bowl running back Ricky Williams. Ricky was the team's most valuable player. Without him, that team would be in big trouble.

The year before, 2003, Ricky had been one of the best players in the league. He was the guy they relied on to carry the offense on his shoulders. He did not have a good offensive line to block for him or a good quarterback to force defenses to respect the pass. Opposing defenses were going to key on Ricky and all the pressure was on him. The problem was that Ricky wanted a new contract and the Dolphins, who already had a contract with him for several more years, refused to give him a big raise. Ricky couldn't handle the stress of the situation and abruptly retired the day before the start of training camp.

In doing so, he left the team in a terrible position. They were completely unprepared to replace him at running back. If this had happened back in March, the Dolphins could have signed a good running back in free agency. If it had happened in April, they could have drafted a replacement. Even in June, there might have been an opportunity to find a good running back. However, by late July, no good running backs were available. Ricky could not be replaced—not without a trade. And guess which Dolphin player was hoping the team would trade him away to get a new running back!

The Dolphins needed to trade a good player to get a good running back. Since they had a good backup to replace Wale, we thought we'd caught our break. The situation looked encouraging.

On July 28, 2005 ESPN.com reported: "The day after the abrupt retirement of tailback Ricky Williams, ESPN.com reported the Dolphins would likely use Ogunleye as trade bait to upgrade their offense. Miami officials denied that was the case and consistently insisted they would not trade the prized defensive end."

Much to our disappointment, the Dolphins told me they were still not going to trade Wale. Nevertheless, we waited and waited. Yet, after a few weeks went by, the team would not budge. If the most bizarre event of the season, Ricky Williams's retirement, hadn't caused the Dolphins to trade Wale, it looked like nothing would. Still, we stayed the course, relentlessly searching for our opportunity.

The Dolphins played two preseason games without Wale and the defense looked very good. The offense, however, did not look good at all. We needed another break to tip the scales in our favor and time was running out.

Finally, by the third preseason game, we got it. The Dolphins lost two important wide receivers to injury. Without Ricky and those two receivers, their offense was doomed. With their defense so stout, they could afford to trade Wale. Also, that late in the preseason, it became clear that Ricky was not coming back. The Dolphins were running out of time and options. If they wanted a good offensive player, they had to trade Wale, and that's what they did.

On August 21, the team called to tell me that there was an agreement with the Chicago Bears in place. They had agreed to trade Wale for starting wide receiver Marty Booker and a third-round pick in next year's draft. The Dolphins could then trade that third-round pick shortly thereafter in order to get St. Louis Rams running back Lamar Gordon. However, for all of this to happen, the Bears and I first had to agree upon a contract.

Wale was tremendously excited that the Bears wanted to trade for him.

News of the possible trade was reported that day by the *Palm Beach Post:* "The Dolphins have agreed to trade defensive end Adewale Ogunleye to the Chicago Bears in exchange for wide receiver

Marty Booker and a third-round draft choice, if agents Drew and Jason Rosenhaus can work out a contractual agreement with the Bears today."

The situation was tricky. The Bears told me that they wanted to trade for Wale, but their long-term contract offer was disappointing. Nothing worthwhile comes easy in this league. We could have taken the one-year offer from the Bears or their disappointing long-term contract, but we didn't. We stood our ground.

Rather than hang up the phone, I kept the deal alive and negotiated with the Bears throughout the night. Both sides wanted to do the deal.

Keeping things positive, we went back and forth in marathon negotiations until both sides were happy. By the time we said okay, Wale would receive the richest deal in history for a restricted-free-agent defensive end. The contract was a six-year deal worth over $34 million with a $15 million bonus. Wale would make $20 million during the first three years of the deal. He was the happiest man on the planet.

We fought hard for what we wanted against the impossible and still made it happen. We never yielded no matter how bleak it looked. Maybe we got lucky with Ricky retiring and the Dolphins needing tremendous help on the offensive side of the ball, but as the saying goes, luck is when preparation meets opportunity. By hanging in there, we were in position to be prepared to take advantage of the opportunity that finally presented itself. The deal was truly a win/win/win—for Wale, the Dolphins, and the Bears. Marty Booker turned out to be a productive receiver for the Dolphins. Wale helped the Chicago Bears make it to the 2007 Super Bowl, and along the way, he pocketed a cool $20 million.

On August 24, ESPN.com covered the situation best, reporting:

After twice extending the negotiating deadline, the Miami Dolphins and Chicago Bears late Saturday night completed a blockbuster deal… The teams had reached a conditional trade agreement earlier in the day, but completion of the deal hinged on the Bears' ability to sign Ogunleye to a contract by a 7 P.M. deadline. That deadline was first extended to 8:30 P.M., and then beyond, as agent Drew Rosenhaus and Chicago officials frantically negotiated.

In the end, the Bears accomplished in one day what Miami could not in nearly seven months this offseason, agreeing with Ogunleye to a six-year contract worth about $34 million, with signing bonuses essentially worth $15 million.

One of the league's premier dealmakers, Rosenhaus told ESPN.com as the first deadline approached that he was "very pessimistic" an agreement could be reached. But he and the Bears chipped away throughout the evening and finally reached a deal.

It is believed the Bears initially offered about $4 million in bonuses, but having negotiated the eight-year, $66 million that unrestricted free agent Jevon Kearse signed with Philadelphia this spring, which included a $16 million signing bonus, Rosenhaus had a demonstrated knowledge of the market at the position.

Not to be outdone, the *Miami Herald* reported:

A whirlwind negotiation via an airplane phone ended in a stunning contract for Pro Bowl defensive end Adewale Ogunleye and a new wide receiver for the Dolphins' sagging offense.

The Dolphins and Bears agreed in principle to the deal Saturday afternoon. The Bears, who imposed a Saturday night deadline to get the deal completed, initially offered only $4 million in guaranteed money. However, they changed quickly and it was apparent they were intent on doing the deal.

That 2004 season, something happened to Wale that often happens to players who miss training camp: he got injured. He severely injured his ankle toward the end of the season and missed five games. It took him the entire 2005 off-season to recover from the ankle surgery. The key point is that if Wale had taken the one-year deal and then gotten injured, he might never have gotten the big contract. He would have missed his chance just as he did coming out of college. Wale was very smart in knowing what he wanted and fighting for it. Additionally, at no time did he ever make Jason or me insecure as his agents. Jason and I knew Wale had our back and was loyal to us. That allowed us to focus more effectively on getting the job done.

The Bears were very smart as well. When we first did the deal, they actually brought in insurance guru Jim Edgeworth to insure Wale in case he got hurt. When this occurred, the Bears were reimbursed in accordance with their policy.

Wale's contract made big news across the NFL. It showed every player that I knew how to make the impossible happen. The players watched and were very impressed. Given Wale's happiness with my performance as his agent, he recommended us to several of his teammates, including linebacker Lance Briggs, defensive tackle Tommie Harris, running back Thomas Jones, wide receiver Bernard Berrian, and special-teams linebacker Brendon Ayanbadejo—all of whom later developed into Pro Bowl–caliber players. When I first signed Wale to the Bears, he was my only Bears client. It didn't take long for that to change.

I remember calling Wale to let him know that I'd signed another player who wasn't on his team but whom Wale had recommended.

"That guy stinks!" he told me.

"What do you mean? He's a great player. You told me so," I said in shock.

"No, I mean he stinks. On one play, I tackled him and the way it worked out, my face mask got shoved into his butt. It smelled horrible. He crapped his pants!"

After laughing my head off, I told him, "It's a good thing we got you that big bonus. You earned your money, Wale, every penny!"

CHAPTER 11

THE VALUE OF RELATIONSHIPS

WHEN JASON WAS A COLLEGE STUDENT AT UM, HE BECAME close friends with two players. The first was Robert Bailey, who, after eleven years in the league and two Super Bowl championships, became our partner. The second player was Jessie Armstead.

Jessie was the top high school recruit in the nation when Jimmy Johnson recruited him to sign with the Hurricanes in 1989. He was a stud linebacker coming out of Dallas Carter High School in Texas. One day while I was still a law student at Duke and was at UM on spring break, I visited the guys on campus with Jason. As a true freshman, Jessie had made a name for himself and I was familiar with him. I was hanging out with some of the guys I knew from when I was a student there and Jessie was around. I introduced myself to him and joked around a bit. I teased him by saying that I heard guys from Texas were soft wimps. Considering that Jessie looked like a body-builder and I was a Jewish law student half his size, he laughed.

That first year, it was Jessie's turn to be hazed. And as a junior,

Robert Bailey was all too eager to be the senior enforcer. One afternoon at the apartment complex where all the guys stayed, Robert was the ringleader of a group of juniors and seniors who were looking to haze Jessie. Robert was talking tough and, with an electric razor in his hands, told Jessie that he was going to shave his head bald whether Jessie liked it or not.

Jessie wasn't happy about it but understood that's the way it goes when you're a freshman. But Robert, who was half Jessie's size, was talking just too much trash for Jessie to take. Jessie stood up to him and Robert grabbed him and tried to wrestle him down. Robert was tough, but Jessie was too strong for him. As they were grappling, the other seniors grabbed Jessie and shaved his head. They were best friends five minutes after.

Jason told me about this and about a rumble that had gone down at UM. There was a lot of pride among the guys from the state of Florida and the guys from the state of Texas. Even though they were all teammates at UM, the Texas guys all hung together. They were always eight strong. The Florida guys, although they were a much bigger group, traveled in smaller packs. Some of the Texas guys ended up fighting some of the Florida guys and it flared up into a brawl. Jessie and wide receiver Kevin "K-Dub" Williams were the ringleaders of the Texas crew.

As Jason and I were messing with Jessie and K-Dub that afternoon, I joked with them that there was going to be a rumble now between the Texas dudes and the Jew boys (obviously meaning Jason and myself). They jumped up and acted like they were going to wrestle but were only kidding around. Jason and I surprised them by jumping on them. We didn't get very far and survived only because they were laughing so hard.

A few years later, both guys were gearing up for the 1993 NFL draft. K-Dub was a top prospect and ended up being the second-round pick of the Cowboys. Coach Johnson, who'd recruited him to UM and then became the Cowboys head coach, drafted him. As for Jessie, he had a rough career at UM. He blew out his knee after playing brilliantly as a freshman and then the next year tore his shoulder apart. He never had a chance to get healthy and make it back to form. Consequently, he was not highly rated going into the draft.

That year we signed linebacker Marvin Jones from FSU, who was the fourth overall pick in the 1993 draft. Between Marvin and K-Dub, it was a tremendous year for us. The year before we were dead and buried with no rookies, following the Randal Hill trade.

In '93, we were set and didn't need any more clients. As for Jessie, we signed him for only one reason—he was Jason's friend.

A lot of teams told us that Jessie was too small and not durable enough to play in the NFL. They said he lacked the size to be a linebacker and wasn't fast enough to be a safety. He was a "tweener"—someone in between positions. His senior year at UM, Jessie had been only a part-time starter. The coaches rotated him with Rohan Marley—the son of Jamaican singer Bob Marley. Jessie was the forgotten man, the one who fell between the cracks.

As I was trying to get my career going, I wanted to work with players who were going to be high draft picks. Taking on a client is so much work and responsibility for us, and we get so emotionally involved. We want to be with guys who are going to have long, positive careers. We get so close to our clients that it becomes very painful to work with a player who isn't going to be successful. When I asked the teams where Jessie stood, they graded him out as a guy who wasn't going to make it over the long haul. That was very disappointing to me.

When the time came to sign the rookies, Jason told me that he didn't care what the NFL experts said, he believed in Jessie. He had watched every game and seen every play Jessie made. He knew Jessie had the athleticism and mental toughness to succeed. He was convinced the NFL scouts were wrong. Jason didn't have the heart to turn his back on Jessie.

I gave Jason the green light, and since I already represented a linebacker in the draft, Jason represented Jessie himself with me as his partner.

On draft day, Jason was at Jessie's house in Dallas with his family and it was extremely painful to watch over twenty other linebackers get drafted ahead of Jessie. Jason and Jessie waited all the way until the eighth round for the New York Giants to take him. He went in the last round—they don't have eight rounds anymore.

Being fiercely proud and determined to make it in the NFL, Jessie was very angry about being treated like a bottom-of-the-barrel player. Most eighth-round picks didn't make it in the league.

Not Jessie; he made the team his first year by playing special teams. On kickoffs and punts, Jessie ran downfield full speed and made the tackle on the return man. He was fearless and smart, becoming a top special-teams guy in his second year. Fully healthy, Jessie started to get some playtime his third year on passing downs at the linebacker position. He played well in those special situations. His fourth year, Jessie became a starter and we got him a nice contract. From then on, he exploded. Beating all the odds against an eighth-round pick, Jessie became a five-time Pro Bowl linebacker and one of the best in the league. He was without a doubt the most respected player on the team by his peers and became the leader of the Giant defense. He led the team to the Super Bowl against the Ravens. It was fun for us to have both Jessie and Robert Bailey (then with the Ravens) in that game.

Jessie was one of our highest-grossing clients for many years. It's a good thing Jason had believed in him and persuaded me to sign him—for more reasons than you know. Let me explain...

When Jessie was a team leader on the Giants, he recommended us to one of his teammates, receiver Ike Hilliard. Ike was looking for a new agent since his old agent turned out to be a crook. We signed Ike, thanks to Jessie, and from there Ike introduced us to his friend and fellow Florida Gator Fred Taylor. Fred was an outstanding young running back from UF who'd been drafted by Jacksonville in the first round. Like Ike, he was looking for a new agent and Ike referred him to us.

It turned out that Fred was close friends with a young UF graduate named Jeff Rubin. Jeff was an aspiring financial planner who discovered that agent Tank Black had defrauded Fred and other players out of millions of dollars using a Ponzi scheme. Tank created dummy corporations and had his clients invest money in them. He was later decertified by the NFLPA and incarcerated for his crimes. After seeing Fred lose millions of dollars, I was thrilled to negotiate a long-term contract for him in 2003 that would pay him an up-front $8 million signing bonus.

I first had the chance to meet with Fred during the summer of 1999. He was staying at a house with a bunch of other NFL players in a beautiful area of Golden Beach, Florida. One of the guys staying at the house was Jevon "The Freak" Kearse, who was Fred's best friend and former teammate at UF. At this time, the Freak was a rookie Pro Bowl sensation defensive end for the Titans and one of the most exciting young superstars in the league. I hung out with those guys and it was a lot of fun.

Shortly thereafter, Jevon's representatives had a major breakup and Jevon was no longer comfortable with the situation. With Fred's recommendation, I became Jevon's new agent.

When I signed Jevon in 2000, he was still under contract with the Tennessee Titans for several years. At the time, he was best friends with offensive guard Zach Piller, also from UF. When Jevon called me to tell me that he'd recommended me to Zach, I was happy for two reasons. First, I was happy that Jevon thought enough of me to refer me to his friend. Second, I was happy to meet with Zach, who was a very good starting lineman. When I met with him, I was impressed not only with the player but with the person as well.

There are so many different personalities in a locker room. As an agent, you deal with them all. There are some guys who are considered arrogant. There are some who are quiet and keep to themselves. There are the locker-room lawyers who are overly opinionated and always complaining about something. And then there are the guys who make everyone laugh and are always in a good mood. Those are the guys that everyone loves and respects. Well, Jevon and Zach were everybody's favorite around that Titan locker room.

That's why I was so surprised that the Titans didn't try harder to keep Jevon. As I said before, Jevon was all world in his first three years. Unfortunately, he got bitten by the injury bug, missing fourteen games over the fourth and fifth years of his contract. The Titans made us offers to extend his contract, but they were far below what we felt his value was. The team expressed serious concerns over his durability.

With free agency scheduled to start on March 3, I met with the

Titans general manager Floyd Reese at the Indianapolis Combine in late February. He told us that they felt Jevon's value was between $5 million and $6 million a year. Floyd wasn't comfortable going higher than $10 million on the bonus. I was confident Jevon would do better on the open market—if we could get there. The big question was whether the Titans would keep Jevon off the market by making him their franchise player and offering him a one-year deal around $5 million. I was very concerned that they were going to franchise him. When I met with Floyd in Indianapolis, he was playing it close to the vest, but said they were leaning toward not franchising him.

The problem with franchising a player is that it prevents him from testing his value by seeing what other teams would pay for his services. This leads to a difference of opinion over what a fair deal is between the team and the player. If an agreement is not reached, the player can either hold out or take the one-year tender. As I know all too well, that causes heartache for everyone.

So when Floyd told me that the team was not going to franchise Jevon, I was thrilled. On February 25, 2004, the Associated Press reported: "The Titans decided that their best chance to keep Jevon Kearse was by letting him test the free agent market and they decided not to place the franchise tag on him... 'It's almost going to serve as an arbitrator if you will,' Titans general manager Floyd Reese said yesterday. 'Let the market decide what's out there, then go from there.'"

I was very excited for Jevon with free agency on the way. I knew there would be teams coming after him. The next day, February 26, 2004, the *Washington Post* reported: "The Redskins are interested in Jevon Kearse now that he'll become a free agent... 'I think everybody in the league would have an interest in Jevon Kearse,' Redskins head coach Joe Gibbs said. 'I think what happens most of the time is a guy like that who is unrestricted, you figure everybody in the league is going to be talking to him. So it's going to be a matter of who wins out.'"

The NFL does not permit teams to talk to agents prior to free agency about other teams' players, but an agent has to find a way through hypothetical conversations to know in advance what his client's market value is going to be. Therefore, while still allowing the teams to follow the rules, I had numerous hypothetical conversations about Jevon while not specifically discussing him per se.

As free agency neared, there was no point in getting a deal done with the Titans without first testing the market, especially since their numbers were low. I told Floyd we were going to enter free agency, but we would keep him in the loop.

On March 2, 2004, the day before free agency, the *Tennessean* reported: "Jevon Kearse and the Titans aren't even negotiating a contract extension. The start of the free agency period begins at the end of Tuesday, so he appears to be headed out as a free agent. 'Jevon is going to test the market,' said Kearse's agent, Drew Rosenhaus. 'We are anticipating a lot of action, a lot of interest. We'll just have to see what happens.'"

At the stroke of midnight on March 3, Jevon was at my office. The weeks of discussions and hypothetical negotiations had come to a head. I could finally take the gloves off and get going. The phone rang at one minute past midnight and several teams were soon in the hunt.

I was up all night negotiating. What it came down to when the money was the same between two teams was that Jevon wanted to play for Eagles coach Andy Reid. And so we agreed on a long-term contract with the Eagles to pay Jevon $20 million in bonuses and approximately

$8 million a year. That was a monster free-agent contract for Jevon and a huge feather in my cap.

Shortly after the deal was done, Jevon Kearse told the *News Journal:* "Basically, Drew found out what I wanted and then he got it for me. We had a certain situation in mind and this was it. And once we made up our minds that I wanted to be an Eagle, he got it done real quick. That's why you have an agent like him."

I busted my butt for Jevon and Zach Piller and they appreciated my hard work and results. The next year, in March 2005, I negotiated a $15.5 million contract for Zach.

Following Jevon's lead, Zach recommended me to a bunch of his teammates: offensive lineman Justin Hartwig, quarterback Billy Volek, and offensive lineman Jacob Bell. That's how this business works—you do a great job for a guy and he is so happy with you that he goes out of his way to return the favor. Just like that (well, there was a lot of work involved) I picked up three awesome new clients.

As for Fred, he didn't stop with Jevon when it came to recommending me. Fred appreciated how hard I worked on his 2003 contract, so when his teammate and stud Pro Bowl defensive tackle Marcus Stroud asked him about us, Fred gave us two thumbs-up. And he didn't only do this with Marcus Stroud. He also recommended us to his close friend Plaxico "Plex" Burress. Both situations were complex. Neither deal was an easy one.

The way I see it, a deal never should be easy. If it turns out to be easy, then the agent didn't try hard enough. If it's easy, that agent didn't push the team to their limit and beyond. An easy deal is one where the agent left money on the table.

I wasn't going to do that. Marcus had one year left on his five-year rookie contract with the Jaguars. We didn't want to play that one year out. Jason and I visited with the Jaguars general manager Paul Vance repeatedly, working hard until we closed on the six-year $31.5 million contract Marcus deserved. That deal made Marcus one of the highest paid defensive tackles in the NFL.

As for Plex, he was in a pickle as a free agent. For whatever reason, although he had all the physical ability in the world as a receiver, teams weren't knocking on the door. After being in free agency for several days and unhappy with the results, Plex spoke with Fred. Guess what happened from there? That's right—he hired us.

Plex had an offer from the Giants, but his previous agent and team never got on the same page and the Giants pulled their offer. As soon as I could jump into the action, I met with the Giants general manager Ernie Accorsi and their negotiator Kevin Abrams to not only get the deal back on the table but to sweeten the pot. Shortly thereafter, we negotiated a $25 million deal with the Giants.

Just three seasons later, Plex was a huge part of the Giants' stunning Super Bowl upset of the Patriots and will be due for a new contract extension. That's what happens when you catch the Super Bowl winning touchdown.

The bottom line is that we get the job done that the client hires us to do. He appreciates it and recommends us to the next guy with a tough negotiation on the horizon.

Our clients really go to bat for us because we go to bat for them. Over the years, Fred recommended us to the following Jaguars: Pro Bowl defensive tackle Marcus Stroud, wide receiver Ernest Wilford, fullback Greg Jones, defensive end Paul Spicer, quarterback Quinn Gray, and punter Chris Hanson. Wale Ogunleye really championed for me as well, recommending me to the following Bears: Pro Bowl defensive tackle Tommie Harris, Pro Bowl linebacker Lance Briggs, running back Thomas Jones, wide receiver Bernard Berrian, and Pro Bowl special-teams linebacker Brendon Ayanbadejo. I would go on to negotiate monster new contracts for all those guys...so when Wale goes out to dinner with me you know who is picking up the check.

And as much credit as Fred and our clients deserve in going to bat for us, it's not like they put on a PowerPoint presentation with numerous persuasive bullet points. It's because of what we accomplished for Fred Taylor, Jessie Armstead, Willis McGahee, Clinton Portis, Jeremy Shockey, Warren Sapp, and Adewale Ogunleye that the players around the league know us. The players around the league see my face all the time...everywhere. And they see me smiling with my clients—victorious in the end. They all know that one way or another, I am going to come through for them.

Sometimes players just see your work and knock on the door— that is the ultimate compliment. Darnell "Doc" Dockett, a rookie defensive tackle out of Florida State University hired me out of college in 2004 primarily because he was very impressed with the job I did for Willis the year before. I had tremendous respect for Doc because I knew he'd overcome horrendous tragedy and adversity as a young man to make it in this league.

Would you believe that at the age of thirteen on the Fourth of July holiday, young Darnell walked into his kitchen and found his mother lying dead on the floor from a gunshot wound to the head. As if that wasn't hard enough to cope with, his father died four months later from pancreatic cancer. Mercifully, Darnell's uncle Kevin Dockett, a successful businessman and wonderful person, took his departed brother's son under his wing and raised him as his own child. Today, Darnell is a Pro Bowl player.

So when Dockett told me that he respected what I'd accomplished in my career, it meant a lot to me. He understands the real meaning of Friedrich Nietzsche's words—"That which does not kill me makes me stronger."

Once I came through for Doc and negotiated a big extension for him, he recommended me to his teammate and fellow defensive lineman Antonio "Scoobie" Smith. I gotta tell you that both those guys are super fun to hang with. They are both great guys, great clients, and make this business fun. And that's the way this business works. When Doc or Fred or Jevon or Zach Piller say, "Drew is awesome. He works hard for you, calls you every day, and will get you paid," the players come knocking on my door. And when I get the call from an interested player who is unhappy with his agent—after he initiates the communication about hiring me (pardon the legal disclaimer that Jason insists on)—I am on a plane the next day meeting with him face-to-face.

For instance, when Jessie Armstead called me late in the 2004 season to say that relatively unknown Washington Redskin linebacker Antonio "AP" Pierce had talked to him about me, I was excited. Whenever Jessie calls about a player, I know it is legit. Late in the season in 1996, Jessie called me about someone I never heard of. His name was Olindo Mare, he was a kicker from Syracuse University who was on the practice squad with the New York Giants. Jessie told me that even though he was a backup kicker, he was a good guy and could really kick. On Jessie's word, I signed Olindo. The next year, I brought Olindo to work out for his hometown team, the Dolphins. The year before Jimmy Johnson had released our client kicker Pete Stoyanovich—one of our all-time favorite guys and a longtime fan favorite of the Dolphins. When Jimmy decided to give Olindo a chance to compete with the kicker who replaced Pete, we were excited. Olindo would go on to kick for the Dolphins for ten seasons, from 1997 through 2006. As a Pro Bowl kicker, he became the highest-paid kicker in the history of the NFL. He was not only a great kicker, he was also a great client, recommending us to stud fullback Rob Konrad, punter Donnie Jones (who has to be the funniest guy in the NFL), and punter Chris Hanson.

So when Jessie called me about Antonio "AP" Pierce and told me he was a baller, I bought into it. Then I watched him play and knew he was the real deal. Even though AP was not drafted and didn't play his first three years on the team, that fourth year he emerged as an impressive starting linebacker.

By the time AP called me, I knew his whole story. He told me that the Giants had offered him a deal that his agent recommended, but he wasn't comfortable with. He told me he was letting that agent go and looking for someone more aggressive. I told him I was that guy. Just a few months later, I almost doubled the amount of money he turned down and landed him a deal with the Giants for $25 million.

It was largely because of strong-character Pro Bowl players like Jessie, Olindo, and Sapp, guys who were loyal friends and made us successful together, that I was able to rise to the top. That's why when I saw that Jessie was trying to get into coaching in March 2008, I asked him to join Rosenhaus Sports instead. He just seemed perfect to work with our clients and help them be successful on and off the field the way he was. Jessie is a leader who commands respect and I know that our clients will greatly benefit from the wisdom of a five-time Pro Bowl New York Giant linebacker who made it the hard way as a Miami Hurricane from Dallas and was able to walk away from the game with his dignity, health, and financial security. Every player should strive to accomplish what Jessie did as an NFL player, a businessman, and a family man.

As for Rosenhaus Sports, with Jessie we are ready to grow again like we did in 2003. Largely because of what I pulled off with Willis in the April 2003 draft, players took notice and wanted me to deliver for them. High-profile players like running back Clinton Portis and Dolphin tight end Randy McMichael, guys who became landmark clients for me, gave me the opportunity in late 2003.

From that point on, I would go on an unprecedented tear signing new clients and building an empire. After the 2004 draft, where I represented safety Sean Taylor, defensive lineman Darnell Dockett, defensive end Bobby McCray, safety Guss Scott, cornerback Keiwan Ratliff, and linebacker Darrell McClover, we signed Pro Bowl defensive tackle Tommie Harris, Pro Bowl linebacker Lance Briggs, cornerback Mike McKenzie, Pro Bowl receiver Anquan Boldin, Pro Bowl defensive tackle Marcus Stroud, Pro Bowl linebacker Antonio Pierce, Pro Bowl kick returner Eddie Drummond, safety Yeremiah Bell, safety Dwight Smith, receiver Taylor Jacobs, and running back Reuben Droughns. That 2004 season we negotiated thirty-seven contracts worth more than $315 million. (It's too bad for my clients and me that NFL contracts aren't guaranteed and players typically only see the first few years of long-term contracts.)

In 2005, a year after I delivered for Randy, Clinton, Jevon, Sapp, and Wale, players saw it all over ESPN and wanted me to do the same for them. That's why in 2005, my roster of clientele exploded, with great new players like Pro Bowl receiver Terrell Owens, Pro Bowl receiver Chad Johnson, Pro Bowl running back Edgerrin James, Pro Bowl receiver Plaxico Burress, first-round-pick receiver Donte Stallworth, Pro Bowl linebacker Dan Morgan, Pro Bowl cornerback Sam Madison, receiver Ernest Wilford, first-round-pick cornerback Phillip Buchanon, receiver Roscoe Parrish, quarterback Billy Volek, center

Justin Hartwig, punter Donnie Jones, quarterback Quinn Gray, full-back Najeh Davenport, cornerback Travis Fisher, center Chris Myers, running back Vernand Morency, defensive end Dan Cody, and defensive tackle Gabe Watson. That 2005 season we negotiated thirty-one contracts worth more than $324 million.

And 2006 proved that 2005 was not a onetime wonder. I rode the wave of success through the adversity of the "Next Question" press conference to sign more great players: Pro Bowl running back Frank Gore, first-round-pick running back Thomas Jones, linebacker London Fletcher, cornerback Drayton Florence, guard Jacob Bell, quarterback Drew Stanton, linebacker Lawrence Timmons, receiver Sinorice Moss, offensive tackle Eric Winston, fullback Jameel Cook, Pro Bowl special-teams linebacker Brendon Ayanbadejo, defensive tackle Fred Evans, fullback Darian Barnes, tight end Buck Ortega, and Pro Bowl special-teams safety Hanik Milligan. That 2006 season, we negotiated thirty-nine contracts, worth $260 million. (We actually had a better year in 2006 despite the lower totals because the contracts were more front-loaded and short term, which means the player takes home more but the long-term totals are less.)

In 2007, we signed NFLPA president and Pro Bowl cornerback Troy Vincent, Pro Bowl tight end Kellen Winslow II, Pro Bowl running back Marion Barber, cornerback Bryant McFadden, receiver Bernard Berrian, defensive end Antonio Smith, offensive tackle Luke Petitgout, cornerback Will Allen, running back Earnest Graham, safety Renaldo Hill, tight end Greg Olsen, receiver Aundrae Allison, receiver Jason Hill, linebacker Antwan Barnes, running back Darius Walker, tight end Anthony Becht, defensive end Ebenezer Ekuban, defensive end Demetric Evans, linebacker Lemar Marshall, defensive end Michael Myers, safety Mike Doss, receiver Glenn Holt, running back Michael Pittman, fullback Moran Norris, linebacker Nate Harris, running back Rock Cartwright, and Pro Bowl special-teams receiver Kassim Osgood. That 2007 season, we negotiated forty-six contracts, worth approximately $362 million.

Through the first half of 2008, we've already signed linebacker Jon Beason, safety Kenny Phillips, linebacker Dan Connor, receiver Devin Thomas, tight end Kellen Freeman-Davis, running back Kevin Smith, cornerback Jack Ikegwuonu, linebacker Stephen Tulloch, defensive end Matt Roth, defensive tackle William Joseph, cornerback Fernando Bryant, safety Dominique Barber, receiver Kerry Reed, running back Chad Simpson, and safety Greg Wesley. Only midway through March 2008, we have already negotiated forty-five contracts, worth $532 million, with a lot more contracts to come.

The ascent that began in 2003 has a lot to do with the emergence of Jason, Robert, and Danny Martoe, all of whom exceeded my expectations. We have worked extremely cohesively as a team to succeed for our clients. Remember, it's one thing to sign a client, it's another to deliver for them and keep them happy enough to stay with you and recommend you to their friends. And now I can't help but think back to all the predictions from my critics and competitors during the 2005 "Next Question" era when I was supposed to be finished. It didn't exactly happen like that. Our crew is loyal, hardworking, and all about winning, which explains a lot about our success.

But there's another reason I have yet to discuss that explains how I signed superstar after superstar over the last several years—I was a good loser. Keep reading and you'll understand.

CHAPTER 12

BE A GOOD LOSER

I AM A GOOD LOSER. IN FACT, I TRY VERY HARD TO BE ONE. What do I mean by that? Well, do you remember the story about how Grand Master Young Soo Do used to make Jason fight his rival student? Jason and that other kid hated each other and couldn't wait to beat the hell out of the other on Tuesdays and Thursdays, the days the students would spar. But whenever my dad came to the school, our karate teacher would announce, "Special fighting today," and in the last few minutes of class, no matter what day of the week it was, the two would fight.

Jason and that kid tore into each other like crazed dogs. When Jason lost one of the battles, he was so angry he pushed the guy in the back of the head after the fight was over. Our karate teacher never got mad at Jason, except for that one day. He punished Jason severely. But we learned something about sportsmanship and character.

Being a good sport means being a gentleman in defeat and not lowering or dishonoring yourself. Being a smart sport means realizing losing is temporary. Being a good loser means recognizing that by being a good sport and keeping your composure, you may get the chance to have another shot at the title. Being a good loser gives you the chance to win in the long run. Being a bad loser means you lose because you not only lowered yourself by letting your emotions get the best of you but you also blew any chance you had down the road of getting another opportunity to win.

Believe it or not, as I was writing a draft of this chapter, a client called me to complain about another agent. He told me that another agent who'd recruited him was harassing him because he was pissed off about the player hiring me. The night before, at four o'clock in the morning, the agent sent the player a text calling him a "bitch!"

My client Greg Olsen, the 2007 first-round-pick tight end of the Chicago Bears from UM, would say, "How dumb was that!" And Greg would be right.

The agent was obviously upset that he lost the battle and felt very bitter. By being so stupid, the agent killed any chance he had of getting my client down the road. He also made the mistake of crossing us and we'll make him pay for that. He'll be sending more angry texts to more players before long.

It doesn't bother me when something like that happens. I actually love it. That agent is no longer a threat to my relationship with my client. Stupid move by the competition—but what else is new.

Being a good loser has been instrumental to my success. UM running back Edgerrin "EJ" James, who in 1999 was the top running back in the draft, is a textbook example of that.

By 1999, it had been five years in a row that I dominated at UM, signing Sapp and other top Hurricane rookies. The year before, I signed UM cornerback Dune Starks, who was the tenth pick in the first round by the Baltimore Ravens. I was determined to keep my streak going and that meant landing EJ.

I recruited him hard. At the time, I focused on signing one rookie—the best player at UM. EJ was my one and only target. I had to sign him and went all out.

Unfortunately, no matter how hard I tried, no matter what I did, no matter how close I got to him, month after month went by and I couldn't persuade him to sign with me. Most rookies sign with their agent the first or second week in January. All of them have their agent in place by the April draft. EJ was the exception to the rule and didn't hire an agent until July; I devoted six months of my life to signing him.

On draft day in late April, I was there at his draft party with several other agents who were also recruiting him. EJ was the fourth pick in the first round of the draft to the Colts. It felt strange to celebrate because he wasn't my client. That made me even more determined to win. I worked and worked, only to lose.

All along, my instincts told me I wasn't going to succeed. But all I know how to do is keep going and work hard. EJ and I both knew that I was going to come up short and yet he saw me and Jason bust our asses. I knew he respected that.

As for me, I kept telling myself to stay the course and I would be the choice. EJ had a group of advisers assisting him with the decision. I recruited them as well. When I got the call on the day they made their decision, I was told, "Good news...you are the first runner-up."

I got super excited when he said "good news" thinking I'd been chosen. When I heard runner-up, I was in pain—a lot of it. I reacted by picking up the phone to call EJ. Being a stand-up guy, he took my call rather than avoid me out of awkwardness. I told him no hard feelings, that I had a lot of respect for him, that I wished him nothing but the best, and to keep me in mind down the road if things didn't work out. I hung up the phone with nothing to show for my efforts—nothing except good sportsmanship.

I then called Pierre Rutledge, EJ's primary adviser, and was very positive toward him as well. I genuinely harbored no ill will, but I was in agony over losing out on a great player from my home turf. Pierre, always a professional, explained the reasoning behind the decision and I took it like a man. I told him to feel free to keep in touch and that is what he did.

In the end, I spent a lot of time and money recruiting EJ without anything to show for it. Other agents recruited him as well, and when they came up short they bad-mouthed EJ to the media. My approach was obviously very different.

Of all the players who have come out of UM, I don't think anyone is more loved by the players than "Uncle EJ." He's a fascinating young man. He's as clever as any attorney I've crossed paths with and as tough as any gangster out there. He always governs himself by a code he learned growing up in his hometown of Immokalee, Florida. He had it rough early on and survived by hustling here and there to get by. He is a serious guy who never crosses anyone first and is always loyal to his friends and teammates. I have never met anyone who had a bad word to say about him—other than scorned agents.

In the NFL, most players like to have an "event" in the off-season. Having a lot of UM teammates in the NFL and friends on his current NFL team, EJ went to a friend's charity event almost every weekend. Being an agent, I would go to all of my clients' events. Since EJ and I were both UM guys, we were often at the same events.

One event that I recall in particular was a celebrity basketball charitable fund-raiser put together by my client Anquan Boldin—the

Pro Bowl wide receiver for the Arizona Cardinals. Anquan hired me in August 2004—after a tremendous rookie season. I had just gotten Portis a new deal and Anquan's situation was very similar to his. Anquan had a Pro Bowl rookie year. Like Portis, he'd been Rookie of the Year and signed a four-year deal coming out of college. Anquan saw that Portis got a new deal after the second year even though he had two years remaining on the rookie contract. Anquan wanted to get a new deal, too, even though he was under contract for two more years, and he hired me to get him that new deal. The next year, by the start of his third year, he got his new contract.

Anquan and EJ were friends. They have a lot in common. Both guys are from very small towns no one ever heard of (Immokalee and Pahokee) and those towns are not far from each other. More importantly, both men are tough, stand-up guys who command the respect of every teammate and NFL player they've ever stepped onto the football field with.

So when Anquan had his annual charity basketball game in Pahokee, Florida, EJ was sure to be there. So was I—Anquan would have me introduce the starting lineups and emcee the game. Every time I saw EJ, he was very friendly toward me and always threw in a line or two about me being the best in the business, and if he were to go with someone else, it would be me.

It wasn't just talk. EJ had been saying that for years. In fact, for the 2000 draft, he recommended me instead of his own agent to his best friend, UM junior linebacker Nate Webster.

Nate was a lot like EJ in that he was tougher than anyone, but Nate was crazier than EJ. Nate was too fearless for his own good. I think the only player on the UM team he didn't fight was EJ.

Let me take a step back for a minute. Former UM wide receiver

Santana "Tan" Moss was only five-nine and 180 pounds coming out of college. And yet he was remarkably fearless and tough as a rookie in 2001. Tan is a funny and friendly guy, but he has that street-thug toughness in him. When he got to the NFL and was drafted by the New York Jets in the first round, a few offensive linemen thought they could haze him. They thought wrong. Tan, outweighed by a hundred and fifty pounds, took on a Jets offensive lineman and scared the crap out of the guy. Tan is just street tough like that. And as tough as Tan is, he'll tell you he won't mess with Nate.

When Tan was in middle school, he and Nate were classmates. He told me that Nate was the bigheaded bully who beat everyone up in school. Tan and everyone else were scared of him. Nate eventually went to Northwestern high school, which is the top football high school in Florida. Nobody messed with Nate there, and when he got to UM, he made a name for himself real quick.

Nate was famous for his sleeper hold. That's right—he actually used a sleeper hold on other UM football players. When he first got there, he fought a big, ugly three-hundred-pound offensive lineman who outweighed him by a hundred pounds. Nate was short and light for a linebacker, at five-eleven and two hundred pounds as a freshman. And yet Nate got his thick forearm and biceps around the guy's neck and squeezed like an anaconda until the guy blacked out. While the lineman was unconscious, Nate laughed, slapped him into consciousness, and cussed him out.

Throughout his tenure at UM, Nate was still a bully, putting the sleeper hold on ten other teammates. When he was drafted by the Bucs, former Hurricane Warren Sapp took him under his wing and loved the guy.

Jason and I developed a great relationship with Nate, too. In fact,

Jason once asked him to put the sleeper hold on him just out of curiosity. I was nervous and told Nate I'd fire him if he didn't let go, but he laughed it off and let Jason go without putting him out. Jason said it was the most helpless feeling he'd ever experienced.

What Jason and I learned is that when you fail, when you lose, as heartbreaking and painful as it is, even though you feel as helpless as you'd feel in Nate's sleeper hold, you are not. You can still win in the long run if you lose with class.

Permit me to return to EJ to continue making my point.

EJ's rookie contract was due to expire after the 2004 season. The Colts had a choice to either offer EJ a long-term deal or let him be a free agent to test the market. The team did not want to offer a long-term deal because their philosophy was to invest in young running backs not veterans. Remember that when EJ was drafted in 1999, the Colts traded away All-Pro veteran running back Marshall Faulk in order to get the fourth pick of the draft, which they used to select EJ. The Colts did not want to pay Faulk since he was a veteran, and several years later, they did not want to make a long-term investment in EJ now that he was a veteran. However, they did not want to part ways with EJ, so rather than lose him to free agency, they franchised him and retained his rights for the 2005 season by offering him a one-year $8.081 million contract with a $1 million incentive.

EJ and his associate Pierre knew that striking a long-term deal with the Colts and dealing with the franchise would be extremely challenging. There was a great deal of uncertainty regarding what was going to happen. Year in and year out, I saw EJ at numerous events. We had maintained a very genuine relationship and he knew how much respect I had for him. He also saw me get the job done for Portis, Willis, Wale, Sapp, Zach, and Jevon. He knew everything there was to know about me. He paid meticulous attention to how I handled each of those situations and the ensuing results. So did Pierre.

Therefore, when I got the call from Pierre and EJ to come in and handle his negotiations, it was unbelievably rewarding. First of all, EJ could have hired any agent in the business and he chose me. Second, he is respected by everyone for being street-smart and handling his business. Third, I had worked so hard to get him in 1999. Fourth, I dealt with the pain of him signing with a rival agent and kept my composure. And fifth, I waited and waited for years on that phone call. The old saying "If at first you don't succeed, try and try again" could not have been more true.

It made big news that EJ hired me, and when asked about making the move, he said to the *Miami Herald,* "Drew to the rescue... Y'all know how fast Drew can talk. If there's potential for him to make it happen, he will."

I wanted to prove EJ right. In 2005, a one-year $9 million salary for EJ plus $1 million in incentives with the Colts. In March 2006, he was a free agent. The Colts did not offer him a long-term contract because they knew the kind of money he deserved and they were not prepared to pay him that. Ironically, the Colts went on to win the Super Bowl that year without EJ. Don't cry for EJ, though; he received a $30 million contract with the Arizona Cardinals, earning $20 million his first two years. If you include his 2005 compensation with the Colts, he grossed approximately $30 million in three years—something no NFL running back had ever done!

So while it was special for the Colt players to win a Super Bowl, it was also pretty special for EJ to bring in $30 million. Like I said, don't feel sorry for EJ. One thing about him, he sure takes care of business.

To illustrate that point further, let's compare the two top running-back contracts negotiated in the 2006 market. The first involves Shaun Alexander. During the 2005 season, Shaun set an NFL rushing record, scoring twenty-eight touchdowns and rushing for 1,880 yards; he was also voted NFL MVP. What more can an NFL running back do? How about leading his team to the Super Bowl (the Seahawks lost to the Steelers) and getting on the cover of the Madden NFL 2007 video game?

EJ had a very good year with the Colts in 2005, rushing for 1,506 yards and thirteen touchdowns, but it was not an MVP year. Logically, you would conclude that Alexander had more leverage and should have been the higher-paid player. Well, you might think that, and it would have been true if you remove agents from the equation. But Jason and I pride ourselves on being the best negotiators in the business. EJ didn't hire us for our looks. We were brought in to get him a superior contract and that is what we did.

The numbers don't lie. Over the first two years of his contract, Shaun Alexander earned $18.525 million. EJ earned $20 million. Over three years, Shaun would be at $23 million and EJ at $25 million. EJ did a four-year deal totaling $30 million. Shaun did an eight-year deal, and over four years would earn $28.56 million. EJ's contract is better. Now, Jason and I can take a lot of credit for that, but not all of it. EJ flew out to Arizona with me and was intricately involved in the face-to-face negotiations. He was tremendously helpful and I could not have done it without him.

Now let me ask you a question. What if I hadn't been a good loser back in 1999? What if I insulted EJ and Pierre to the media the way other agents did? What if I didn't genuinely maintain my high regard for EJ every time I saw him in the off-season for a period of six years?

Because I was a good loser and waited six years, from 1999 to 2005,

I was able to win on a four-year $30 million contract for EJ that is as impressive as any contract I've ever signed my name to. That's why I advise you to be a good loser. It can be a temporary situation.

Antrel Rolle, the defensive back from UM who was a top ten draft pick (eighth overall) of the Arizona Cardinals in the 2005 draft, was recommended to me by EJ this past year. I recruited Antrel coming out of UM and was very disappointed when he went in another direction, but I was a good sport about it. So two years later, in the middle of the 2007 season, he asked EJ about me, gave me a call, and the next day I was in Arizona meeting with him. That's how well the principle can work.

And what happened with EJ was not an isolated incident. When Sean Taylor fired me to hire EJ's agent right after Sean was drafted with the fifth overall pick in the April 2004 draft, I was humiliated and extremely upset. But I kept my composure, and in July 2004, he rehired me. Although I never got to negotiate Sean's next deal, the time I had with him was worth more than the commission I could have earned—much more.

Oddly enough, sometimes it works out for the best that you don't get a player you want. When Ogunleye recommended us to Bears running back Thomas "TJ" Jones, we were ecstatic. TJ is as cool as they come and a real tough guy at the running-back position. He is a strong-character guy, built like a bodybuilder, and is a lot of fun to hang out with. We were thrilled to represent him because we knew he would be an outstanding client. Additionally, there was one other factor. When we signed TJ in 2006, his brother Julius Jones was the starting running back for the Cowboys. Although Julius expressed an interest in working with us, in the end he decided to stay with his original agent. We would have liked to sign Julius and it was disappointing when it didn't work out. But a year later, in 2007, another Cowboy running back expressed an interest in us—Marion "The Barbarian" Barber. We signed Marion early in the 2007 season, and coincidence or not, he exploded to become a Pro Bowl stud. That would not have happened if we'd signed Julius because those two were competing for the starting position with the Cowboys. Sometimes it's funny how things can work out for the best.

You would think that representing the family member of a recruit, and having the family member give you a great recommendation, would make it a lock to get the recruit. You would think that, but in this business nothing is automatic or easy. Things tend to happen the hard way for me, so it's a good thing I am a hard worker. Case in point—Phil Buchanon. I recruited Phil hard coming out of UM in 2002. He was cousins with Jevon "The Freak" Kearse, so I really thought I would get him. Instead, he went in another direction. Three years later, he made the move to hire me. Now Phil is starting at corner for the Tampa Bay Bucs.

There was a very similar situation in 2004 when I recruited Chicago Bears superstar defensive tackle Tommie Harris coming out of Oklahoma. Tommie was cousins with two of my clients—Stockar and Jerome "Jerry" McDougle. I was very close with both Stockar and Jerry. Stockar, a first-round-pick offensive tackle from Oklahoma University in 2000, went to the same school as Tommie. Jerry went to UM and was a first-round pick in 2003. Having both of them as my clients and big advocates, I thought Tommie would want to sign with me, but it didn't work out that way.

I liked Tommie a lot. He was extremely unpredictable and humorous in a very entertaining way. I was heartbroken when I didn't get him because I knew he was a great kid and great player. But I stayed on good terms with him and handled the disappointment like a gentleman. A year later, Tommie called me and asked me to meet with him. Shortly thereafter, I signed him while he was back in Oklahoma visiting friends. Jason and I went out to a farm with him.

On the farm, a baby cow had just been separated from her mother. The baby cow was crying out for her and I realized that cows were intelligent animals with feelings. At the time, my dog had just died, and to me, it was like losing someone in my family. After that day, Jason and I stopped eating red meat and pork. We came to the conclusion that we would no longer eat mammals of any kind. To this day, we have kept our word and haven't eaten any mammals—but we still like to chew up and spit out sports agents.

The same year I initially recruited Tommie—2004—I also recruited Kellen Winslow II. Kellen had succeeded Shockey at UM as the next great tight end, and they were very close friends. Jeremy really went to bat for me with Kellen.

I remember this one night in January 2004, Shockey came back into town after the Giants' season was over. I told him that Jason and I were going to meet with Kellen and he came along. I thought Jeremy was going to have a serious, professional conversation with Kellen, going over in detail how hard Jason and I worked for him and how happy he was with his contract. Instead, Jason and I had to jump in between those two.

Kellen and Jeremy are as macho as two dudes can get. They are two extremely energetic guys and are always up for action. Well, get them in the room together after they haven't seen each other for a year and something interesting is going to happen. They are going to wrestle. It's a friendly thing, but a manhood thing as well. Those two are very competitive, and as much as they respect each other, they each want to challenge the other guy in something. Don't get me wrong; they are true friends and neither would want to be in a foxhole with anyone else, but they like to test each other.

During the 2007 off-season, when Kellen was rehabbing his knee after a serious motorcycle accident, Jeremy helped push him to the limit and Kellen pushed Jeremy in turn. They are two of the most fun-loving guys you'll ever meet and it is awesome to hang with the two of them—except for that night in early 2004. I don't know about you, but seeing two monsters wrestle right in front of you and getting caught in the middle of it when you try to break it up is not my idea of fun. If one of those elbows goes flying my way, I would be in big trouble. Fortunately, Jason and I survived the clash of the titans that night.

Unfortunately, Kellen didn't sign with us out of college in 2004. He signed with the same agent Willis had initially chosen. And like Willis, he later made the move to hire us.

When word broke that he hired us, it made news. Kellen told the *Plain Dealer Reporter,* on July 29, 2007, "When I went down to Miami in the off-season, I wanted a guy working hard for his client, and I think [Drew]'s the best out there. Being that he's based in Miami, he has connections down there and he's a good friend as well. I just felt it was the right thing to do."

Well, it took three years, but we love representing Kellen now. We didn't have to wait as long for linebacker Jon Beason. Jon was a first-round-pick linebacker in the 2007 draft with the Carolina Panthers. We represented another first-round-pick Carolina Panther linebacker and that player was Dan Morgan. Dan came out of UM in 2001 and was the eleventh pick in the first round by the Panthers. That same year, we represented the twelfth pick, defensive tackle Damione Lewis from UM, and receiver Santana Moss, who was the sixteenth pick by the Jets.

We knew Dan and his dad pretty well when they were going through the agent selection process. We had the ultimate respect for Dan and his dad as true tough guys. We'd known Dan Sr. for several years because he was Dan Marino's bodyguard. Although he worked for Marino, they were close friends. Dan Sr. is a big guy but not a giant. He wasn't as tall as Marino and probably weighed less, but nobody, and I mean nobody, messed with Dan Morgan Sr. Dan had been a real badass soldier in the Special Forces who'd been trained in hand-to-hand combat. He was the real deal. Dan Jr. was, too.

Dan won just about every award a college linebacker could win and deserved it. As an All-American, he was the first NCAA player in history to win the Bronko Nagurski Trophy, the Dick Butkus Award, and the Chuck Bednarik Award. He was absolutely fearless and would run through a brick wall with or without a helmet. I had a lot of respect for both father and son, and since I represented Dolphin linebacker Zach Thomas, I thought I made a lot of sense for Dan. To my disappointment, Dan went with another agent in 2001. However, when I negotiated a contract for Damione Lewis, who was the player taken immediately after Dan, that rivaled Dan's in value, his dad called me to say they were interested in hiring us down the road for his next contract.

Down the road came on April 28, 2005, when Dan hired me to be his agent. Dan had played four seasons when I came on board. The 2005 season was the last year of his contract. He did not want to play out the last year of his contract. He wanted a new deal before the season started. He had a sense of urgency and wanted an agent with that same urgency to get him a new deal.

As the start of the 2005 season approached and we were looking for the new deal, Dan had this to say about me to the *Charlotte Observer:*

> I've known Drew forever...My dad worked for Dan Marino and we always used to go to Dolphins games and I'd see him then. I always had a good relationship with Drew, but for one reason or another, I didn't sign with him coming out of college. I always had it in the back of my head that I wished I would have signed with him because we're actually friends. It's not just a business thing. I'd see him around and I finally just pulled the trigger. I was coming up on a contract year and I felt like he'd do a good job...That's what Drew does best and I've got a lot of confidence he'll get something done."

We had to get something done because Dan had missed nine games in 2003 and 2004. Despite this, he was coming off two great seasons overall and didn't want to play the fifth year out and risk injury. I told him that in this business, you can get hurt at any time, and if you get hurt that fifth year, you could lose millions. He agreed, and we got a new deal shortly thereafter for $28 million over six years. The key to the deal was the $11.5 million Dan would earn in 2005 and 2006. That turned out to be the key because Dan got injured in 2005 and 2006. He suffered severe injuries that would have killed his leverage had we not gotten the deal when we did. Timing is everything. You gotta know when to pull the trigger and get the deal. If Dan had played out that fifth year of his original contract, he would have lost millions.

After Dan missed part of 2006 after suffering a concussion, and 2007 with a torn Achilles tendon, he and the Panthers agreed to part ways. Dan is all heart and is as tough as they come. Sometimes a change of scenery is a good thing. But before Dan left, he had some advice for one of his teammates—sign with Drew.

In 2007, Dan's last year with the Panthers, the team drafted his replacement—ironically, it was UM linebacker Jon Beason. I'd recruited Jon coming out of college and it didn't work out because I signed FSU linebacker Lawrence Timmons. I viewed them as playing two different positions, with Jon being inside and Lawrence being outside, but Jon felt there was a conflict of interest. Interestingly enough, the agent he ended up hiring turned out to have an even bigger conflict of interest.

A few months after negotiating Jon's deal, the agent left the business to become the commissioner of a new football league. Once that happened, Jon did not have an agent. He talked with Dan Morgan and Dan told him that I would get the job done for him. When the season was over, I met with Jon, and based partly upon Dan's recommendation, Jon hired me.

The other part of the equation involved another Dan. Instead of Dan Morgan, it was Dan Martoe. Who is Dan Martoe? He is the one guy out of the thousands of people who came up to me, called me, wrote me, and e-mailed me about coming to work for me who impressed me enough to hire him.

Danny went to West Virginia, not Harvard. While in high school and college, he worked at a Taco Bell, rode a jackhammer, was a bouncer and a garbage man. After college, he worked in a boiler room in New York and made countless cold calls every day. He went to work for UBS Financial and displayed a talent for increasing assets.

He then went into business for himself and managed the financial affairs of a few NFL players.

I crossed paths with Danny time and again while we were recruiting. Danny would be recruiting a player to be his financial manager and I was recruiting the player to be his agent. He was very respectful, likable, and hungry. Most of all, like me, he was first and foremost a hard worker. I liked his hustle.

Instead of being arrogant, he was humble. Instead of being intimidating, he was intense. Instead of being nervous, he was focused. Instead of being an outsider, he made you believe he was "one of us." He reminded me a lot of my dad because he was emotional, aggressive, and a good person. Being a self-made professional, having worked from the bottom up, Danny earned my respect.

I had been looking for a guy I could trust to help me, Jason, and Robert grow our company. The time had come to recruit beyond the University of Miami. The time had come for Robert to have a partner with the marketing and endorsements. Danny could spearhead both.

When I told him that I wanted him to come work for me, he flew down from New York the next day and showed up at my doorstep with his suitcase. He didn't have much, but he had everything I was looking for—determination. He didn't ask what the pay would be (that came later); he just said okay, I'll be there.

He started working for me in November 2005, just after Terrell got suspended. At that time, I was a tough sell to rookies because my competition told them that I had ruined Terrell's career and he was finished. And I didn't help the cause with the "Next Question" press conference. That hurt me with recruiting. Dan began to work for me too late in the game to be much of a factor in recruiting that year. Nevertheless, we still had a good year, signing Sinorice Moss, the receiver from UM who went in the second round to the Giants; Eric Winston, the offensive tackle from UM who went in the third round to the Texans; and Gabe Watson, the defensive tackle who went in the fourth round to the Arizona Cardinals. Out of that rookie class, Sinorice signed with us because his brother Santana had recommended us, Jason delivered with Eric, and Danny was helpful with Gabe.

Recruiting Eric was great. Since the Hurricane season ended before New Year's, Eric flew out with his financial planner, Matt Cassano, to Vegas. There was a big New Year's party at the Ghost Bar in the Palms Hotel. It was a wild scene. I flew in to visit with Eric and also got to hang with Terrell Owens. Jason stayed a bit longer with Casie. That was some New Year's party. A smart guy, Eric was a lot of fun. He's as down-to-earth as a Hurricane football player can be; I guess that's the blue-collar Texas in him.

The next year Danny said we would get back in the first round and he was right. We signed linebacker Lawrence Timmons from FSU, who went in the first round with the fifteenth pick to the Steelers, tight end Greg Olsen, who went in the first round to the Bears, and quarterback Drew Stanton, who went in the second round to the Lions. Drew was our first rookie-quarterback draft pick and Danny played a huge part in his signing.

Danny did good, and not just with the rookies. He became very close with a lot of our veteran clients as well. I wasn't looking for an Ivy Leaguer. I was looking for a guy with guts, street smarts, and mental toughness. Most of all I wanted a fixer, a guy who got the job done, and that was Danny.

I now had a good crew in place and was ready to grow. How I made that happen is what comes next.

CHAPTER 13

PUT YOURSELF IN POSITION FOR OPPORTUNITY AND SEIZE IT!

I'VE KNOWN A LOT OF EXTREMELY INTELLIGENT PEOPLE who never became successful. And I've known a lot of very talented people who also never became successful. But I've never known any hard workers who didn't eventually make it. What too many Harvard graduates never get is that it's not enough to be smarter or more talented than the next guy; you have to be a worker to succeed in the real world.

That's why the most important advice I can give is to work hard. What does it mean to work hard? It means constantly putting yourself in a position for opportunity to come your way, always hustling and giving your best effort. It means always finishing your kicks, as Grand Master Young Soo Do taught me to do.

I worked hard to bring in new clients, using three techniques. The first approach was to target rookies and directly recruit them. The second approach was to recruit veteran players who approached my clients and contacted me. The third approach, which has been just as successful as the first two, was to simply do everything I could to be "Johnny-on-the-spot"—putting myself in the right place at the right time for opportunity to present itself. It's all about putting yourself in position for business to come your way.

Perhaps you've heard of a wide receiver named Chad Johnson— aka Ocho Cinco. I first met Chad in May 2003 when I was at a Miami Dolphin off-season minicamp. At the time, he was entering his third season with the Cincinnati Bengals, an up-and-coming player but not yet a superstar.

He and I were sitting in the stands not far from each other. I was in my usual spot, planting my flag and being highly visible. I didn't know much about Chad and was caught off guard when he came up to introduce himself. He was from South Florida, knew a lot of my clients, and was familiar with me. We made small talk and nothing happened, but I would later bump into him from time to time and he was always friendly.

Nothing came of it until I saw Chad in January 2005 at a client's charitable event. He had become a superstar All-Pro receiver for the Bengals but had a terrible contract. Signed in 2003, it locked him up for seven seasons. Although he was considered by many to be the best, he wasn't among the top twenty-five highest-paid receivers in the league and still had five seasons to go. He was, to say the least, unhappy with this contract and looking to make a change.

It just so happened that as he was asking himself which agent out there would be the best fit for him, there I was, right in front of him. While I was hanging out with my clients at the event, Chad initiated a conversation with me about his contract. He confided in me that he thought it was time to make a change. I didn't disagree.

By me hustling and being everywhere, by being visible and accessible, and because Chad was aware of the success I had the year before with McGahee, Ogunleye, Kearse, and Portis, I was in the right place at the right time.

Chad and I bonded right away. He is one of those rare personalities who is charismatic, entertaining, dynamic, and most of all likable. In 2006, a year later, Jason and I were able to get him a new contract and place him near the top of the receiver market—a tough feat to accomplish considering he still had four years remaining on his contract.

All that happened because instead of being out to lunch or sitting on the couch or playing golf, I was working, hustling, and making the effort. It also happened because once I was in a position for opportunity, I had the guts, talent, and ability to sell myself.

I respect nothing more than someone who works hard on weekends or late into the night. As Don Corleone said in *The Godfather,* "It makes no difference to me how a man earns a living." Few things are more noble than working hard to make a better life for your family. In all aspects of life, when adversity comes, I respond by working hard.

The situation with Pro Bowl Chicago Bears linebacker Lance Briggs is a perfect example. Lance signed a four-year deal as a third-round draft-pick rookie in 2003 out of Arizona. In his second year, he emerged as a starter. That was Wale Oguneleye's first year with the Bears. While watching Wale, I couldn't help but notice that Lance was making plays all over the field, from sideline to sideline. I was very impressed with him. So when Wale told me that Lance had asked about me and said he was going to call me, I was staring at my phone, waiting for it to ring.

When Lance called, I instantly clicked with him. Jason and I got on the first available plane to meet with him and signed him as soon as it was permissible. Jason saw Pro Bowl potential in him and he was right. Following the 2005 season, his third year in the league, Lance made the Pro Bowl. That off-season, with one year remaining in his contract at the minimum salary, we approached the Bears about doing an extension.

Because I was something of a high-profile personality during the Terrell Owens drama, Lance's negotiations were of significant interest to the Chicago media and fans. When asked about hiring me, Lance said to the *Chicago Sun-Times* on July 27, 2005: "He's a guy that gets it done... Guys go to him because he's a shark. He's going to go in there and take care of business. He's not going to leave anything on the table. He allows a player to see his value more so than most."

Lance hired me to negotiate a long-term contract with the Bears. He knew how aggressive I'd been in making it happen for Wale, and wanted me to do the same for him. When the Bears made us a long-term offer, though, he was very disappointed. The offer was too low and they would not budge. While on the one hand, Lance did not want to play out his final year at the minimum salary and risk injury, on the other hand, he did not want to do a below-market deal. As a young Pro Bowl player, he felt he deserved to be among the top players at his position in salary, and he was right. The Bears, however, had a different value in mind and we could not reach an agreement. Therefore, Lance decided to play the season out for the minimum and then get the big deal as a free agent.

This was during the same season—2005—when T.O. was suspended by the Eagles. Needless to say, I was catching a lot of heat. The fans did not want Lance to be a holdout. I took a lot of criticism from the Chicago media. They put me in their crosshairs and took aim at me. Note the following:

Linebacker Lance Briggs is signed through 2006 and has said he won't hold out for a contract extension next training camp. But his agent, Drew Rosenhaus, is known to use such tactics.

[Bears general manager Jerry] Angelo downplayed any concern, pointing out an extension isn't a necessity. But it would preclude Briggs becoming a free agent.

"Drew's a good agent," Angelo said. "We have no problems with him at all. That gives us hope.

"Every player has his own set of circumstances. We have to address each one individually. We certainly want Lance here." (ChicagoSports.com, January 2006)

"When I was in Tampa, we had many of Drew Rosenhaus' players, so I'm not treating that as an obstacle," Angelo said. "He's done a lot of good deals over the years and hopefully this will get done as well." (ChicagoBears.com, March 2006)

As I said before, we did not reach a long-term agreement and Lance reported for training camp at the start of the 2006 season. Although he did not hold out, he wasn't happy about playing out the final year of his contract at the minimum salary.

Nevertheless, he came in and had an outstanding year for the Bears. He was again voted to the Pro Bowl. At the Pro Bowl in Hawaii, Jason hung out with him a little bit. Believe it or not, what Lance wanted to do most of all was to go to the Marine base out there and train as a marksman. He and Jason jumped into a military jeep and received U.S. Marine instruction in firing an M-16 assault rifle. Lance was an outstanding shot, slightly better than Jason—Lance would say a lot better—and was a natural. The guy had the time of his life there.

Lance came back to the mainland expecting to be a free agent and shop his services to the highest bidder. He hoped the Bears would be in the mix because he loved his teammates and the fans. But instead of allowing him to hit the market and let it dictate his value, the Bears franchised him, making him a one-year offer at $7.2 million. They did not offer him a long-term deal.

While $7.2 million is a great deal of money, Lance was extremely upset and disappointed with the offer for two reasons. First and foremost, he wanted to play for the Bears for the long haul. He was a three-year starter and had helped that team reach the Super Bowl. He was a core player and believed in and bled for his teammates. He was a true team player and had the support of every single one of his teammates. No one is more respected, loved, and admired by his peers than Lance. So when the team did not offer him a long-term deal and prevented him from getting one from another team, he felt that the team had betrayed him.

The $7.2 million deal also upset Lance because we felt he could get a deal similar to what two other free agent linebackers, Adalius Thomas and Joey Porter, had gotten. They signed multiyear deals that they are only likely to see the first three or four years of—Porter will be lucky to get through year three. After three years, by 2009, Thomas and Porter will be at the $23 million to $24 million range, and over four years, at the $28 million to $29 million range. They were guaranteed approximately $20 million. Lance was guaranteed $7.2 million. Should Lance play out the 2007 season and get hurt, he was risking getting nothing and losing out on the $13 million he could have been guaranteed had he been a free agent.

The fact that the Bears did not make him a long-term offer and wanted him to be a one-year mercenary infuriated him, and he let his anger with management be known. He said he loved his teammates and the fans, but did not want to play for the organization anymore. He threatened not to play for the Bears.

Despite being upset, Lance did not blame me and try to throw me under the bus, and stayed loyal. One thing about Lance, his character is impeccable. He is a loyal guy and is like family to me. Not once did he turn on me when things looked bleak. He's a good guy on a team full of good guys, which is why the Bears went to the Super Bowl that year.

After we were franchised and prevented from hitting the market, I could have told Lance that the fight was over and to surrender. I could have sat around and called it quits. I could have hit the couch and watched TV or played golf. I could have done a lot of things—but instead, I did what I always do, which is work hard to put myself in a position to make something happen.

So after we missed the frenzy of free agency and things were looking hopeless, I decided to try to do something creative. The annual NFL owners' meetings were taking place at the end of the month at the Biltmore Hotel in Phoenix, Arizona, near Lance's neck of the woods. I told Lance to meet me out there and see what we could drum up. As ridiculous as it sounds, I told him to walk around with me, let me introduce him to the owners and GMs, and see if we could stir up some interest in him. With nothing to lose, Lance met me out there and we hustled. What I hoped for was that a team would try to trade for him and give us the contract we were looking for.

After we'd met and greeted a dozen GMs and owners, all of whom behaved like gentlemen to Lance, it seemed like no one was interested in trading for him. And then around 5 p.m., I came across Washington Redskin owner Dan Snyder and Vinny Cerrato, his astute executive vice president of football operations. They were sitting outside in the patio area having a drink.

I walked up to them and introduced Lance. I told Dan to picture the two-time Pro Bowl linebacker at six-one and 240 pounds in a Redskin uniform. Extremely articulate, intelligent, and charismatic, Lance was an easy sell. One thing about Snyder, he wants to win as much as, if not more than, any other owner. While cash is king to most NFL owners, Dan is all about winning. Football is his passion and he loves nothing more than making the big move to improve his team.

After five minutes of talking to us, Dan turned to me and said, "Call [Bears general manager] Jerry Angelo and tell him I want Lance. Offer to swap my sixth pick for Lance and his thirty-first pick in the first round."

He told me that if the Bears would do the deal, he would offer Lance a similar contract to those of Thomas and Porter. I called Jerry and proposed the deal. He told me he would need some time to evaluate the offer. Fox NFL insider Jay Glazer was right there and found out the scoop. The media was all over it.

Shortly thereafter, the *Chicago Sun-Times* reported:

"As I've come to find out," Jerry Angelo said, "really we have two commissioners: the one that runs the NFL and the one that runs the things that happen to the NFL."

That obviously was a reference to Rosenhaus, whom Angelo visited last week at the owners meetings in Phoenix.

I tried and tried, but the Redskins and Bears could not agree on the terms of the trade. A deal did not get done. At the start of training camp, Lance signed a one-year deal and played out the 2007 season. During the season, the San Francisco 49ers were close to trading for him, and in my opinion, we had an excellent chance of landing the kind of contract we were looking for, but the trade never materialized. It was not for a lack of effort on our part.

Once again Lance had a Pro Bowl season, his third in a row. This time, because we added a clause to the 2007 contract that said if Lance played 75 percent of the downs the Bears could not franchise him, he was a free agent in March 2008.

In the end, after hitting the market and evaluating all Lance's options, we did what Lance wanted most to do—stay with the Bears on a long-term contract. The deal was for six years, for $36 million, but he would earn $14.905 million over two years (by 2009) and $21.6 million over three years (by 2010).

At first, it looks like Lance lost money and didn't get Thomas and Porter dollars (recall that they were at $23 million to $24 million over three years and $28 million to $29 million over four years), but that would be an inaccurate conclusion.

Remember that Porter and Thomas signed in 2007, when we were looking for a contract similar to theirs. That year, we took the franchise contract at $7.2 million. Factor in Lance's 2007 earnings, and by 2010, after the first four years of Thomas's and Porter's deals, their earnings would be at $27.8 million to $29 million to Lance's $28.8 million. In the end, Lance got what he wanted—the big money and to stay with the Bears. We were able in the negotiations to make that happen, largely because of our efforts with the Redskins at the owners' meetings. That is what happens when you work hard to put yourself in position for something to happen and then work to make it happen. In Lance's case, it couldn't have happened to a nicer guy.

During the week of the 2008 Super Bowl festivities, I found myself back in Arizona. I was in a tough spot. I was battling the flu, a kidney infection, and had an angular tear in the disks of my L4 and L5 vertebrae that hit a nerve, sending shooting pains down my legs. Rather than be in the hospital or in bed like everyone urged me to be, I went to Arizona. I went there because my clients were there, free agency was on the horizon, and other agents were whispering in my clients' ears that we had too many clients and weren't paying attention to them, etc.

I was hurting. The burning-hot pains shooting down my legs were the worst at night and prevented me from getting any sleep. The lack of sleep was not allowing me to get better and beat the flu. The stress caused a kidney infection that had me urinating blood. Other than that, I was fine.

I was fine until Jason called me and said that Chicago Bears wide receiver Bernard Berrian was in the process of letting us go. Losing a client is my worst nightmare. It hurts in many different ways. First, getting fired causes ripples and you have to do immediate damage control with your other clients. Second, it is embarrassing, aggravating, and painful for a long time. Third, the money you would earn goes into your rival's pocket.

To me, losing a great player with whom I have a great relationship is the worst. I'd rather have lost my kidney than Bernard. He was a superhot upcoming free agent and I knew I was going to get him a blockbuster deal. I hadn't lost an active NFL client for two years, and desperately wanted to keep my friend on board. We were good friends and I was caught off guard. Normally my instincts let me know when a guy was on the brink and I am able to talk to him and nip things in the bud. With Bernard, because he was such a strong-character guy, I didn't see it coming. I found myself entrapped in the perfect storm.

I called him and couldn't get through. The word was that his previous agent and a rival agent had told him that he wasn't a priority to me. Unable to get him on the phone, and barely able to walk, what could I do?

I did what I had to do. I did all that I could do, which was to suck it up, get on a plane to Fresno, and hope that Bernard would be impressed with the heart I showed. Although it was a long shot, I decided to put myself in position to have a chance. I arrived in Fresno in agony, but as soon as I landed and text-messaged him that I was there, Bernard called me. He couldn't believe I'd gone out there. Impressed to learn that with everything going on I still flew out to see him, Bernard knew I was his guy. He told me he was staying with me and he kept his word. Suddenly I felt a lot better.

Within weeks, I negotiated a monster $36 million contract for him with the Minnesota Vikings. He would earn $19.2 million in the first two years. Now he and I are both very happy that we stayed the course and got it done.

The principle of working hard to put yourself in position to get lucky has served me my entire career. That was how I started out. I used to be at Dolphin camp all the time. In August 2002, even though he was not a client of mine, Tim Ruddy, an outstanding veteran center for the Miami Dolphins, had this to say about me to the *Miami Herald:* "You really don't even talk to your agent. I mean he's not here. Unless it's Drew Rosenhaus—then he's here every day."

Tim knew what everyone knew about me: I was always working. That's why Pro Bowl cornerback Sam Madison called me in October

2005 and told me he wanted to meet with me. When I showed up at his house, he didn't want me to make him a presentation or say much of anything at all. He told me that he had seen me around training camp almost every day since he was drafted by the Dolphins in 1997. He knew his contract was coming up and there was a lot of uncertainty ahead. And he was right. When his contract expired, I negotiated a deal for him with the Giants and now he has a Super Bowl championship ring.

Two years later, I got a similar phone call. This time it was from NFLPA president Troy Vincent. If you remember, in 1991, the Dolphins traded away my client Randal Hill to Arizona for their first-round pick in the 1992 draft. With that pick, that Dolphins took Troy. Fifteen years later, Troy hired me to represent him.

That news sent shock waves around the NFL. In March 2007, the *Philadelphia Inquirer* wrote:

A few weeks ago, the Washington Redskins released Vincent the cornerback. He subsequently hired Drew Rosenhaus as his agent in a move that stunned—and scared—many in the league who expect Vincent to follow Upshaw as head of the union. If that happens, Rosenhaus will have an influential ally who only will bolster his standing as the most powerful agent in the NFL.

"People shouldn't be surprised, because Drew negotiates good contracts, if not the best contracts," said Vincent, who acknowledged that Rosenhaus had been pursuing him for 13 years. "I have a lot of opportunities on and off the field, and I don't like negotiating for myself. I just felt like now and in the future, he needs to be someone that is part of my team."

While he was president of the NFLPA, Troy could have hired any agent. Being the president of the NFLPA at that time, he was privy to all the contracts and had the inside track on what was really going on in the business. His vote of confidence was the ultimate compliment.

That's what happens when you work hard. But sometimes hard work isn't enough. Sometimes it's the smart work that makes the difference. In negotiations, this makes all the difference. In the next chapter, I am going to take you into the negotiating room with me. I am going to sit you right next to me along with Jason, across the table from the toughest negotiators in the business. Together, we are going to take them on and I'll show you how we win in this business.

CHAPTER 14

BE A LEADER

THIS CHAPTER IS ABOUT NFL NEGOTIATIONS. THEY CAN be complex—they should be a battle. When they are not, it is because the agent surrendered. What comes next is not a fast-paced, thrilling story—unless you like numbers and negotiations. If you are business-oriented and thrive on finding challenging solutions, then this chapter is for you.

One of our most challenging negotiations started on draft day April 28, 2007, with our client Greg Olsen. To help Greg and our two other rookie clients be as comfortable and relaxed as possible, we threw a private draft party at South Beach's exclusive Shore Club. We had three clients we expected to go in the first two rounds. Each player had a deluxe, two-story bungalow suite for him and his family.

Our first client to be drafted was Florida State University line-backer Lawrence "LT" Timmons. LT was picked by the Pittsburgh Steelers with the fifteenth pick in the first round. Next up was Miami Hurricane tight end Greg Olsen. I knew he would either be a late first-

or early second-round pick. The pressure was on for him to get into that first round. From my discussions with Chicago Bears general manager Jerry Angelo leading up to the draft, I knew the Bears liked Greg. With the Bears having the thirty-first pick (there are thirty-two overall in the first round) and with the thirty-second pick belonging to the Colts, who did not need a tight end, the Bears were our last chance to make it.

Since each team had fifteen minutes to make their pick, we were counting the seconds, waiting for the phone to ring, when it was the Bears' turn. And when it did ring, and Cliff Stein, the negotiator for the Bears, was on the line, I knew Greg was going to the Bears...but there was a catch. Cliff told me he wanted my word that we would get the deal done by the Fourth of July. I told him he could count on me and Jason to give it our best shot and act in good faith. He said okay and the whole room went wild.

Shortly thereafter, we were celebrating again as our third player at the Shore Club, Michigan State University quarterback Drew Stanton, was drafted early in the second round by the Detroit Lions. With Drew being from Michigan and having played at Michigan State, the Lions were a great fit for Drew. We were thrilled for Drew and his father Gaylord, who'd been instrumental in the decision to hire us. Drew was our first rookie quarterback, and is not only an outstanding quarterback, but an even better person. It's something special to celebrate the drafting of our clients with their families at their sides. To see these kids from wonderful families get rewarded for their hard work is a great feeling. The stakes are so high and the pressure is incredibly intense, so when you win on draft day, the elation is tremendous.

Once the player gets drafted, Jason comes into play. Rookie contracts are the most complex and quantitative negotiations in the business. Jason's background as a certified public accountant and attorney gives us a big edge because it is largely a numbers game with rookie contracts.

There are numerous mathematical rules, values, and computations that I do not want to bore you with that pertain to rookie contracts. That's Jason's department. Suffice to say, he and I had our work cut out for us because the Bears asked us to strike a deal by the Fourth of July. Training camp started for Chicago on July 26. So why ask us to agree before then?

The reason is that in the past, Bears first-round picks did not sign until well after the start of training camp. The negotiations often stalled. This led to the players holding out, missing extremely valuable practices, and falling behind. It is terribly counterproductive for a player to miss the first few days of training camp, let alone the first few weeks. The Bears' previous first-round pick, running back Cedric Benson, held out for thirty days because he wanted a better offer. It didn't work. Chicago did not budge one penny and the holdout gave everyone a black eye. As a result, the Bears decided to take a proactive position to prevent any further holdouts and instituted the new policy to make every effort to sign rookies by July 4. Greg was the Bears' first-round pick the first year of that new policy. He was, you could say, the guinea pig. Why was that a problem? It was a problem because no first-round pick had signed by or before the Fourth of July in several years.

Pardon me, I stand corrected. In years past, only the *very first* overall pick had signed prior to July 4. Typically, the team with the first overall pick strikes a deal with the player by draft day in April to make sure there will not be a holdout. That's what happened the year before—2006—when the Houston Texans surprised everyone by taking defensive end Mario Williams instead of running back Reggie Bush. What teams typically do is leverage the top two or three players against one another by stating that they will select the player who agrees to the team's offer. Every player wants to be the first overall pick, so they are tempted to accept the team's deal.

Year in and year out, the team with the first pick in the draft signs its player by April's draft day. In 2007, it was different. The Raiders selected Louisiana State University quarterback JaMarcus Russell, but did not agree on a contract. Why couldn't the Raiders and Russell strike a deal on draft day?

There was a new NFL ruling that changed rookie contract negotiations. The new decision ruled that if a player was given an option bonus and later got into trouble or held out, he did not have to repay the option bonus. The teams did not like this rule at first.

What is an option bonus? Before answering this question it is necessary to discuss the structure of bonuses for rookies. First, there is the signing bonus. The signing bonus is a guaranteed bonus that a player gets upon signing the contract. If a player retires after signing the contract or forfeits the contract down the road, he has to pay back a portion of the signing bonus. Second, there is the roster bonus, which is a bonus a player gets for being on the team (the active roster) the day he signs the contract. Signing bonuses and roster bonuses are very similar in substance—both are given when he signs the contract. The primary difference is that the roster bonus counts in full against the salary cap that year and the signing bonus is allocated over the term of the contract. The roster bonus is treated the same as salary in that it counts in full that year against the salary cap.

For instance, if a player signs a five-year contract with a $5 million signing bonus, a $500,000 roster bonus, and a $1 million salary, the player's compensation will count $2.5 million against the salary cap that first year. This is because only $1 million of the $5 million signing bonus counts against the salary cap each year, the total amount of the bonus being allocated evenly over the five-year period of the contract. The $500,000 roster bonus and the $1 million salary count in full that year, so the total charge against the cap is $2.5 million.

The option bonus comes into play in March of the second year of the contract. It is like a signing bonus, but instead of getting it the first year in July, the player gets it in March of the next year. It is also allocated over the remaining term of the contract. Say for instance a player receives a $4 million option bonus in year two of the five-year deal. Since the option bonus is in year two of the five-year deal, there are four years remaining on the contract, so the $4 million option bonus is allocated over the four years to count $1 million each of the remaining four years.

The new legal ruling stated that of the salary, signing bonus, option bonus, and roster bonus, only the signing bonus has to be paid back to the team if the player forfeits the contract after the initial year the bonuses were earned. Prior to this ruling, the player had to pay back roster and option bonuses as well. Therefore, the ruling initially upset the teams because they paid players big option bonuses, and if a player got into trouble—as Michael Vick did—or held out for a new contract several years into the deal, the team could only get back the signing bonus. Teams want the leverage of being able to get back the bonus monies in order to force players to honor their contracts and at the same time provide incentive for the players to not get into trouble or hold out.

The teams reacted to this by declaring that they were no longer going to give big option bonuses, only big signing bonuses. That was a huge problem for the players because due to the intricate accounting rules of the salary cap, they could get better contracts under the same cap number by receiving big option bonuses instead of big signing bonuses.

The reason is the rookie pool restrictions. The NFL assigns each team a specific amount of money they can spend on rookies—the rookie pool. Out of that rookie pool, which could be $3 million, each draft pick on a given team has to carve out his piece of the pie. The more one player gets, the less money that remains for the others.

If the first-round pick does a deal worth $1.5 million against the salary cap, that leaves only $1.5 million for the other six rookies. Conversely, if the other rookies do their deals and eat up $2 million of the rookie pool, that leaves only $1 million for the first-round pick.

Therefore, the bigger the salary-cap number you can get for your client, the bigger his contract will be. Additionally, by using option bonuses instead of signing bonuses, you can squeeze out a million dollars more while still keeping the cap number the same. So the key to negotiating a rookie deal is to get a big rookie number and then get the big option bonus instead of a big signing bonus.

Why is the option bonus better than the signing bonus? Consider the chart below, which provides two different approaches using the same cap number of $1.399 million.

In example #1, the signing bonus amount of $5.570 million is allocated over the five-year term of the contract, so it counts $1.114 million against the salary cap. When you add in the $285,000 salary, the total cap number is $1.399 million. The bonus in this example comes to $5.57 million. That is the maximum signing bonus permissible using this structure at a cap number of $1.399 million.

EXAMPLE #1	ALL SIGNING BONUS	
Cap Number $1,399,000	2007	2008
Signing Bonus	$5,570,000	
Option Bonus		$0
Roster Bonus	$0	
Salary	$285,000	$370,000
Total	$5,855,000	$6,225,000
Total Bonus	**$5,570,000**	

EXAMPLE #2	ALL OPTION BONUS	
Cap Number $1,399,000	2007	2008
Signing Bonus	$0	
Option Bonus		$5,515,000
Roster Bonus	$1,114,000	
Salary	$285,000	$370,000
Total	$1,399,000	$7,284,000
Total Bonus	**$6,629,000**	

Max Option Bonus Total	$6,629,000	Example #2
All Signing Bonus Total	$5,570,000	Example #1
Difference	$1,059,000	
Total—All Option Bonus	$7,284,000	Example #2
Total—All Signing Bonus	$6,225,000	Example #1
Difference	$1,059,000	

Example #2 uses the option bonus instead of a signing bonus. In this structure, there is a roster bonus of $1.114 million and a salary of $285,000 in year one. Both count in full against the salary cap, so the cap number is the same total as in example #1—$1.399 million. However, the rules allow for an option bonus that maxes out at $5.515 million in the second year. The rule in particular is the 25 percent rule, which states that each year of the contract cannot increase the cap number by more than 25 percent of the first year's cap number. This rule precludes the second-year bonus that is permissible in example #1 because there is no room left in the 2nd year cap number. You derive the $5.515 million bonus amount by taking the cap number in year one at $1,399,999 and increasing it by 25 percent to get to $1,748,750. You then subtract the second-year minimum salary of $370,000 to get to $1,378,750. This is the maximum amount of bonus allocation permissible in year two, so to derive the maximum bonus you multiply the $1,378,750 times four (years remaining on the deal from year two) to get a maximum option bonus in year two of $5.515 million. Add that to the first-year roster bonus of $1.114 million and the total bonus in example #2 amounts to $6.629 million.

The structure in example #2, which utilizes the option bonus instead of the signing bonus, yields $1.059 million more in bonus monies than in example #1. When you factor in that the signing bonus is partially deferred a year, there is no advantage to using the signing-bonus approach in example #1.

I've put you through all of the above boring calculations to demonstrate that utilizing the option bonus instead of the signing bonus can add big money to the deal. Maybe I should have asked you to just take Jason's word for it . . . The funny thing about Jason is that because he has a beautiful wife (Cassandra) and adorable baby girl (Aubrey), he is proud to characterize himself as a numbers geek.

The point is that the option bonus allows you to have a bigger total bonus than the signing bonus. Rookies can get millions more using the option bonus. Given the increase in rookie-contract values over the years, teams have been looking for ways to lower them. The new ruling was exactly what they wanted because it gave the teams the excuse to say no more option bonuses, which meant the players were going to have to take smaller bonuses. The teams had the leverage to force players to use the structure in example #1 instead of example #2.

That's the position the Raiders took with the first pick of the 2007 draft and that's why he wasn't signed on draft day. Russell refused to take a smaller bonus than the previous year's first overall pick. In fact, Russell would be the last rookie to sign, as he did not sign his contract until September 12 after missing training camp since July 26. So if the first overall pick didn't get done early, how were we supposed to get it done early for Greg with the Bears?

To complicate matters, during the 2007 off-season, Lance Briggs was franchised, as you may recall, and said since the Bears did not want to give him a long-term deal, he did not want to play for them anymore. The fans, of course, hated on me for this action and that's what I preferred. It's my job to take the heat for my client. Thus the media went around saying that the Bears, in drafting Greg, had picked the right player but the wrong agent. The media predicted that Greg would be a holdout primarily because I was his agent.

Never mind that not one of my players had held out in years. Because of the whole "Next Question" press conference and what was going on with Lance, the media took their shots at me. Showing a lot of character, Greg wasn't fazed by the media's criticism and had total confidence in Jason and me.

Looking for the latest information I could get my hands on, I called Mark Levin, the contract guru for the NFLPA. Mark is there to counsel and assist agents about negotiations. When I asked him if there were any new developments, he told me he was hearing there were going to be thirty-two holdouts (the number of first-round picks) because of the option-bonus problem.

As if the assignment of getting Greg done early wasn't tough enough, it was just our luck that we had to deal with the Bears. There are teams that are more than reasonable and happy to overpay to get the deal done. And then there are teams like the Bears who never overpay and almost always underpay.

The Bears' negotiator, Cliff Stein, is respected by agents as one of the toughest, most knowledgeable, and well-prepared negotiators in the business. He doesn't do deals that reflect poorly on the organization. His job is to negotiate contracts on behalf of the club that allow him to show General Manager Jerry Angelo and President Ted Phillips how much money he saved them. And he is damned good at what he does. Jerry handpicked him because he wanted a savvy negotiator who could manage the salary cap in a profitable manner.

Year in and year out, Cliff crushed the agents for their first-round picks and forced brutal deals down their throats. This led to holdouts and players missing valuable practices in training camp, but in the end, they took the Bears' deal.

The way Jason and I saw it, the holdouts were counterproductive. We wanted to get Greg signed on time, but we weren't going to take a bad deal. So when we got Cliff's first offer on June 1, we were not encouraged. The offer had a bonus that was $485,000 less than what the player in Greg's slot (number thirty-one) got the previous year. The total package was $835,000 less than what the thirty-first pick got in 2006.

Cliff's reasoning for offering less was that the first-round players in 2006 had taken smaller bonuses and overall totals than the players in 2005. He put together a chart showing what the twenty-fourth through thirty-second players got in 2006 versus 2005. Now, Jason is a statistical and chart fanatic. He didn't just take Cliff's word for this. He read every first-round draft pick's contract for the last three years, read the Bears' contracts for last five years, and put together an array of entirely different charts with different analyses.

For the most part, players did take smaller bonuses and totals in 2006 than in 2005, but some got increases. The bottom line is that some agents are more effective than others.

Why did numerous 2006 first-round picks take less than what the player in his slot received the year before? Because of another rule change, what else?! This one was easy—teams could only sign players in the top sixteen of the first round to six-year deals. The seventeenth through thirty-second picks could not sign beyond a five-year term. The NFLPA enacted this rule to help the players because teams were forcing mid to late first-round picks to swallow six-year deals. Unless you are a top five pick, it is much better to do a five-year deal than a six. This is because the player is a free agent after the first contract expires. Additionally, most teams won't do an extension unless only one year is left on the contract, so if you have a five-year deal, you have much more leverage to get a new deal after four years.

In the 2006 first round, players in the top sixteen wanted five-year deals, but teams forced six-year deals down their throats. Those who got five-year deals chose to take a bad five-year deal rather than an average six-year one. Neither of those options is acceptable to me. With Lawrence Timmons, the fifteenth pick in the 2007 first round, I was faced with those same options. I'll get to that shortly.

In the meantime, the biggest myth surrounding first-round-pick contracts is that they are slotted—meaning that fifteenth pick should get more than the sixteenth pick but less than the fourteenth pick. In theory, the fifteenth pick should be averaged right in between the fourteenth and sixteenth picks. While that is how it should work, that's not how we work. We don't slot or average our contracts. We try to excel and beat the average. Every year we are criticized by our competition with outright lies that you wouldn't believe. We combat those fabrications by showing how strong our contracts are. It is a key component to our success to be able to show that our contracts are superior. That is why we are more successful than any other agent in this business. It's not smoke and mirrors—it's hard work and smart work.

In 2006, there didn't seem to be much of either in the first round. We didn't negotiate a first-round-pick contract that year. As I said above, LT was the fifteenth pick. The 2006 fifteenth pick took a bonus of $6.409 million, whereas the 2005 fifteenth pick got $7.050 million. It wasn't just the fifteenth pick in 2006 who took less; the majority of first-round picks that year did as well. To make up for the smaller bonus, the teams persuaded agents to take an incentive bonus. This bonus was called the "One Time Not Likely To Be Earned Incentive Bonus" (1*NLTBE). The teams used it because it did not count against the salary cap the first year or in any year until the year after it was earned, if ever.

The 1*NLTBE bonus said that if the player played 35 percent of the downs the first year or 45 percent in any year thereafter, and if the player performed at a certain level or if the club statistically improved in one of three areas, the player would get a bonus. As far as incentives go, it is a relatively easy one to earn. To make it tempting to the agent, the team guaranteed the amount of the 1*NTLBE bonus against the player's salary in the first few years. Thus, if the player got cut in the first three years of the deal, he would be guaranteed to get the bonus.

However, if the player got released in year four or five, the guarantee was worthless. Additionally, if the player didn't play 45 percent of the downs, he never got the bonus. Of if he played the 45 percent but didn't reach the level of performance—say forty-one catches—or if the club didn't improve that particular year in one of three selected categories, the player never got the bonus. I have first-round-pick clients, as does every other top agent, who would not meet the criteria to earn the 1*NLTBE bonus. It is an incentive and is no substitute for a bonus that the player gets for signing his name on the dotted line. It is a perfect example of how teams outsmart agents.

We weren't interested in the 1*NLTBE in lieu of the signing, option, or roster bonus. We weren't interested in a structure with a large signing bonus in lieu of the option or roster bonus. We were interested in a deal that was a good deal for everyone. Unfortunately, the 2006 market was terrible, we were dealing with one of the toughest teams in the business, the legal decision on option bonuses set the stage for leaguewide holdouts, and the Bears' first offer was dreadful. And somehow we were supposed to get Greg signed weeks earlier than any player had signed in the last five years (other than the first overall pick). Given our reputation as tough negotiators as well, every agent Cliff talked to told him there was no way we would get Greg signed by the Fourth of July, let alone the start of training camp. The word on the street was that we would definitely be a holdout and one of the last guys to sign. Clearly, we had our work cut out for us.

And so we went to work. Based on his huge stack of charts, Jason put together numerous statistical points in a voluminous letter to Cliff that quantitatively substantiated our offer. We didn't just say "I'm Drew Rosenhaus—the greatest agent on the planet and my client is the greatest player ever so give me a great contract."

Cliff appreciated the amount of research and work involved in our counteroffer and responded with his own chart, which allowed us to agree on many aspects of the market. Once we were on the same page, Cliff sent us another offer that we did not consider an improvement because he increased the 1*NLTBE bonus in lieu of the option bonus. Additionally, the bonus structure was a mixture of the signing and option bonuses rather than the structure that maximizes the option bonus as in example #2 above.

We responded by putting together another lengthy letter setting forth ten statistical reasons for our position. Greg and his father read and reviewed this letter just like they did the first one. They were ecstatic with both letters. And believe it or not, so was Cliff. Why would Cliff be happy about us making such a strong counteroffer? Because it was based on a tremendous amount of research and reason. Cliff respected and appreciated how hard we were working on this negotiation. Our putting together a letter that numerically justified our position made Cliff understand that we were serious about getting a deal done by the Fourth of July.

As soon as Cliff finished reading our letter, he called to ask us to come to town on July 2 for a face-to-face meeting. Most deals get closed in face-to-face negotiations. It looked like there was a real chance of this deal getting done. This was very hard to believe because of one other reason why no one signs early. I left this one until now.

The main reason the agent with the thirty-first pick will wait is that he wants to see what the thirty-second pick gets. It's a terrific boost if the player drafted after your client gets a great contract. Surely, with the thirty-first pick, you as an agent can't expect to take less than what the thirty-second pick was offered. By seeing what the player in front of you and behind you gets, you know the market. The agent can slot the contract for the thirty-first pick in between the thirtieth and thirty-second pick and eliminate all risk.

What's the risk? The risk is that if the thirty-first pick's agent signs early and the next day the thirty-second pick signs for a better deal, then the client got a below market deal, and that agent looks bad, risks getting fired, and will have a tough time recruiting the following year. So if you are an agent, why take the risk of doing a bad deal and getting put out of business?

Doesn't it seem prudent to wait until you're sure that your client will get a fair deal? Is that really selfish of the agent?

The answer is yes. An agent's responsibility to his client is to act in the best interest of the player. It would have been very easy and safe for us to protect our own ass by waiting for the thirtieth and thirty-second picks to sign regardless of the Bears' request that we sign by July 4. But it would not have been in Greg's best interest and here's why.

First, the teams don't all have the same starting date for training camp. Sometimes, the thirty-first pick starts camp before the thirtieth. If the thirty-first pick wants to sign by the start of training camp, which is extremely important for many reasons, he may not have the luxury of waiting for the thirtieth and thirty-second picks to sign. If the agent wants to get the player signed on time, he often has to agree to a contract before the player in front of his client and/or behind his client signs. It's not worth it for the thirty-first player to hold out and wait to see if the thirty-second player gets $100,000 more to sign than he does. But it is worth it to the agent who doesn't want to be undone by the competition. Thus, too often, agents do what's best for themselves and not the client.

Second, what if the thirtieth and thirty-second picks come in low? By waiting to slot the player and cover his own ass, the agent ends up lowering his client's market value and loses leverage. As long as the deal slots in between the thirtieth and thirty-second pick, the agent is protected; but in the meantime, if the agent had more confidence, courage, and foresight, he could have gotten a better deal for his client.

Third, there is a rookie pool. A team has a fixed amount of money in the rookie pool to sign its seven rookie picks. For example, if the rookie pool is $3 million and the first-round pick waits to sign while the other six picks sign and eat up a big chunk of this money, there is no room to negotiate the rookie-pool number for the first-round pick anymore. Teams can fix the cap number for the first-round pick by signing the other rookies first. If he waits, an agent can't protect his client's getting a maximum slice of the pie.

Fourth, as the player's representative, the agent has to be a leader and dictate to the market, not let the market dictate to him. The key to being a good negotiator is knowing when to pull the trigger. That means having the courage to act on your convictions rather than playing it safe. Jason and I knew that the time to pull the trigger was on the Fourth of July for three reasons. First, it would be very valuable to the Bears to set a precedent of signing a Rosenhaus first-round pick by the Fourth of July. If we, the agents with the reputation of being the toughest in the business signed that early, other agents will have no excuse not to do so as well. Second, if a strong-character kid like Greg, who comes from a great family and is extremely intelligent, agrees to a Fourth of July deal, no other player has an excuse not to do so as well. To set these two precedents, the Bears would pay an extra premium to close the deal. And third, Cliff would be a hero in the Bears front office and around the league for closing a deal three weeks early, with the toughest agents in the business, at a time when everyone else is bracing for lengthy holdouts. All three of those reasons expire on July 4 if we don't pull the trigger. Once that deadline passes, we knew the

Bears would no longer have that extra incentive to do the deal. Conversely, we knew, for those same three reasons, that the Bears would pay more on the Fourth of July than they would afterward.

Okay, so we knew we wanted to close the deal by the Fourth of July, which meant, technically, getting it done on the third, since no one except us works on the Fourth. And we also knew that Cliff wanted to close the deal on that day as well. The problem was that we were still very far apart. They wanted a big signing bonus, which has the effect of lowering the total bonus. We wanted a big option bonus and small signing bonus, which had the effect of increasing the total bonus. The key from there was coming up with the big idea—how to get the Bears to accept the big-option-bonus structure.

The way I saw it, this was Jason's problem. He's the numbers guy. We discussed the whole situation at length and I told him it was his job to come up with a bonus formula that would work for both sides. My job was to persuade the Bears to do whatever Jason would propose.

Thus far, we have talked about being creative in coming up with the big idea and knowing when to pull the trigger. That's not just talk. That's the creed by which we live. Jason had a puzzle to solve. It was as simple as this: The Bears did not want to give a big option bonus because if the player forfeited his contract in later years, the team would not be able to get back a portion of this bonus. The solution: even simpler. Jason came up with the idea of creating a special bonus in the third, fourth, and fifth years of the contract. This bonus would be paid to the player if he was a good boy and did not forfeit his contract. That was the solution. Seems elementary, my dear Watson, doesn't it? And yet no one had ever done it before. When Jason presented the idea to Mark Levin of the NFLPA, Mark thought it was excellent.

Why it was such a good solution is that the new bonus was, in fact, a bonus—not an incentive that requires playtime or performance at a high level. A player could be injured the entire year or never play a down and still receive the bonus. It was like a regular roster bonus or salary in the sense that if the player is on the team, he gets the bonus. Best of all, the bonus had no effect on the rookie cap, so the contract could be front-loaded. We could get the big option bonus and still provide the team owner with protection if the player forfeited his contract. It was a win/win idea.

Now that we had the winning idea, we had to get the Bears—one of the most conservative and traditional organizations in the NFL—to do something that was completely unique and unprecedented. What we had to do for the Bears was make a precedent. How? We had another first-round pick—Lawrence Timmons.

Lawrence was the fifteenth pick of the Pittsburgh Steelers. It just so happened that the Steelers were, for the first time in many years, in a state of change and uncertainty. Their longtime, iconic head coach Bill Cowher had just retired. The Steelers brought in a young, unproven head coach, Mike Tomlin. I knew it would be imperative to the organization to get things going on the right track and that meant they had to get their first round pick signed on time. Their negotiator, Omar Khan, is no pushover, but he was looking to get a fair deal done on time. So Jason and I proposed the new bonus concept to him. Seeing that it was a reasonable proposal, Omar agreed to move forward in the negotiations with our structure, a big option bonus up front and the new bonus in years three, four, and five.

So when we went to meet with Cliff face-to-face, we didn't just show up with empty pockets. When Cliff said he would be willing to give us a fair bonus but his owner needed protection in case of forfeiture, Jason proposed the new bonus structure and I emphasized that the Steelers had already agreed to do it.

After hours of going back and forth, discussing and examining in great detail every aspect of our proposed structure, we were able to agree to move forward. We gave Cliff numerous reasons why the new structure was a smart move for the team. Now, we aren't any smarter than Cliff, who sees all the angles, but we had had a week to put together our position as to why this structure was mutually beneficial. We didn't demand it or else. We pointed out numerous valid reasons. Once Cliff agreed, we decided to meet again first thing in the morning to work out the numbers.

Having passed the toughest hurdle, we were very hopeful that we could reach a deal on the dollar amount. Starting early in the morning and working twelve hours straight, we went through a dozen different dimensions of the deal. Hammering out one aspect after another, we pressed on, stayed positive, and worked through until we finally could agree on all twelve parameters.

We advised Greg to sign the deal and he did. We executed a five-year contract worth approximately $10.7 million. The player the year before got $9.7 million. Greg was thrilled, the Bears were thrilled, and we were thrilled. We had the courage to be leaders and set the market, as Greg was the first of all the 2007 first-round picks to sign.

We had the confidence in our ability as NFLPA contract advisers to know that we had a good deal from the Bears, that it wasn't going to get any better, and that it would hold up very well when the thirtieth and thirty-second picks signed. And we were right. Greg's contract had significant increases across the board compared with what the player in his slot the previous year had received, and in many respects was superior to the contracts of several players in front of him. That's not to say we got the best of the Bears. It was a great deal for both sides because it addressed the Bears' concerns, set a tremendous precedent for their future first-round picks, and allowed for positive momentum at the start of training camp.

Shortly thereafter, we closed Lawrence Timmons's deal as well. Do you remember I stated earlier how the 2006 first-round pick in LT's spot (fifteenth) took a bad five-year deal instead of an average six-year deal? That was the market for 2006 mid-first-round picks. They took a beating.

We were not going to wait for the deals to come in around LT at numbers fourteen and sixteen. We decided to be aggressive and set the market for five-year deals. Working very hard with Omar Khan of the Steelers, we put together a five-year deal with a major increase in the bonus and the overall package compared to 2006. Lawrence signed a five-year contract worth $15 million. The player the year before got $12.6 million. It was a great deal for the Steelers because it addressed their concerns, it was fair, and the deal got done early. Lawrence was the first player in the top twenty-five to sign. And then, when the middle-of-the-first-round deals came in, given how high we had set the market, those players fared much better in 2007 than their counterparts had done in 2006.

In the end, we negotiated superior contracts for Greg and Lawrence because we were leaders. We didn't wait for other agents to set the market. We didn't wait to slot our client in between the two players around him. We did our homework, came to negotiations prepared, found a creative solution to a challenging problem, and then worked hard to agree on the structure and dollars. We were proactive. We took command of the situation and led the way.

CHAPTER 15

BE A KID AT HEART

THE THING ABOUT ME THAT SOME PEOPLE FIND A BIT unusual is my affinity for superheroes. Walk into my house and you will actually find posters of Rocky, 300, Batman, and Conan the Barbarian. I don't want to be confused with the Forty-Year-Old Virgin, but you will also find a collection of small sculptures of comic-book heroes by artist Randy Bowen. Yes, as kids, Jason and I had collected comics and baseball cards. Yes, we still have them. And yes, I still read comics today. Occasionally I enjoy reading a Stephen King novel and Jason reads an Albert Einstein biography or physics book every chance he gets, but we are still seen from time to time reading comic books on our airline flights.

Too often in the professional world, as you mature, you become dehumanized. I know doctors who perform surgery on a patient and attorneys who argue a case on behalf of a client. They view the person as a patient or a client, not as a mother, a father, a husband, etc. They do not get emotionally involved.

The day that happens to me is the day I will get out of this business. I don't want to mature. I want to stay a kid at heart. When my dad took Jason and me to see *Rocky* in 1976, we cried our eyes out. Watching Rocky get knocked down, seeing him struggle to get up while Mickey yelled at him to stay down after taking an inhuman beating, still gets me. Throughout my childhood and teens, I watched that movie and will always be inspired by the story of someone who was down on his luck and, when he got his chance, overcame the odds with sheer heart and toughness.

Call me corny, I don't care. I like comic books. They are fast and fun reading. Reading about Batman, I saw an ordinary human defeat opponents possessing superpowers. Batman won because of his intellect and discipline.

I loved Conan the Barbarian. Watching the sheer courage and brutality of a fearless warrior was awesome. His courage was as extraordinary as his fighting skills.

And today, as an adult, I am still in awe of the heroics of the 300 Spartans, led by King Leonidas, who took on thousands and thousands of the enemy. They fought with honor and courage, and never quit.

Hey, I realize that's the movies and comics, but I've seen even greater heroism with the firemen on 9/11 and in our soldiers overseas. When I read about U.S. Army private Johnathon Millican being posthumously awarded the Silver Star for jumping on a grenade to save his four friends, I felt sorrow for his family's loss and a surge of pride in being an American.

I had always looked at Grand Master Young Soo Do as invincible. Sean Taylor was as indestructible as an athlete could be. I've learned the hard way that any cowardly seventeen-year-old punk can pull a trigger and mortally wound the most noble, powerful person on the planet. Over the years, I've come to realize that in real life, if you get punched in the face fifteen times, you don't all of a sudden get mad and decide to beat the guy in a fight. In real life, bones break, ligaments tear, and careers end prematurely.

I've seen giant defensive linemen like Warren Sapp, Tim Bowens, and Jeff Cross go through painful surgeries and grueling physical therapy from the abuse they took playing in the NFL. And if the bodies of these giants break down from the wear and tear of playing football, I marvel at what the little guys have to endure.

Knowing what NFL players sacrifice and risk, I don't desensitize myself to what's at stake. My clients can fire me at any time for any reason. What stops them from doing this is their confidence that I am the best agent in the business, and our friendship. I work hard every day to maintain their confidence, earn their trust, and cultivate our friendship. And it's because we talk all the time about everything, because we stick together during the good times and bad, and because we are friends, that I don't become like so many doctors and lawyers out there. We don't have an attorney-client relationship. I am not their boss and do not speak down to them like in a father-son relationship. We are partners.

It's the kid in me, who has so much fun working with these guys, that keeps us as peers. Sure, I put on the suit and tie, but I'd much rather be hanging out in a pair of shorts like I did back in my college days, enjoying the sun and fun at the beach. Twenty years later, that hasn't changed. Let me tell you a story about linebacker Dan Connor, the all-time leading tackler at Penn State.

When Danny Martoe first asked me to take a flight to meet with Dan Connor's parents in Pennsylvania, I was very skeptical. First of all, we have never represented a Penn State rookie in the draft. And second, as a result of the "Next Question" press conference, I wasn't very popular in that neck of the woods. I thought our chances were very unlikely. Still, if they were willing to meet with us, there was a chance. Making the disciplined decision, I flew out with Jason, Robert, and Danny Martoe. When Danny Martoe mentioned the Connor family lived near Scranton, I got a kick out of it because I enjoy the Scranton-based TV show *The Office*.

We pulled up to the house dressed in our best suits. Would you believe about an hour later, Jason and I were in shorts, swimming in the lake? It turned out that Dan Connor's brother was there and he'd recently lost his wedding ring in the lake behind the house. Being a kid at heart, I volunteered to jump in and look for it. Jason, as always, backed my play but was not a happy camper swimming in the murky, cold water. Robert and Danny Martoe, staying warm on the shore, were very helpful, pointing out where the brother was swimming when he lost the ring. We didn't find the ring, but Dan Connor's parents, Jim and Carol, were very surprised and impressed that we helped out.

Once we dried off and went back into the house, Jim and Carol had their own take on us and dismissed everything they'd heard or read about me. I could tell that they were giving us a clean slate and had decided to take a good look at our track record and contracts. From there, we went into great detail about the Greg Olsen and Lawrence Timmons negotiations. Since they were both high school teachers, they appreciated the strategy and numbers involved in the deals.

We then showed them our current list of Pro Bowl linebacker clients like Zach Thomas, Lance Briggs, Antonio Pierce, Dan Morgan, London Fletcher, etc. We highlighted their contracts and discussed our plan to promote their son to the NFL teams in the April 2008 draft.

Come January, it was between us and another agent. Dan's parents screened all the agents, presented their top two to Dan, and left it to him to decide. Fortunately, he chose Rosenhaus Sports, which caused quite a stir in the Philadelphia area.

An article in Phillynews.com quoted Dan Connor's father saying:

> Philadelphia fans absolutely hated this guy. We thought it would be interesting just to talk to him. It was more or less on a whim. But once you do talk to him, you put all that other stuff aside.
>
> One, he knows his stuff and two, he cares only about his clients. This is our son. We wanted someone who we knew would really look out for him.
>
> We wanted to keep Dan out of it until after his bowl game. The idea was to bring him the last two guys and let him make the final decision.

I love it when the parents are involved in the agent selection process because they are going to make the right decision based upon what is best for their son. Too often, when the kid makes the decision, it's for all the wrong reasons. That's why I told that same reporter: "It's always nice dealing with people that pick agents on a professional basis and not for all the other nonsense you see in this business."

When a family picks you to represent their son, they are placing their trust in you. Everything is in your hands, and I put a tremendous amount of pressure on all of us to come through for them. That's why I try so hard to fight for every penny and win for my players. But negotiations are a battle. Teams don't just say okay. Too often, when things reach an impasse, both sides get heated, and the negotiations become antagonistic, offensive, and negative. Being a tough negotiator doesn't mean holding out for what you want. And it doesn't mean walking out the door in the middle of negotiations.

It means being a closer. It means getting the deal done, and not just any deal, but the deal you were looking for all along that you strategically positioned yourself to get.

When you suggest a compromise, it's not just in order to compromise. It's because the midpoint between where you are at and where they are at is actually where you want the deal to be. That's when you compromise. But sometimes both sides are intransigent. Sometimes you have no choice but to walk out. But before you do, you better know what's at stake and do it as a last resort. The enemy is not the people sitting on the other side of the table, the impasse is. The key to finding a way to get to the promised land in negotiations is to be a leader. Rather than have the tempo of negotiations dictated to you, a leader will dictate the tempo. In my opinion, the most productive way to lead the negotiations is to keep them positive. Case in point, Frank Gore.

I first met Frank in the fall of 2001 when he was only eighteen years old. I was at the University of Miami to give a speech to a business class about negotiating in the NFL. I, of course, notified the compliance office at UM and was cleared to address the class. Frank had made a name for himself as a big-time high school recruit in South Florida, breaking all kinds of records as a running back. When I was introduced to him, I expected him to be bigger, leaner, and more muscular. He didn't look all that impressive. He looked to be five foot nine and less than two hundred pounds. With those numbers, I didn't have high expectations.

And then I watched the kid play. He was spectacular as a true freshman in 2001, running for 562 yards with five touchdowns on sixty-two carries. Frank earned my respect, averaging an astounding 9.1 yards per carry. Jason was enamored with Frank's talent. We knew that the kid had a bright future.

We also had inside information on the guy. Former UM tight end Jeremy Shockey, whom we signed as a client in February 2002, told us that Frank was special. The 2002 season looked extremely promising for Frank, as he had won the starting running-back job as a true sophomore.

Unfortunately, shortly after we signed Jeremy, Frank injured his left knee in practice. It was not a minor injury. From a brutal collision with safety Sean Taylor, Frank tore the anterior cruciate ligament (ACL) and cartilage in his left knee. That was a nasty, season-ending injury.

Fortunately, Dr. John Uribe, the outstanding orthopedic surgeon I mentioned earlier, reattached the ACL and stitched up the torn cartilage in the knee to preserve it. Typically, when that happens, a player who is an exceptional athlete can come back to be very good but doesn't regain the same degree of athleticism. Consequently, Frank missed the 2002 season rehabilitating his knee.

In Frank's absence, running back Willis McGahee had an incredible season for the 'Canes. Unfortunately, Willis suffered a horrific knee injury late in the fourth quarter of the final game of the season. To everyone's surprise, including my own, Willis declared he was going to come out early and enter the 2003 draft despite suffering the torn ACL.

Hurricane fans wanted to know who was going to be the next stud running back for UM in 2003. UM had a long line of outstanding running backs, such as Edgerrin James, Najeh Davenport, Clinton Portis, and Willis. Everyone wanted to see Frank come back from the injury and be the special player that he was before getting hurt. The question was, would he be the same player that Jeremy Shockey once called "Freaky" Frank?

Frank started out the 2003 season getting better with each game. In his first four games, he rushed for 118 yards, 127 yards, 134 yards, and 74 yards. Frank looked good but not great. The type of injury he'd suffered takes time to heal, so there was reason for optimism that Frank could eventually return to form. However, that fifth game, Frank blew out his right knee—the other knee. The ACL tear was truly devastating.

No player I had ever seen came back from two surgically reconstructed knees. It appeared to be over for Frank. Maybe, at best, he could rehabilitate the rest of the 2003 season and be ready for 2004. Maybe he could be good enough in time to make it back, but he had almost no chance of being the superstar he'd once looked like he could be.

Frank made it back in 2004 as a redshirt junior and performed remarkably well, considering the circumstances, but didn't look special. He still had one year of college football to return to form.

From time to time, when I was visiting a client at the rehabilitation facility, I would see Frank working on his knees with Ed Garabedian, who is the best physical therapist I have ever seen. Ed is tremendously knowledgeable and has an instinctive ability to recognize the optimal point to work muscles, ligaments, tendons, scar tissue, cartilage, etc. The guy is a miracle worker and the perfect complement to Dr. Uribe.

Every time I saw Frank there, I felt bad for him. The guy was always rehabbing with Ed, working up a sweat. He didn't say much, he's not a talkative guy. He wasn't flashy or cocky. He was blue-collar all the way.

From time to time, Jason and I would tell Frank to keep his chin up and that we had confidence he would be a big-time NFL running back like Edgerrin James, Willis McGahee and Clinton Portis. Jason still believed Frank could make it back and saw promise in his 2004 performance. He and I hoped that Frank would be the man in 2005 and have a monster year. And then a strange thing happened...

Frank called us to say that he was skipping his final year at UM to enter the NFL draft, and wanted to meet with us about being his agent. Jason and I were shocked. We thought for sure he'd stay in school because one big year would give him the chance to be a first-round pick. We knew that if he came out early, he didn't have much of a chance to be a first- or second-round pick.

Frank said that he wanted to come out because his mother was suffering from diabetes and other serious ailments. He wanted to make money as soon as possible in order to take care of her. Frank came from one of the poorest neighborhoods around. Without expensive health care and nutrition, his mom would not last long. He didn't care that it was in his best interest to stay in school, he had to make money now to help his mom. And that's what he did.

At the time of Frank's call, I had already signed another college running back, Vernand Morency out of Oklahoma State. As much as Jason and I wanted to work with Frank, we had already committed to another running back. Since it would have been a conflict of interest to represent both running backs, we had no choice but to honor our commitment to Vernand.

Nevertheless, Frank called in the months leading up to the draft to keep in touch. He enjoyed conversing with me and picking my brain. Since the NFLPA regulations governing agents permitted us to talk with Frank so long as Frank initiated the communication, I continued my relationship with him. It turned out that he'd lost about twenty pounds to maximize his speed and quickness under Pete Bommarito's training. Light, lean, and quick, Frank ran very well for the teams at the UM workout prior to the draft. He was very impressive and consequently was drafted in the third round by the San Francisco 49ers.

On July 29, 2005, Frank signed a three-year deal with an upfront signing bonus of $599,500. His salary in all three years, as was usual for a third-round pick, was $230,000 the first year, $350,000 the second year, and $435,000 the third year. However, to protect their interest, the team inserted a clause that would lower Frank's salary by almost half if he suffered a season-ending injury during the preseason in either of the first two years.

Frank was worth a third-round pick since he had a lot of upside. If he could stay healthy, he might return to his freshman form. Or he could take a bad hit to either one of his knees and his career would be over. With first- and second-round picks being seven- and eight-figure investments, the $599,500 third-round bonus was a good gamble for the 49ers.

There was a lot of uncertainty surrounding Frank—concerning his performance, not his heart or his toughness—as he got off to a slow start that rookie season, and missed two games in the middle of the season with a minor groin injury (is there such a thing?). However, toward the end of the season, he won the starting job and played well. Frank managed to lead the team in rushing with 608 yards on 127 carries and scored three touchdowns. By the end of the season, he had established himself as a solid running back who the 49ers felt could be their starter heading into the 2006 season.

Unfortunately for Frank, during the season he had injured both shoulders but managed to play through the pain. As soon as the season was over, he underwent surgery on both shoulders.

Despite the injuries, the 49ers saw enough in Frank to believe in him. They didn't draft or sign anyone to replace him. Head Coach Mike Nolan made the determination that Frank was his guy.

Frank returned to Miami during the summer of 2006 and trained at the UM facility. Since Jason and I represented a bunch of his friends in the NFL from UM, we bumped into him regularly. Each time I saw Frank, he would say to me that he was going to be a Pro Bowler and that he wanted me to negotiate his next contract.

Frank had earned my respect. He won the starting job with the 49ers and had a chance to become a big-time starting running back in 2006. From time to time, he would call me and I was happy for his success. Nevertheless, because I had so much history with Frank, it just didn't seem right that we weren't working together.

At the start of the 2006 season, I was anxious to see how he would do as a starter. A lot of scouts I talked to didn't think he was fast enough or durable enough. Jason and I were convinced he would have a breakout year.

Frank started off playing well for the 49ers. The first six games he ran for 520 yards on 112 carries, averaging 4.6 yards per carry and 87 yards per game. At that point, he had proven he could get the job done as a starting running back. Watching him play, we saw flashes of a player who could make the jump from a good starter to Pro Bowl player, like he told me he would be. Jason and I were convinced that Frank was ready to take it to the next level and be able to command a monster contract.

Frank's plan all along was to do what Clinton Portis had done—renegotiate after playing only two seasons in the NFL. Remember, Frank signed a three-year deal and was scheduled to earn the minimum salary of $435,000 the third year. He wanted to get an awesome new contract in his third year, as Portis had done. However, Portis had been a Pro Bowl player his second season and he was the only running back to ever get a new big contract so quickly. Most players have to wait four or five years to get the big contract. Since Frank was under contract for one more year and since he had two reconstructed knees and shoulders (unlike Portis), getting a new contract would require two things. First, he would have to play at a dominant level for the remainder of the season and become a Pro Bowl player. And second, he would need a very talented agent.

Leading up to the bye week, Frank had been communicating with me about switching agents. Once it became evident that his agent would not be able to personally negotiate Frank's contract because of an NFLPA suspension, it became a no-brainer to hire Rosenhaus Sports.

And so on October 27, 2006, Frank hired me. We both had extremely difficult jobs ahead of us. Frank would have to do what Portis did—rush for 1,500 yards and make it to the Pro Bowl. In the first six games, Frank had gained 520 yards, so he needed to get 980 more yards in the remaining ten games. To ensure that he made the Pro Bowl, he would have to lead his conference (the NFC) in rushing yards. Most of all, before he could accomplish any of the above, he would have to stay healthy.

Frank's hiring me sent a message around the league that he meant business about getting a new contract. Not for nothing, ESPN's Tony Kornheiser had this to say about me on *Pardon the Interruption* in April 2005: "You don't hire Drew Rosenhaus to restructure...you hire Drew Rosenhaus to rip up and get more." The media jumped all over the move and asked Coach Nolan, a stand-up guy, the kind of person you root for in this business, about me. Coach Nolan had this to say: "I know his agent very well. I've known him for a long time and I don't have a problem with [him]. I assured Frank, 'I know your guy. He's represented a lot of guys I've coached over the years...'"

For the next ten weeks, I watched Frank play and held my breath every time he took a hit to the knee. But the kid just kept getting up no matter how hard they hit him. The team's entire offense was built around him and opposing defenses focused on stopping him above all else. Yet Frank ran for 1,175 in those remaining ten games, totaling 1,695 yards overall. He went from averaging 87 yards per game to averaging 117. He led the NFC in rushing yards and led the NFL in average yards per carry. Frank did it! He was spectacular. He broke team record after team record. He did everything we could have asked of him to provide us with the leverage we needed at the negotiating table.

Frank did his job and it was now our turn to get him a new contract. Despite his stellar performance, Jason and I had our work cut out for us. Why was it mission impossible to get a new contract for Frank? Put yourself in the 49ers' shoes.

They had Frank under contract the next season at a salary of $435,000. The following year Frank would be a restricted free agent and they could keep his rights by paying him a salary of $2.017 million. So they basically had Frank under contract for the next two years at a cost of $2.452 million. That is very inexpensive for a starting running back and would be a great bargain for the team.

Most NFL players have to play four years in order to get their second contract, which is where the big money deal is. Frank was two years away from free agency. Teams are very reluctant to renegotiate a player's contract after only two years. They want players to play at least three or four years under their original contract. Otherwise, every player would want a new deal and it would create chaos. That's why it was so rare and special for Clinton Portis and Anquan Boldin to get new deals after only two years. To make matters worse, both Portis and Boldin had two Pro Bowl–caliber seasons. Frank had only

one. And neither of those players had two knee and shoulder reconstructive surgeries.

If you were the 49ers, why wouldn't you force Frank to play out
the two remaining years at salaries of $435,000 and $2.017 million?
Over 2007 and 2008, we wanted a new deal that would pay him more
than $12 million, not $2.452 million. From the 49ers' perspective, why
pay him the extra $10 million when he was under contract anyway?

The biggest drawbacks were the two season-ending injuries to his
knees that Frank had already suffered. Why pay him $12 million and
risk him getting hurt again? Coaches and general managers get fired in
this league for doing deals that don't work out. From the team's perspective, Frank should play out the two years under contract, become a free
agent, and then break the bank. Why should the team take the risk?

The reason is that some teams are more committed to winning
than to just making a profit. The 49ers are such a team. They will go
out and spend the money necessary to win. All that being said, the
49ers negotiator, Paraag Marathe, signs players to smart deals. He is
part of the new generation of negotiators who do tremendous research
and know all the angles. He is super sharp and you better come prepared to the negotiating table when you sit across from him.

After the 2006 season, my assignment was to get Frank the big
money. He did not want to play out the 2006 and 2007 seasons for the
minimums. There was no way we were going to risk him getting hurt
and missing out on his big opportunity. No sir, the time had come to
make a deal. Our goal was to get the same kind of contract Portis had
gotten. Paraag and I hit an impasse. Jason and Paraag had exchanged
offers with all kinds of charts and analyses, but after months of negotiations, we were not making any progress.

So at the end of March in 2006, while I was at the owners' meetings in Arizona, we arranged to set up a meeting between all parties. Jason and Frank came in on my side of the table. As for the 49ers, Paraag was accompanied by Scott McCloughan, Lal Henegan, and Head Coach Mike Nolan. We met in a conference room at the Biltmore Hotel for hours and got nowhere.

The meeting started off with Paraag putting on a PowerPoint presentation and making numerous statistical arguments as to why his offer was fair. It was very impressive and lasted for an hour. He had obviously spent a great deal of time on it. I could see that Coach Nolan was impressed.

I also noticed that Paraag was stating his position to Coach Nolan. Jason and I quickly realized that Coach Nolan was there to act as a mediator. We knew that if we could win him over, he would okay the deal we were looking for and give Paraag the green light to compromise. It was easier said than done.

Throughout Paraag's presentation, Jason took meticulous notes, as if he were back in law school at a professor's lecture. Going through his notes, point after point, Jason countered Paraag's arguments. But in the end, after Jason and Paraag had gone back and forth over the numbers, we were still at a stalemate. Scott McCloughan took a hard line, saying that the reason he was opposed to doing our deal was that he couldn't justify to his owner giving Frank the big bonus and then risking a career-ending injury.

After hours of debate, Frank was becoming upset. Although throughout the process, the 49ers had been very complimentary toward Frank, he felt they didn't believe in him. Since they'd drafted him, he spent more time at the facility than anyone. He spent all day and all night doing everything he could to be the best player he could be. He was 100 percent devoted to the 49ers and delivered a great year that helped them improve. He was the key to their successful 2007 season and that was our leverage.

When it looked like Paraag and the others were there only to state their case and not to do a deal, I had no choice but to remind them what would happen if we got up and walked out. While being respectful, I made it clear that if we walked out, Frank would not participate in the 49ers' off-season and would not report to camp. I made it clear that failure today would lead to disaster tomorrow.

The key though was not being a tough guy. The key was that when things got ugly, and they did, as tempers flared, Jason and I could have gotten up with Frank and walked out. Too often in the NFL, deals don't get done because egos get involved and the atmosphere turns nasty. Jason and I knew what was at stake. We knew how much adversity Frank had gone through and how much heart he had to become such a great player. We knew we couldn't let this deal fall apart. We couldn't let Frank go home, have a counterproductive off-season, hold out, and then come back in with our tails between our legs. Most of all, we couldn't let him work out another day and risk injury.

So rather than get pissed off, Jason and I both urged the 49ers to join us in avoiding the negative, ego-driven road. We told Coach Nolan that he had the power to get this deal done and prevent disaster. It wasn't too late.

At the same time, Jason proposed a solution: if we could get the money we were looking for, Frank would pay for an insurance policy that would protect the team if he were to suffer a season-ending injury.

We did everything we could to keep the meeting going in a positive direction. Jason's solution removed the last obstacle to the deal, if the 49ers were sincere about wanting to do right by Frank. At this point, Coach Nolan suggested we break so they could talk among themselves.

Frank, Jason, and I waited for their response. We knew they were either going to stand firm or do our deal. There was no in between. Either Frank would finally get the financial security he deserved or he would have to risk injury and play out another year for the minimum. Everything was on the line.

When Coach Nolan opened the door and told us to come in, we sat down and waited for his answer. He turned to Frank and said that they had decided to do the deal. Yes! At that point, Paraag and I negotiated the final details.

When we all walked out, I thanked Coach Nolan, Scott, Paraag, and Lal. It was a smart deal for both sides. Frank signed a five-year contract worth $28 million. Considering that the team had his rights for two more seasons and he only gave up three years of free agency, it was, in effect, a three-year extension. He will only be twenty-eight years old when the deal expires and will be young enough to get a new deal before this one expires.

As Coach Nolan and I were talking, Jason went to find Frank, who had disappeared. When he found him, he was in a phone booth. He was talking to his mom and had tears in his eyes. It was one of the most rewarding, memorable moments of my career to see a good kid, who worked so hard, who overcame so much heartache, finally make it big.

That deal happened because Frank was a great player and a great person and because we kept the negotiations positive. That's what leaders do. When things are going in the wrong direction, they take action to get them back on track.

I cared too much about Frank to let this deal fall apart. Six months later, Frank's mom passed away, but not before seeing her son become a huge success. As he spoke at her funeral, I could see that he kept his composure because he knew in his heart that he'd been a great son to her and made her happy.

I was proud to be a small part of that. I like to think that in a way, agents can be like comic-book or movie heroes. I like to think agents are the good guys. Over the years, I have been the subject of more cowardly personal attacks by anonymous fans than I can remember. I have received countless prank phone calls. My parents have had to hear radio and read newspaper attacks on their son's character. There have been times when it seemed like the entire agent community was working in unison to come after me. That's what one agent urged at the annual NFLPA agent meeting that all agents are required to attend. He proposed that the NFLPA stop me because I was stealing clients. When he was done speaking, the entire auditorium stood up and applauded. In recruiting battles, other agents tell a recruit that if he is not going to pick him, whatever he does, don't pick Drew Rosenhaus. They actually tell the recruits to pick any agent but me. Sometimes I feel like it's us versus the world.

I like to think that despite overwhelming adversity, in our own way, we responded like King Leonidas and the 300 Spartans did at Thermopylae, by standing our ground and fighting. I think the toughest thing about being an agent is that you don't get to put on the pads and play the game. Your battle is one of wits and will, not of strength. Then again, we don't get broken bones or arrows in our chests.

But at some point in everyone's life, I think they are given an opportunity to be a true hero. For years I had developed thick skin over the cheap insults from other agents, the media, and fans, but it still bothers me to be viewed as the bad guy. I know my clients and their families don't see it that way, but a lot of people do. The summer of 2005 was particularly tough for me. I was a constant object of criticism from the Philadelphia media and fans, which fueled my competitors' fires.

To take a break, I decided to visit my client Antonio Pierce, who was doing an appearance set up by Robert Bailey at Disney World in Orlando, Florida. I was staying at the Grand Floridian Hotel with my girlfriend at the time. She and I were having a fun afternoon. We went waterskiing, walked around the Magic Kingdom, and took it easy at the hotel. Sipping on a virgin piña colada and playing some Ping-Pong with my girlfriend, I was enjoying a relaxing afternoon. And then I heard terrible screams.

I saw that a crowd had gathered along the edge of the pool. I ran over there and saw a four-year-old African-American boy lying lifeless on the side of the pool. His father was yelling his son's name, shaking him, doing anything he could to wake him up. I asked the father what happened and he told me that he pulled his son out of the pool and he didn't know how long he'd been under. I checked the boy's pulse and he wasn't breathing. His eyes were closed and his body felt cold.

With his mother screaming and people crying all around me, I felt a rush of adrenaline and instinctively started performing CPR on the boy. While I was pumping his chest, I told his father to breathe air into his son's mouth.

After what seemed like an eternity—one or two minutes—the boy remained unresponsive. The father became even more distraught and I didn't know what to do but keep on going. It looked like no matter what I did, I couldn't bring him back. And then out of nowhere, the boy coughed up water, opened his eyes, and started to breathe. At that moment I knew he was going to make it and I felt sheer elation.

The paramedics arrived shortly afterward and took the boy to the hospital. The police interviewed me and took my statement. When I found out where they took the kid, I went to visit him and his family. While I was there, the doctor told me that I had revived the boy just in time and he was going to be fine.

I've accomplished a lot in my life, but that incident changed me forever. Even though the media made jokes at my expense, saying that in between performing CPR, I stopped to call the media, I didn't care. Their cowardly insults meant nothing to me but should be shameful to them. In saving the life of four-year-old Maurice Hill, I became impervious to the slings and arrows of my critics. I know deep in my heart that I was the hero I always wanted to be. I knew that I did what Batman, Rocky, Conan, and Leonidas would have done. That didn't make me special, but it was special to me because I believe that I did what you and anyone else would have done in my position. I'm not here to say how great I am and how much I love myself. I've got my flaws and make my share of mistakes, but they are all well intentioned. It may surprise some readers that I don't think this book is about me. This book is about the principles that will help you to succeed in any endeavor.

Like me, you are going to face your share of critics and adversity. But amid the fear, chaos, and adversity, if you press on and apply these principles, you will make it through the valley and ascend to the mountaintop. While Jason, Robert, Danny, Jessie, my dad, Uncle Howie, Adam, and I stand at the top, you can count on us to defend our Thermopylae. There's room for more, if you adhere to the code of "Next Question."

ACKNOWLEDGMENTS

We would like to acknowledge the individuals who met with us, looked us in the eyes, listened to what we had to say, shook our hands, believed in us, trusted us, and agreed to bestow upon us the honor and privilege of being their NFL Contract Advisors. And so to you, all of our past and current clients and their involved family members, we thank you for giving us the opportunity to work for you and be a part of the NFL dream.